◢ KU-308-907

Routledge Author Guides

Byron

Routledge Author Guides

GENERAL EDITOR: B. C. SOUTHAM, M.A., B.LITT. (OXON.)
Formerly Department of English, Westfield College, University of London

Titles in the series

Byron by J. D. Jump, Professor of English, University of Manchester.

Tolstoy by Ernest J. Simmons, sometime Professor of Russian Literature, Havard University.

Browning by Roy E. Gridley, Professor of English, University of Kansas.

Routledge Author Guides

Byron

by

John D Jump

Professor of English
University of Manchester

Routledge & Kegan Paul
London and Boston

B

First published 1972
by Routledge & Kegan Paul Ltd
Broadway House, 68–74 Carter Lane,
London EC4V 5EL and
9 Park Street,
Boston, Mass. 02108, U.S.A.
Printed in Great Britain by
Cox & Wyman Ltd., London, Fakenham and Reading
© John D. Jump 1972

No part of this book may be reproduced in
any form without permission from the
publisher, except for the quotation of brie,
passages in criticism

ISBN 0 7100 7334 8 (c)
ISBN 0 7100 7393 3 (p)

821.7
JUM

To Barbara

General Editor's Preface

Nowadays there is a growing awareness that the specialist areas have much to offer and much to learn from one another. The student of history, for example, is becoming increasingly aware of the value that literature can have in the understanding of the past; equally, the student of literature is turning more and more to the historians for illumination of his area of special interest, and of course philosophy, political science, sociology, and other disciplines have much to give him.

What we are trying to do in the *Author Guides Series* is to offer this illumination and communication by providing for non-specialist readers, whether students or the interested general public, a clear and systematic account of the life and times and works of the major writers and thinkers across a wide range of disciplines. Where the *Author Guides Series* may be seen to differ from other, apparently similar, series, is in its historical emphasis, which will be particularly evident in the treatment of the great literary writers, where we are trying to establish, in so far as this can be done, the social and historical context of the writer's life and times, and the cultural and intellectual tradition in which he stands, always remembering that critical and interpretative principles are implicit to any sound historical approach.

BSC

Contents

Contents

Preface

In the Notes on the Text on page xiii I have listed the editions of Byron's prose and verse used in the present volume and have explained the abbreviations I have adopted. References to these editions have been inserted in the body of the text, as have also my occasional references to other primary sources. A list of the principal publications of work by Byron appears on pp. 189–90.

I have reserved the Bibliographical Notes at the end of the book mainly for acknowledging what I owe to those who have written before me on the subjects I discuss; and I have tried to indicate whether my indebtedness follows from assenting to or dissenting from their views. The Bibliographical Notes contain a description of secondary sources for each chapter in turn. For the convenience of the reader who likes an alphabetical arrangement, I have included references in the Index to all mentions of authors' names in the Bibliographical Notes.

I have incorporated in the text, after some slight revision, virtually the whole of three papers previously published by me: 'Byron's Letters' in *Essays and Studies 1968*, edited by Simeon Potter, London, Murray, 1968; 'Byron's *Vision of Judgment*' in *Bulletin of the John Rylands Library*, li (1968), pp. 122–36; and 'Byron's *Don Juan*: Poem or Hold-All?', The W. D. Thomas Memorial Lecture, Swansea, 1968. My chapter on *Cain* derives from an unpublished paper read to the Manson Society in the Faculty of Theology of the University of Manchester in 1968. In addition, I have taken shorter passages from the essay 'Lord Byron' which I contributed to *A Guide to English Literature*, v: *From Blake to Byron*, edited by Boris Ford, Harmondsworth, Penguin, 1957; from the essay 'Byron' in *English Poetry: Select Bibliographical Guides*, edited by A. E. Dyson, London, 1971; and from various book reviews in the *Critical Quarterly*, the *Manchester Guardian, Notes and Queries*, the *Review of English Studies*, and *The Times Literary Supplement*. To the editors and publishers of all of these, I am most grateful for permission to reprint my work.

My debt to colleagues, students, and other friends is now impossible to assess. But I should like to make special acknowledgment of the kindness of Dr W. H. Chaloner, Reader in Modern Economic History in the University of Manchester, who read my first chapter in typescript and corrected me on certain matters of fact and emphasis; of the cheerful readiness with which Miss Diane Cansdale typed the greater part of the book; and of the shrewd and helpful criticism to which my wife subjected my manuscript at every stage in its composition.

Notes on the Text

I have employed the following abbreviations throughout this book:

Correspondence   *Lord Byron's Correspondence*, ed. John Murray, 2 vols., 1922.

Letters and Journals   *The Works of Lord Byron: Letters and Journals*, ed. R. E. Prothero, 6 vols., 1898–1901.

Poetry   *The Works of Lord Byron: Poetry*, ed. E. H. Coleridge, 7 vols., 1898–1904.

Most of my quotations from Byron's prose are taken from *Letters and Journals*. When I quote from any letter contained in that collection, my reference consists simply of the date of the letter; when I quote from a journal or diary, the date of the entry is accompanied by the word 'Journal' or 'Diary'; quotations from 'Detached Thoughts' are identified by serial numbers following that title; and, when I quote from any of the documents printed in appendices or notes, I name *Letters and Journals* and supply volume and page numbers. When I quote from a letter not included in *Letters and Journals*, I associate with the date the title of the collection in which the letter does appear: e.g. '*Correspondence*, 21 September 1813'.

Quotations from *Don Juan* are taken from *Byron's 'Don Juan'*, ed. T. G. Steffan and W. W. Pratt, 4 vols., Austin (Texas) and Edinburgh, 1957. Quotations from Byron's other poems are taken from *Poetry*.

I

An Age of Revolutions

Byron belongs not merely to English but to world literature. His poetry made him famous at the age of twenty-four; his fame quickly spread throughout Europe as far as Russia and to America; and wherever it spread it brought him ardent disciples. He was sufficiently representative of his society to attract a multitude of readers, and he was sufficiently critical of it to win the allegiance of many of the young.

All ages are ages of change. But in some the rate of change increases, or at least men's consciousness of change grows more acute. The age of Byron was one of these. It was an age of revolutions. The American Revolution slightly preceded his birth in 1788, the French Revolution occurred during his early years, and the Industrial Revolution was accelerating throughout his life. As an aristocrat, Byron inherited political privileges and responsibilities in this changing world. While in England, he supported the opposition party, the Whigs, believing it to be the party of freedom and humanity. These concerns explain his lifelong sympathy with movements of national liberation and his hostility to the kings and generals whom he held responsible for unjust wars. Nor did his opposition manifest itself only in political forms. His poems projected upon the public imagination a type of hero who was the very embodiment of revolt.

At the same time, Byron was in some ways highly orthodox. He rarely lost sight of his own status as an English aristocrat, and he retained to the end certain of the traits he had developed as a young Regency dandy. His literary tastes were conservative, and an old-fashioned eighteenth-century empiricism usually made him impatient of the metaphysical speculations that attracted his more Romantic contemporaries. These leanings, evident from the start in his private conversation and his letters, became dominant in the major poems of

I

his later years. They did not nullify his protest, but they made it more realistic and more practical.

To understand such a man, we must review the conflicting forces that played upon him and contributed to his becoming what he was. We must review the political disturbances and revolutions of his time, the aristocratic society and to some extent the more general society in which he spent his years in England, and the nationalist movements with which he became closely associated during the eighteen-twenties.

George III, Wilkes, and America

For all but the last four of Byron's thirty-six years (1788–1824), George III was King of England. He had succeeded to the throne in 1760 at the age of twenty-two on the death of a grandfather whom he stigmatized as 'unworthy of a British Monarch'. He was a solemn and conscientious young man with a tendency to melancholia. Striving against a deep sense of inadequacy, a profound self-distrust, he wished as a 'Patriot King' to purify political life, exaggerating both the extent of the corruption and his own ability to remedy it. His well-known obstinacy followed naturally from the effort he had to make to conquer his misgivings. These misgivings were to triumph during his phases of madness in later life.

As King, he intended to follow a non-partisan, patriotic line. But he had the misfortune to reign during a period when a series of important issues divided even the most sincere and disinterested of his subjects one from another. American Independence was one of these, and the French Revolution was another. At home, Catholic Emancipation and Parliamentary Reform were two more. Conflicts of opinion on these and other issues gradually led to a sharper definition and a more co-herent organization of political parties.

The career of John Wilkes, remembered by Byron in *The Vision of Judgment* (1822) half a century later, provoked such conflicts of opinion. It also helped, whatever may have been Wilkes's intentions, to estab-lish certain of our basic civil rights. Wilkes first gained prominence in 1763 when in the *North Briton*, a paper he had started in the previous year, he described as a falsehood the statement in the King's speech that the peace concluding the Seven Years' War (1756–63) was 'honourable to my Crown and beneficial to my people'. A complicated legal battle ensued. During this, Wilkes represented himself as defending not merely the liberty of the upper classes but 'what touches me more sensibly, that of all the middling and inferior set of people'. Despite initial success, the battle went against him. To the charge of seditious libel was added one of obscenity. By the time the trial came on, Wilkes had fled to France. In consequence of his non-appearance, he was outlawed.

Wilkes was above all an adventurer. A cross-eyed womanizer and a jaunty wit, he had a reckless love of flying to extremes in everything he undertook. Only four years after the events that had apparently ruined him, he made what must have seemed a desperate gambler's last throw by returning to England to offer himself as a candidate in the general election of 1768. Assisted by John Horne, a combative Radical[1] parson who had wished to be a lawyer and who in 1782 extended his name to John Horne Tooke, he stood for Middlesex, representing himself as a freedom-loving individual persecuted by authority. He showed his wit as he canvassed for votes. 'I'd rather vote for the Devil,' one elector told him. 'Naturally,' replied Wilkes, 'but if your friend is not standing, may I hope for your support?' In due course, he headed the poll. The outlawry was subsequently cancelled.

But the government was not prepared to have him in Parliament, and in February 1769 he was expelled from his seat. He was re-elected and re-expelled, re-elected and re-expelled, and once more re-elected. On this fourth occasion, the House of Commons resolved that he was ineligible for election and that the seat should go to the runner-up. The Radicals with whom Wilkes had allied himself denounced this as a violation of the voters' rights. For a while Wilkes led a popular protest movement. In 1771 he defied efforts to suppress the reporting of parliamentary debates. In 1774 he became Lord Mayor of London and yet once again won a Middlesex election, being allowed this time to take his seat. He introduced the first bill for parliamentary reform two years later but withdrew it without a division. The Gordon Riots of 1780 completed his conversion to respectability.

Support for the Americans had been a feature of the popular protest movement Wilkes had briefly led. The thirteen American colonies were growing ripe for independence. By 1770 most of the inhabitants of European origin had been born there, and with Boston about six weeks' sailing distance from Liverpool, they felt very remote from England. The British government was acting within its legal rights in

[1] Only in the nineteenth century did this become a usual term for one who held advanced political views of a democratic kind. Its convenience will perhaps excuse its use with reference to eighteenth-century affairs.

its various proposals for their taxation. But the colonists' resistance was hardly surprising, and it won the sympathy of an articulate minority in England. This was recruited more especially from the Radicals and the Dissenters, and some of its members during these years received the training that was to make them leaders in future political movements for the redress of grievances.

In a strictly military sense, the War of American Independence (1775–83) was an inconclusive business. But the massive British majority originally in favour of disciplining the colonists eventually lost heart at the logistical difficulties of subduing a recalcitrant population occupying a vast territory some thousands of miles away. One of the last to lose heart was George III himself. Finally, the British government ceded the independence which seven years earlier the colonies had claimed with a Declaration that was soon recognized as a classical formulation of democratic ideals:

> We hold these truths to be self-evident, that all men are created equal, that they are endowed by their Creator with certain unalienable Rights, that among these are Life, Liberty and the pursuit of Happiness. That to secure these rights, Governments are instituted among Men, deriving their just powers from the consent of the governed. That whenever any Form of Government becomes destructive of these ends, it is the Right of the People to alter or to abolish it, and to institute new Government, laying its foundation on such principles and organizing its powers in such form, as to them shall seem most likely to effect their Safety and Happiness.

These doctrines were before long to prove explosive in France. England resisted them fiercely throughout the twenty-two years of the French Revolutionary and Napoleonic Wars (1793–1815). In the end they made headway there too.

Another cause that made headway, at least among some of the young writers, during the American and French conflicts was the protest against war itself. John Scott of Amwell, a Quaker poet of whom Dr Johnson was fond, published in 1782 a volume containing 'The Drum':

> I hate that drum's discordant sound,
> Parading round, and round, and round:
> To thoughtless youth it pleasure yields,

And lures from cities and from fields,
To sell their liberty for charms
Of tawdry lace, and glittering arms;
And when Ambition's voice commands,
To march, and fight, and fall, in foreign lands.

I hate that drum's discordant sound,
Parading round, and round, and round:
To me it talks of ravag'd plains,
And burning towns, and ruin'd swains,
And mangled limbs, and dying groans,
And widows' tears, and orphans' moans;
And all that Misery's hand bestows,
To fill the catalogue of human woes.

To be sure, John Scott was not the first to voice the pain and misery of war. They find expression, for example, in Shakespeare's *Henry V*. But so also do the virtues of courage and loyalty which can shine in the circumstances producing the pain and misery. What makes Scott's poem exceptional for its time, despite its conventional phrasing, is that it is totally given up to his sense of the pity of war.

William Blake felt this pity. It is evident not only in poems and drawings produced by him during the American war but also in the work he did during the subsequent French Revolutionary wars. William Wordsworth and Robert Southey felt it, too, and gave utterance to it in some of the poems they wrote early in these French wars. A generation later, Byron was more ready than they had been to find something admirable in the military virtues. But his stanzas on Waterloo in *Childe Harold's Pilgrimage*, Canto III, and his elaborate account of the siege of Ismail in *Don Juan*, VII and VIII, are dominated by his grief and abhorrence at what he describes.

In Byron's *The Vision of Judgment*, both Wilkes and the anonymous political journalist 'Junius' see George III as their enemy, while Satan describes him as the opponent of liberty in America and in France. The King was undeniably of a conservative habit of mind. But historians sometimes suggest that he furthered his own policies by keeping the 'King's Friends' in power against the real will of the country. They recollect that in 1780 John Dunning, a member of the opposition, moved a famous resolution, 'that the influence of the Crown has increased, is increasing, and ought to be diminished.' But recent investigation makes it very doubtful whether this increase occurred;

and J. Steven Watson, the historian of the reign, has little difficulty in seeing George III as anxiously but deliberately exercising precisely the powers that he had inherited, and no more.

Within constitutional limits he did, however, make his views known and felt. He abhorred Wilkes; he urged strong action in America even when discouragement was overtaking his people; he refused to sanction Catholic Emancipation, exclaiming, 'The most Jacobinical thing I ever heard of! I shall reckon any man my personal enemy who proposes any such measure'; and by this refusal he deepened the already profound Irish suspicions of England. His resort to the term 'Jacobinical' to stigmatize a proposal to allow papists to enjoy civil rights which had long been withheld from them reflects his hostility – which was after all an occupational hostility – to the chief political movement of his time, the French Revolution.

Other men found it less easy to take a simple and consistent stand in the face of a movement which seemed as momentous in the decades following its outbreak as the Russian Revolution was to seem in the decades following 1917. Some observers were both fascinated and repelled from the start; some began as sympathizers but were alienated by the way things developed across the Channel; some deplored these developments but continued to cherish the democratic ideals that they had once hoped the Revolution would realize. For Byron, born one year before the crucial sequence of events began, the French Revolution and the career of Napoleon constituted the political background of his whole conscious life to the age of twenty-seven, and a vitally important political memory for the rest of his days. They merit some attention here, more especially as they were seen, and as they affected political developments, in Great Britain.

Reform and Revolution

The seventeen-eighties saw a continuing movement for parliamentary reform. A great deal was wrong. The pattern of representation was irrational and unjust. There were villages that returned members because they had once been towns, and there were thriving towns that were denied representation because they had recently been villages. Only a small minority of the population had the right to vote – about 300,000 out of eight millions – and the qualifications entitling those composing it to do so varied from place to place. Most members of the House of Commons owed their seats either to the landowners in whose areas of influence their constituencies lay or to the little groups of borough electors from whom they had purchased them.

In May 1782 the Commons rejected a proposal by the young William Pitt for an inquiry into the state of the representation. Two years earlier, there had been founded the Society for Promoting Constitutional Information. The purpose of this body was to educate public opinion: 'To convince men of all ranks that it is to their interest, as well as their duty, to support a free constitution, and to maintain and assert those common rights, which are essential to the dignity, and to the happiness of human nature'. A few days after Pitt's defeat, the leading members agreed on the indispensable necessity of bringing public opinion to bear on Parliament for the reform of the House of Commons. Petitions were prepared and presented.

Pitt tried again in May 1783, and once more, as Prime Minister, in April 1785. On each occasion, his defeat was heavier than in 1782. For a time, Reform seemed dead. The Constitutional Society, which had at first grown steadily, began to wilt.

But the movement for Reform received a fresh stimulus when news arrived of the events leading up to the French Revolution. The irreparable breakdown of the financial system of his country had compelled Louis XVI to accede to a widespread demand for a meeting of the old States-General, the national Parliament of France, which had not been summoned for nearly two centuries. As soon as this met, the third estate asserted its claim to predominate over the other two, the clergy and the nobility. Its members constituted themselves into a National Assembly and set about making a fresh national settlement in agreement with the King. Louis resisted and yielded, resisted and yielded. Meanwhile, on 14 July 1789, the people of Paris showed their spirit and their strength by storming the Bastille, the fortress-prison that symbolized the arbitrary power of the monarchy. Similar actions took place throughout France, causing many of the nobility to emigrate.

During 1789 rapid, and in the circumstances surprisingly peaceful, progress was made towards a new constitution. The nobility surrendered many of their feudal privileges, and the National Assembly published a Declaration of the Rights of Man. Even the march to Versailles, in which the women of Paris took a prominent part, and the triumphal bringing back of the royal family to the Tuileries did not greatly cloud what seemed to many observers a miracle of radical but orderly political change. An absolutist régime was being quickly transformed into a constitutional monarchy.

7

No doubt many Englishmen were jubilant to see their traditional enemy, who had recently helped the American colonies to gain their independence, embarrassed by these internal shifts and strains. Some rejoiced at the popular challenge to absolutism and in so doing conceived new hope for Reform at home. The Dissenters, who still suffered under grave legal disabilities, observed that the National Assembly had recognized the equal rights of all citizens. This went further than any British government had managed to go during the whole century since the Glorious Revolution of 1688, which was supposed to have secured civil and religious liberty for all.

The London Revolution Society, one of many formed to commemorate the achievements of 1688, met in November 1789 and heard a sermon by Richard Price, a well-known Unitarian minister and writer on political questions who had been influential at an earlier date in the cause of American Independence. On this occasion Price observed that he could almost repeat the *Nunc dimittis* as an expression of the high hopes the French Revolution inspired in him. The sermon was to draw from Edmund Burke his hostile *Reflections on the Revolution in France* (1790). Following it, a general meeting of the Society adopted unanimously on Price's motion an address congratulating the French National Assembly on the victory of liberty and justice over arbitrary power and on the encouragement given to other nations to secure their inalienable rights.

Price looked forward in his own country to the removal of the legal disabilities under which the Dissenters suffered and to a more equitable system of parliamentary representation. Reform seemed once more to have become a practical possibility.

Sympathy with developments in France, and even enthusiastic hopes for a political millennium, affected many British men of letters. The middle-aged recluse William Cowper, despite his Evangelical disbelief in the efficacy of merely human transformations, felt a thrill at this 'wonderful period in the history of mankind'. Robert Burns, in one of his best-known songs ('For a' that'), asserted his democratic faith in equality and fraternity:

> Then let us pray that come it may,
>   As come it will for a' that,
> That Sense and Worth, o'er a' the earth
>   Shall bear the gree, and a' that.
> For a' that, and a' that,

> Its comin yet for a' that,
> That Man to Man the warld o'er,
> Shall brothers be for a' that.

Even when he became convinced that French expansionism had to be resisted, his song composed for the volunteer regiment that he joined ('The Dumfries Volunteers') ended with the lines:

> But while we sing, GOD SAVE THE KING,
> We'll ne'er forget THE PEOPLE!

His contemporary William Blake is said to have worn the red cap of the Revolution in the streets of London and to have given Thomas Paine, the fighter for American Independence whose *Rights of Man* (1791) was a reply to Burke's *Reflections on the Revolution in France*, timely warning that the authorities would be trying to arrest him. Blake embarked upon a visionary poem in favour of liberty, in which

> the dens shook and trembled: the prisoners look up
>   and assay to shout; they listen,
> Then laugh in the dismal den, then are silent, and a
>   light walks round the dark towers.

But fear of government action apparently prevented the publication of his poem 'The French Revolution'.

Among some of the youngest poets, those between fifteen and twenty years of age when the Bastille fell, the enthusiasm was for a time quite overwhelming. They were responding to a call which P. A. Brown, the historian of the influence of the French Revolution in England, rightly describes as 'irresistible to the young. It had the wonderful sanction of modernity, and was indeed an appeal to the faith which each generation adopts, champions, and betrays; that things are possible, dreams come true, that its day is an exception to all other days.' Wordsworth later recollected his feelings at this time in lines that have become famous (*The Prelude* [1805-6], X. 693-703; [1850], XI. 108-18):

> Bliss was it in that dawn to be alive,
> But to be young was very heaven: O times,
> In which the meagre, stale, forbidding ways
> Of custom, law, and statute took at once
> The attraction of a Country in Romance;

When Reason seem'd the most to assert her rights
When most intent on making of herself
A prime Enchanter to assist the work,
Which then was going forwards in her name.
Not favour'd spots alone, but the whole earth
The beauty wore of promise ...

While still a schoolboy, Samuel Taylor Coleridge celebrated in verse the storming of the Bastille; while still an undergraduate, Robert Southey wrote the revolutionary drama, *Wat Tyler*, that was to be published without his permission, and to his embarrassment, some twenty-three years later when he was Poet Laureate and a confirmed Tory. Though all slightly younger than the three 'Lake' poets, William Hazlitt, Henry Crabb Robinson, and Walter Savage Landor were old enough to experience in differing degrees the mood of elation and optimism of the brief period inaugurated in 1789.

Of the principal British politicians, Pitt, the conservative Prime Minister, took the French changes coolly at first. His leading opponent, Charles James Fox, rejoiced at the fall of the Bastille: 'How much the greatest event it is that ever happened in the world, and how much the best!' His belief in freedom was strong, but he was no extremist. Opposed alike to absolute monarchy, absolute aristocracy, and absolute democracy, he favoured a mixed and balanced constitution. In England he was willing to remedy the grievances of the Dissenters, and to reform the system of Parliamentary representation, but as a sound, liberal-minded Whig and not as a Radical. Burke, however, parted company with his old friend Fox and denounced the revolutionaries for having repudiated tradition in their devotion to abstract political theorizing. He predicted bloodshed, war, and tyranny.

His eloquent *Reflections on the Revolution in France* provoked many retorts. Mary Wollstonecraft's emotional *Vindication of the Rights of Men* (1790) reached the public first, but Paine's simple, shrewd, and vigorous *Rights of Man* was the most influential. William Godwin in *Political Justice* (1793) stood on the same side of the question as Paine and shared with him an optimistic confidence in the almost unlimited power of reason to promote human well-being. Godwin's name became one that nearly twenty years later could still excite 'feelings of reverence and admiration' in the young rebel Percy Bysshe Shelley.

Meanwhile the agitation for Reform was regaining strength. In the spring of 1792, the Constitutional Society began to revive, John Horne

Tooke being among its most active members. In the same season, the advanced 'Foxite' Whigs, though without Fox himself, started a moderate Society of Friends of the People. But more notable than either of these was the London Corresponding Society, a penny-a-week workingmen's Reform club founded in January 1792. Its secretary, a shoemaker named Thomas Hardy, corresponded with similar bodies in Manchester, Norwich, Sheffield, Stockport, and other centres. Horne Tooke gave considerable help. Members of the Society, and of others like it, held that a reformed Parliament would redress the economic grievances that were inevitably a main concern with them. For the first time, Englishmen of the lower-middle and working class were becoming an organized and responsible political force.

If Burke heralded the reaction against the French Revolution, the first practical demonstration of that reaction occurred in Birmingham. There as elsewhere, Dissent commonly went along with a commitment to Reform. On the night of 14 July 1791, a well-schooled 'Church and King' mob burned down the houses and meeting-places of Dissenters, including the laboratory and home of the eminent scientist and Unitarian minister, Joseph Priestley. On the following day the rioters opened the gaols, and only on the day after that did the local magistrates remonstrate against their destruction of property. Two days later still, a military force arrived from London, and the terror stopped. While deploring the disorder, George III learned with pleasure that Priestley had been a victim. Before long, Priestley was to emigrate to America.

The Birmingham outbreak was only one, though distinctly the worst, of many; and the ruling classes evidently regarded with some approval the political prejudices of the rioters. The authorities began to put pressure on tavern-keepers to refuse hospitality to the Reform clubs and increased the number of spies on their pay-roll. Prosecutions started. Paine was accused of seditious libel and, prompted perhaps by Blake, fled to France in September 1792. From Paris, he wrote to the Attorney-General, asking: 'Is it possible that you or I can believe, or that reason can make any other man believe, that the capacity of such a man as Mr. Guelph [that is, George III], or any of his profligate sons, is necessary to the government of a nation?' This was merely one incident in a widespread official heresy-hunt.

These developments in England came in response to developments in France. In June 1791 Louis XVI tried to fly from his country but was detained by its people. In 1792 some of his fellow-monarchs sent interventionist armies to his assistance. The French deposed him and, when the allies penetrated into their territory, made the National Convention their supreme governing body and proclaimed the Republic. Under the menace of the allied advance, there occurred the notorious September massacres, which claimed some 1,200 victims in Paris. Early in the new year Louis was beheaded. Already there seemed reason to suspect that France intended to impose republicanism on others by force, and on 1 February 1793 she declared war on England. The Reign of Terror developed during the summer of 1793 and lasted until the fall of Robespierre in July 1794; during the year perhaps 40,000 persons were killed in France. Meanwhile, the Revolutionary armies were scoring remarkable successes against the allies.

Humane Englishmen were appalled by the massacres and the Reign of Terror, and many of them lost the sympathy they had originally felt for the Revolutionary cause. In addition, patriotism and royalist sentiment helped to revive the old animosity towards the French. Animosity towards the Reform clubs was a natural corollary. Some of these had been in correspondence with the French and had sent congratulatory addresses to the Assembly or the Convention or the extremist Jacobin Society; their representatives had looked forward to an English National Convention. No particular government action was required to excite popular hostility against them.

There were trials of supposedly disaffected persons, and harsh sentences of transportation. The Scottish trials over which Lord Braxfield presided were the most sensational. He would even go so far as to charge a jury to note 'that the British Constitution is the best that ever was since the creation of the world, and it is not possible to make it better'. 'God help the people who have such judges!' observed Fox. Braxfield's might be regarded as the true voice of the conservative reaction of these years, a reaction springing from fear of the working class, dislike of the French, and a deep satisfaction with the existing state of things.

In May 1793 the House of Commons once again refused to consider Reform, this time by a larger majority than on any of the last three occasions. Late in the year, delegates from the London Corresponding Society and other similar bodies attended the meetings of a British Convention in Edinburgh. The authorities speedily brought these to a close, and a second series of Scottish trials followed, with a second series of harsh sentences.

Reform seemed dead once more. Coleridge and Southey dreamed of emigrating to establish a primitive utopian community on the banks of the Susquehannah. But Pantisocracy, as they called it, could never have satisfied the more realistic Wordsworth. Though disquieted by the Jacobin terror in France, by the anti-Jacobin drive at home, and by the war between his own country and France, he was discussing with a friend the starting of a Radical monthly paper. Of the clubs, some gave up the struggle, while others, notably those in London and Sheffield, fought on. The Corresponding Society and the Constitutional Society began to draw together, and there was talk of calling another Convention. In Sheffield, arms were being manufactured. Then the government struck.

In May 1794 the Habeas Corpus Act was suspended and thirteen members of the two London societies, including Thomas Hardy and Horne Tooke, were arrested and eventually indicted for high treason. The trials came on in the autumn, and amid intense public feeling the prisoners were found not guilty. This seems to have been a just verdict. While a few of the leaders may have played with the idea of resorting to violence, the overwhelming majority of them were no more than zealous reformers trying to influence Parliament by mobilizing popular opinion.

Despite their happy endings, the trials disheartened the reformers, and especially those from the higher social classes. The Constitutional Society and the Friends of the People faded out. The Corresponding Society carried on for another five years, while the government, which had grounds for fearing rebellion in Ireland and invasion by the French, enacted a whole series of coercive measures.

The year in which it eventually suppressed the Corresponding Society by name, 1799, saw also the beginning of the consulate of Napoleon Bonaparte. The emergence of an aggressive military dictatorship across the Channel strengthened anti-Reform feeling in England and increased popular support for the government's repression of what were considered revolutionary tendencies. This support was further augmented by Napoleon's elevation to the Imperial throne in 1804, and his elaborate preparations for the invasion of England. The overwhelming majority of Englishmen seem to have been animated for a time partly by fear of subversion, whether originating in France or at home, and partly by pride in the stability of their own society and its institutions. These, they felt, had successfully weathered the storm that had devastated France.

Such attitudes, widely shared throughout the country, kept conservative governments in power almost uninterruptedly throughout

Byron's lifetime and for some years after his death. These governments staunchly resisted all political innovation, they equipped themselves to coerce those whom they suspected of promoting it, and they employed spies to direct their suspicions. Wordsworth and Coleridge, for example, while in Somerset planning their joint publication *Lyrical Ballads* (1798), became the subject of a confidential report on 'a mischievous gang of disaffected Englishmen' submitted by one of the secret agents.

The advanced 'Foxite' Whigs still declared for a cautious Reform. But they distrusted and denounced the Radicals; and the orthodox Whigs were too conservative to support them. As a result, they and their successors remained politically ineffective until the Reform agitation became really powerful around 1830.

The Tories had it nearly all their own way. Even the Wesleyan and Evangelical religious revival, though in itself a movement seeking simply to promote a moral and spiritual reawakening, tended to their advantage. It canalized a good deal of working-class feeling and turned it away from politics. The robust William Cobbett noted this fact with some indignation and in 1830 denounced all schemes 'for the purpose of *amusing* the working classes, and *diverting their attention from the cause of their poverty and misery*. The methodist parsons are the most *efficient* tools in this way. They flatly assert, that when a man's dinner is taken away by the tax-gatherer, it is *for his good*, and that he ought to bless God for it. The vagabonds are fat and sleek enough themselves, in the mean while.' Moreover, many Radicals and advanced Whigs were free-thinkers. As a result, devout Evangelicals became readier to associate themselves with the alternative party. William Wilberforce, for example, the great opponent of slavery, was an Evangelical and a Tory.

Despite the general swing towards conservatism, illustrated in the lives of Wordsworth, Coleridge, and Southey among many others, the Reform movement began to revive from about 1806 onwards. Cobbett became its leading journalist, Henry Hunt its leading orator. The shrewd Samuel Whitbread, described by Byron as 'the Demosthenes of bad taste and vulgar vehemence, but strong and English' in his oratory ('Detached Thoughts', 5), brought it back into practical politics in 1809. Three years later, aristocratic sympathizers founded the Hampden Club, and Byron became a member. But the movement became really strong only after the defeat of Napoleon at Waterloo in 1815 had brought the long-drawn-out hostilities to a close, and a postwar slump had caused grave hardship to vast numbers of the people.

Early Regency England

It could be argued that economic developments in Britain during the twenty-two years of war were more truly revolutionary than were the political developments in France that precipitated the struggle. This is no place to describe in any detail matters of which Byron had apparently little knowledge and no first-hand experience. In general, it may be said that the industrial exploitation of new inventions facilitated an expansion of production and of trade that led at once to rapid urban growth and in the long run to a predominance of industry over agriculture.

Industrialization brought material benefits for many, and it promised more of them for all. But there were grave drawbacks. The regimentation of labour that goes with factory life could provoke a violent hostility towards the machines that made factory life possible. Moreover, at particular times and in particular places the introduction of new machines could threaten the very livelihood of those employed in an industry. Forbidden by law to organize themselves in trade unions for their protection, the workers were tempted in such circumstances to resort to illegal action.

Towards the end of 1811, economically the worst year of the war for Britain, outbreaks of organized machine-smashing occurred in Nottinghamshire. The trouble spread to Derbyshire, Leicestershire, Staffordshire, Lancashire, and Yorkshire. The government reacted by making such sabotage, and even the taking of a Luddite oath, punishable by death. In his maiden speech in the House of Lords in 1812, Byron resisted this. He emphasized the 'squalid wretchedness' of the working people, ascribed it to 'the destructive warfare of the last eighteen years', and denounced the bill as unjust, inefficient, and inhumane (*Letters and Journals*, ii, pp. 424–30). The Whigs welcomed him as a promising recruit.

Despite executions and transportations, Luddism outlasted the war and became one of many factors contributing to the social unrest of the first five years or so of peace. But Byron left England for the last time only ten months after Waterloo. The England he knew as an adult was the England of the years from 1811 to 1816, and it is this early Regency England that calls for the closest attention now.

George III lapsed into madness towards the end of 1810 and never recovered sufficiently to resume his duties as King. The Prince of Wales became Regent a few weeks later, and on his father's death in 1820 he succeeded to the throne as George IV.

The middle-aged aesthete who came to power in 1811 had a lively if shallow intelligence and considerable social gifts. At the same time, he was vain, idle, and self-indulgent. Leigh Hunt, poet and Radical journalist, went to gaol for describing him as 'a libertine over head and ears in debt and disgrace, a despiser of domestic ties, the companion of gamblers and demireps, a man who has just closed half a century without one single claim on the gratitude of his country or the respect of posterity'.

But the Prince still retained for some – for 'Monk' Lewis, the terror novelist, for example – the charm that had once won him the regard of many. As a young man he had, like previous Hanoverian heirs, opposed the King. Politics as well as a fondness for similar amusements had made him Fox's companion, and when he became Regent the Foxites naturally expected him to favour them.

They were to be disappointed, The Prince had grown into agreement with the Tories. He thought the war ought to be fought with vigour, he was in no hurry about Catholic Emancipation, and he felt little enthusiasm for Reform. So the Whigs remained in opposition, convinced that their friend had betrayed them. Thomas Moore, the Irish poet, voiced their resentment in verse. The two opening stanzas of his 'King Crack and his Idols' are typical:

> King Crack was the best of all possible Kings
> (At least, so his Courtiers would swear to you gladly,)
> But Crack now and then would do het'rodox things,
> And, at last, took to worshipping *images* sadly.

> Some broken-down Idols, that long had been plac'd
> In his father's old *Cabinet*, pleas'd him so much,
> That he knelt down and worshipp'd, though – such was his taste! –
> They were monstrous to look at, and rotten to touch.

Nor did the poets in opposition spare his physical characteristics. In 'The Devil's Walk', Shelley commented upon his enormous corpulence:

For he is fat, – his waistcoat gay,
When strained upon a levee day,
   Scarce meets across his princely paunch;
And pantaloons are like half-moons
   Upon each brawny haunch.

The Whigs took an active revenge for his neglect of them by espousing the cause of his wife, Princess Caroline, whom he heartily detested. It was a far from immaculate cause. If he had been promiscuous, she had been indiscreet; if he was pampered and self-centred, she was loud and sluttish. Nevertheless, the Whigs gave her their somewhat interested backing, and Byron went along with them. This backing was extended to her unruly daughter, Princess Charlotte, whom the Whigs knew irreverently as 'the young'un' and who was the next in succession to the throne after her father. Princess Caroline had also the boisterous support of the populace, and her husband its contempt.

The country of which he was, so to speak, the acting constitutional monarch was still a mainly agricultural country, and it was still a country of wide though not insuperable class distinctions. Its turbulent and freedom-loving people responded to the leadership of a ruling class which knew how to inspire and evoke their obedience. The men of this class prided themselves on being gentlemen and received admiration for being gentlemen. As such, they placed a high valuation upon a personal honour that would have been sullied by a lie, an act of cowardice, or a failure to face the consequences of any of their deeds; and they recognized an obligation to behave with generosity. They might be Philistines, and they were often selfish. But they did take seriously the values which their code of honour existed to defend. A duel could follow an affront to a gentleman's honour. Pitt, Castlereagh, Canning, Wellington, and Peel all became involved in such encounters. Byron and Moore would probably have taken a shot at each other but for an accidental failure in communications.

In their stately country houses, surrounded by their terraces, gardens, lawns, avenues, and parks, they lived a life which Byron presents mockingly in the final cantos of *Don Juan* but which a popular twentieth-century historian, Arthur Bryant, records in more favourable terms. 'The gentlemen hunted, raced, shot, fished, read, played at billiards, cards and *écarté*, looked after their estates, sat on the Bench, and rode, danced and joined in charades with the ladies; the latter gossiped, sketched, made scrapbooks, embroidered stools, looked at engravings, walked in the gardens and inspected the greenhouses, played with their children in the nursery wings, devoured the novels of Walter Scott or Lady Morgan, constantly dressed and redressed, and displayed their elegant accomplishments to the gentlemen.' They were attended by an army of servants.

Since egalitarian notions had not yet penetrated far, masters remained masters, and servants servants. But their relationship was a personal one, and there were many activities in which both happily shared. Sporting activities were prominent among these. Hunting, for example, provided rôles for both, and on the cricket field the sole superiority was that established by greater skill.

The country was rich. Despite periods of economic peril, such as that already mentioned as having occurred around 1811, it was emerging from the war richer than it had entered it. Trade had expanded, industry had grown, farming had flourished. The hard work of a rapidly growing population – about thirteen millions by 1815, five millions more than in the seventeen-eighties – was achieving extraordinary results. These seemed even more extraordinary when compared with the results on the Continent of the long wasteful period of war.

The more affluent classes aspired to elegance in their dress, their furniture, their conveyances, their gardens, and their buildings. In all things the fashionable Regency style was graceful and just a little showy. The dandies were its most skilful exponents, and G. B. Brummell, the famous Beau, was the chief of the dandies. No mere fop, he dressed with exquisite propriety and scrupulous cleanliness. Aesthete and bantering wit, accomplished dancer and singer, and inveterate gambler, he was at the height of his prosperity during Byron's years in England. Friendship with the Prince Regent gave him, like other dandies, an influential position in society. Lady Hester Stanhope left a vivid record of his appearance 'riding in Bond Street, with his bridle between his fore-finger and thumb, as if he held a pinch of snuff'. Expressing a fondness for the dandies, Byron observed: 'they were always very civil to *me*, though in general they disliked literary people' ('Detached Thoughts', 29).

The social life of these men, and of the great ladies who gave the balls and routs in London's West End during the season, was glittering and extravagant. It could also be narrow and snobbish. Vulgarity was often closely attendant upon even the most elegant Regency achievements.

High society shone most brilliantly during 'the summer of the sovereigns', 1814. Napoleon had just been overthrown for the first time, after the Russian, Prussian, and Austrian armies from the east, and the British army from across the Pyrénées, had successfully invaded France. In June, the Tsar of Russia and the King of Prussia arrived in London, accompanied by the Prussian Field Marshal von Blücher and the Chancellor of the Austrian Empire, Prince Metternich, among others. They dined in splendour at Carlton House with the Prince Regent. Three weeks of ceremony and pageantry followed, three weeks of balls, dinners, and visits to the Opera, to Hyde Park, and to Ascot. Byron sympathized with Napoleon rather than with these representatives of the old régimes. Nevertheless, he threw himself wholeheartedly into the festivities of this summer gala.

Few of those who attended the balls, masquerades, and routs knew much about the other Britain that the Industrial and Agrarian Revolutions were bringing into existence. Factory production in the growing towns of the Midlands and the North, and the larger-scale farming made possible by the enclosure of common land, were expanding the numbers and changing the nature of the urban and rural proletariats. Conditions in the growing towns – Manchester increased its population by 70 per cent in the first two decades of the century – were often nothing less than horrifying. Low-quality housing, inadequate drainage, excessive hours of work in unhealthy and dangerous conditions, and an absence of social amenities made for distressed and eventually resentful workers. The tyranny of individual bosses could aggravate these ills; surviving sets of factory rules seem to us today to be very harsh. Nor was life in the slums in the East End of London any better than life in the least savoury of the industrial areas.

The well-to-do were not all of them ignorant or forgetful of these things. The Wesleyan and Evangelical religious revival had among other effects that of strengthening humanitarian feeling generally. Action was taken not only to abolish the slave trade but also to alleviate domestic evils. Charitable persons visited the poor, provided them with comforts, and instructed their children in the Christian faith. They established Sunday schools, benefit societies, and soup and clothing clubs. They tried to reform prisoners and to protect children against undue exploitation in industry. When particular calamities occurred, they subscribed to the funds that were opened to mitigate them.

Nevertheless, the evils seemed still to grow. A post-war recession, which would in any case have been difficult to avoid, was turned into a disaster by the government's ill-judged economic and financial measures. Moreover, the harvest of 1816 was the worst in living memory. The consequent widespread and acute distress provoked Luddite and other riots to such an extent that Shelley, writing to Byron in Italy on 20 November 1816, declared:

> The whole fabric of society presents a most threatening aspect. What is most ominous of an approaching change is the strength which the popular party have suddenly acquired, and the importance which the violence of demagogues has assumed. But the people appear calm and steady even under situations of great excitement; and reform may come without revolution ... I earnestly hope that, without such an utter overthrow as should leave us the prey of anarchy, and give us illiterate demagogues for masters, a most radical reform of the institutions of England may result from the approaching contest.

For about five years, protest was urgent and reaction sharp. Mass meetings and demonstrations occurred. The so-called Blanketeers in 1817 set off to march from Manchester to London. The Habeas Corpus Act was suspended, and the leaders were imprisoned. Two years later, a crowd of between fifty and sixty thousand persons assembled to hear Henry Hunt in St Peter's Field, Manchester, and came into violent collision with the Lancashire Yeomanry. Nine men and two women were killed and many were injured, with the result that the encounter became known as the massacre of Peterloo. The government which had defeated the French revolutionaries was not going to succumb to English revolutionaries. It introduced the notorious Six Acts against arming and drilling, seditious meetings, and inflammatory political journals. With the failure of the wild Cato Street assassination plot against members of the Cabinet in the following year, 1820, the agitation subsided, to mount again in a more constitutional form ten years later.

There was a continuity between these later movements and those stimulated by the French Revolution in its first phase. Some of the new leaders were disciples of the old, and some of the old leaders reappeared; ideas and methods often corresponded closely with those of the Reform clubs of the seventeen-nineties. At the same time, conditions were changing. Increasing industrialization was bringing new troubles. While most men continued to think in terms of political remedies even for their economic ills, a few of them were beginning to look for economic remedies; and some of them were thinking that they might have to use physical force.

Nationalism: Italy and Greece

From the start of the twenty-two years' war, the advanced 'Foxite' Whigs had been less convinced of its necessity than were those composing the conservative governments that were almost uninterruptedly in power. The Terror did not make Fox withdraw his early praise of the Revolution; instead, he blamed the admitted evils of the French régime on the enmity of the more reactionary European powers. His disciple Charles Grey asserted in 1797 that the Revolution 'in the end ... would tend to the diffusion of liberty and rational knowledge all over the world'. Napoleon's career shook this faith in some and shattered it in others. From the time of the brief Peace of Amiens (1802–3), Grey conceded that the war was just and necessary.

In 1806, during the last few months of his life, Fox was Foreign Secretary. In the previous year, Austerlitz had made Napoleon master of Europe, but Trafalgar had destroyed his hopes of invading England. Fox negotiated to end hostilities. The insatiability of Napoleon's demands forced him to acknowledge that Grey was right. Nine years later, during the hundred days that preceded Waterloo, Grey himself and Whitbread were recommending the recognition and acceptance of the newly reinstated French Emperor, but they could not even carry with them all the members of their own group.

The dramatic spectacle of Napoleon's career dazzled many who were by no means wholly in sympathy with the political forces it represented – or misrepresented. Byron, an advanced Whig with certain limited Radical sympathies, assuredly felt its fascination. His attitude, as expressed in *Childe Harold's Pilgrimage*, III, was too ambivalent to satisfy a Bonapartist as fervent as Hazlitt, but it sufficed to sharpen Byron's own animosity towards two Tories who had contributed greatly to Napoleon's downfall: Viscount Castlereagh, Foreign Secretary from 1812 to 1822, and Arthur Wellesley, from 1814 Duke of Wellington, who had commanded the victorious British forces in the Peninsular campaign and at Waterloo.

Wellington combined aristocratic pride with a painstaking

professionalism as a soldier and ruthless honesty as a man. Byron saw him as the stiff-necked agent of European reaction. He believed Castlereagh to be one of the promoters of that reaction. Nor was he alone in this belief. Most Englishmen of his political complexion shared it, not least Shelley, who wrote in *The Mask of Anarchy*, after receiving news of Peterloo:

> I met Murder on the way –
> He had a mask like Castlereagh –
> Very smooth he looked, yet grim;
> Seven blood-hounds followed him.
>
> (ll. 5–8)

Undoubtedly, Castlereagh acquiesced in the restoration of the old régimes after 1815 in France, Italy, and elsewhere. On what except the principle of legitimacy could a sincere Tory hope to found a stable peace at that date? But Castlereagh was no extremist. The highly reactionary Holy Alliance of Russia, Austria, and Prussia excited his derision as 'this piece of sublime mysticism and nonsense'. He knew well the strength of the new democratic and nationalist faith (quoted by J. Steven Watson, p. 569):

> It is impossible not to believe a great moral change coming on in Europe, and that the principles of freedom are in full operation. The danger is that the transition may be too sudden to ripen into anything likely to make the world better or happier ... I am sure that it is better to retard than accelerate the operation of this most hazardous principle which is abroad.

By accelerating the operation, the French had inflicted on Europe a quarter-century of bloodshed, war, and tyranny. Castlereagh wished to retard it by adjusting the new faith and the old legitimacy to each other; he laboured to persuade the restored Louis XVIII to see himself as a constitutional monarch.

He differed sharply from the devious Austrian statesman, Metternich, with whom he found it expedient to associate himself at times while the peace treaty was being negotiated. Metternich offered an unqualified resistance to the new faith. Just as the Austrian Empire, with its Teutons, Czechs, Magyars, Italians, Serbs, Croats, and Poles, by its very existence denied the principle of nationalism, so its leading negotiator was prepared to re-define European frontiers without respect for it. Nor did his fellow-negotiators in Vienna regard it with anything like the favour that was to be shown to it at Versailles following the First World War.

As a result of their negotiations, the Austrian Empire expanded into Italy as far south as the river Po, the cities of Milan, Verona, and Venice thus coming into its possession. In 1817, the Piedmontese ambassador at St Petersburg described the resulting situation in a memorandum submitted to the Tsar:

> Austria, possessing the richest and most fertile regions of the peninsula, besides nearly a quarter of the total Italian population, and also holding sway over Tuscany, Parma, and Modena through princes of her ruling House, cuts Italy in half and is its actual mistress. On the one hand, by the re-establishment of the entire temporal domain of the Pope, two and a half millions of Italians have been plunged afresh into a state of absolute nullity, and the King of Naples, relegated to the end of the peninsula, has no longer any means of contributing to the defence of Italy; while on the other hand Austria threatens the King of Piedmont on his flank, pressing upon him with all her weight, and by merely calling up her garrisons in Lombardy could sweep down upon him, reach his capital in a couple of marches, and destroy his resources.

Nationalism was a growing force and was eventually to compel the unification of Italy. But it was still weak during these postwar years. Metternich himself observed sardonically to his Emperor in 1817: 'I have for some time been certain of the existence in Italy of several secret fraternities, which, under different names, foster a spirit of excitement, discontent, and opposition. ... In design and principle divided among themselves, these sects change every day and on the morrow may be ready to fight against one another. ... I believe ... that the surest method of preventing any of them from becoming too powerful is to leave these sects to themselves.' The most important of them was the Carboneria.

In 1820, elements of the Neapolitan army, in which the secret fraternities were especially strong, forced King Ferdinand to accept a constitution. Early in the following year, an Austrian force restored his absolute power. Elsewhere in Italy some of the more fervent and sanguine of the nationalists hoped that events in Naples would spark off a general rising. Byron, who had become a Carbonaro and had

23

determined to play an active part in any such rising, did not believe that it could succeed. At all events, it did not occur.

During this same period, there were related stirrings in Piedmont and in Spain. But more successful than any of the movements directed against régimes newly restored by the Congress of Vienna was the struggle in Greece against a Turkish domination that had lasted for centuries. The Greek War of Independence began on 25 March 1821 and ended in effect six-and-a-half years later when the British, French, and Russians destroyed the Turkish and Egyptian fleets at Navarino.

After a slow start, a number of groups in Britain began to organize assistance for the Greeks in their fight for freedom. In March 1823 a London Greek committee was established. Evangelicals, Dissenters, Whigs, and Benthamite Radicals became members. The elderly Jeremy Bentham himself brought his clear and incisive mind and blithe inexperience to its service, and one of his disciples became secretary. J. C. Hobhouse, who had accompanied Byron on much of his Mediterranean grand tour of 1809–11 and who was now a Member of Parliament, gave Byron the first notification that the committee meant to appeal to him to serve as its agent in Greece.

Meanwhile, it was raising funds. Eventually it collected well over £11,000. It spent £4,000 on war supplies; nearly £1,800 on such non-military items as medical supplies and printing-presses; £500 on a plan of Bentham's to educate eight Greek children in England; about £4,000 on advertising, freight and insurance fees, and the expense accounts of representatives in Greece; and almost £750 on 'sundry minor expenses'.

Byron never saw these accounts. If he had, he would surely have protested against the nature and size of some of the items. Even without seeing them, he had to warn the committee against sending articles that were completely useless to the Greek insurgents: mathematical instruments, for example, and trumpets. His well-informed realism constantly conflicted with the committee's high-minded progressivism, and this conflict became acute when a devoted Benthamite, Colonel Leicester Stanhope, was sent out to join him. Byron wished to talk about gunpowder and field guns, but Stanhope was more interested in education and the Press. Byron chose to support the moderate Greek leader, Alexander Mavrokordatos, but Stanhope favoured the unreliable Odysseus, who pleased him by voicing Radical views. The subsequent history of the struggle for Greek independence proved the correctness of Byron's judgment.

Conclusion

Of the matters surveyed here, Byron knew about some by hearsay, he had the opportunity of partially observing others, and he commented at one time or another upon most. But in relation to the Greek War of Independence he played a major part. This will receive attention later.

In two important general respects he bore the imprint of his epoch. First, he was a Regency aristocrat, for a time in his youth a dandy, and he retained to the end an affection for a style of life that he came to deride but never quite outgrew. Second, though too young to share the enthusiasm that many felt initially for the French Revolution, he was old enough to witness, and to react strongly against, the repressive policies at home and abroad that conservative governments adopted in their anger and fright at the course it took. A hater of war, which he could tolerate only when fought by a subject people against its oppressors – by the Spaniards against the Napoleonic armies, for example, or the Greeks against the Turks – and a downright opponent of every kind of despotism, political, religious, or moral, he was in many respects a representative Whig aristocrat with certain Radical sympathies, but, it must be said, with little sympathy with Radicals who had risen from the lower orders. This, however, is only the man in so far as he was a product of his age. Like everyone else, Byron must also be seen as a unique individual.

2

George Gordon, Lord Byron

Early Years

George Gordon Byron was the only child of an unstable union. His father, a gay and extravagant Guards officer, married twice, on each occasion securing an heiress. The first wife bore him three children, of whom only Augusta survived infancy. The second became the mother of the poet. The small fortune which Catherine Gordon brought Captain Byron lasted him about twelve months.

She was a highly emotional Scotswoman of sadly little charm or intelligence. Her attitude towards her husband fluctuated, often for good enough cause, between violent affection and violent rage. In 1790, after five years of marriage, the son being then two years old, the couple separated for the last time. Captain Byron died in the following year.

Until 1798, Mrs Byron and her son lived in Aberdeen in financially cramped gentility. Her pride, her toughness, and her devotion to George enabled her successfully to adapt her life to its changed circumstances. The small boy's nurse, Agnes Gray, and his Presbyterian tutors introduced him to the fascinating and horrifying Calvinist notions of innate evil and predestined damnation. But to his acquaintances at school he seemed a very normal youngster, friendly and spirited, generous and passionate, resentful and plucky. In his eighth year, he was utterly in love with Mary Duff, a distant cousin of his own age; about the same time, he had a memorable holiday in the Scottish highlands; and in his eleventh year, on the death of his great-uncle, the misanthropic old 'Wicked Lord', he became the sixth Baron Byron of Rochdale.

He and his mother then moved to England. They sampled life at Newstead Abbey, the family seat near Nottingham. But before long they let the house and estate for the period of Byron's minority, while he began to receive at Harrow the education that was intended to fit him for his eventual adult responsibilities. After an unhappy start, he came to regard Harrow with affection, not least because it was the scene of a number of those protective friendships with younger and dependent persons that were to remain so important to him.

During the summer vacation of 1803, he fell deeply in love with Mary Chaworth of Annesley Hall, near Newstead. Two years his senior, and already engaged to be married, she became for him, like Mary Duff and Margaret Parker before her, a representative of an ideal, unattainable love. He had been twelve when he had experienced his passion for his cousin Margaret Parker. Earlier than this, May Gray, the sister of and successor to his Aberdeen nurse Agnes Gray, had provoked in him a premature sexual awakening. For most of his life he was to find difficulty in reconciling the ideal with the reality of sexual love, and he was to suggest that this difficulty underlay his recurrent melancholy.

Mrs Byron had taken a house in Southwell, near Nottingham. Her son found the place dull and did all he could to avoid spending his school holidays there. Things improved a little when he met the Pigots and other Southwell families. But his relations with his mother, never easy, were growing more and more unhappy. Though genuinely fond of him, she was emotionally unbalanced and alternated between indulging him and abusing him. Her abuse could be so coarse and so violent that during his last year at Harrow he wrote to his half-sister Augusta (23 April 1805):

> I assure you upon my *honour*, jesting apart, I have never been so *scurrilously*, and *violently* abused by any person, as by that woman, whom I think I am to call mother. . . . Within one little hour, I have not only heard myself, but have heard my *whole family*, by the father's side, *stigmatized* in terms that the *blackest malevolence* would perhaps shrink from, and that too in words you would be shocked to hear. Such, Augusta, such is my mother; *my mother!* I disclaim her from this time.

Shortly before attaining his majority, he was to tell Augusta: 'I never can forgive that woman, or breathe in comfort under the same roof' (30 November 1808). As he lost sympathy with his mother, he drew closer to his half-sister.

At Trinity College, Cambridge, which he entered in October 1805 –

27

the month of Trafalgar – Byron formed a romantic attachment to John Edleston, a choirboy. Living extravagantly, he began to accumulate the burden of debt that in time was almost to cripple him. In the summer of 1806, lack of ready money drove him back at last to that 'execrable Kennel' (26 February 1806), Southwell, and in November he had a small volume of his poems privately printed under the title Fugitive Pieces in the near-by town of Newark. A protest from a friendly clergyman alerted him to the likelihood that people would think some of his verses scandalous. Having recalled and destroyed all but four copies of the book, he had a revised collection printed under the title Poems on Various Occasions in January 1807. Like its predecessor, this volume carried no indication of authorship.

Almost simultaneously with his publication in his own name of a volume of poems, Hours of Idleness (1807), that derived in part from these two private collections, he found himself in a position to return to Cambridge. His acquaintances there must have been surprised to find him much slimmer than when he had left. He had begun to fight his congenital tendency to fatness and had formed habits of strenuous dieting and exercise that he was to maintain on the whole for the rest of his life. Some of his university acquaintances now became intimate friends. Important among these was the level-headed and candid John Cam Hobhouse. He and Byron both inclined to liberalism in politics, and both became members of the Cambridge Whig Club. But at this time their literary interests united them more closely. Byron was doing little about his formal studies but was writing hard. His love of mischief remained strong. Asked why he had lodged a tame bear above his rooms in Trinity, he replied that he meant him to sit for a fellowship.

A scornfully dismissive notice of Hours of Idleness in the great Whig quarterly, the Edinburgh Review, had the initial effect of depressing him and perhaps of driving him more deeply into exhausting dissipations. But anger quickly conquered depression and he sought revenge in English Bards, and Scotch Reviewers, a verse satire in the manner of Pope and, more immediately, of William Gifford. He published this anonymously in March 1809, the month in which he took his seat in the House of Lords.

On 2 July 1809, he sailed from Falmouth on his grand tour. 'The world is all before me,' he wrote to his mother, 'and I leave England without regret, and without a wish to revisit any thing it contains, except yourself, and your present residence [Newstead]' (22 June 1809). In making the first of these exceptions he must have felt serious reservations which it would have been unkind to mention in such a letter. But he was wholehearted in making the second. Since the relinquishment of Newstead by the tenant who had rented it during his minority, he had spent some time there, and the love he had felt for it as a boy had revived in great strength.

The Grand Tour

During the eighteenth century, the grand tour of Holland, Germany, Italy, and France had formed part of the normal education of young Englishmen of good family. In 1809 the regions usually visited were all either in the French Empire or in states dependent upon the French Empire; they were therefore closed to British travellers. But at sea there was no danger from the French sufficiently great to deter Byron from embarking upon a Mediterranean tour.

Accompanied by his Cambridge friend Hobhouse, he visited Portugal and Spain, currently the scene of Wellington's masterly Peninsular campaign and of the Spanish partisans' ferocious resistance to the French. Near Cádiz, a bullfight disgusted both young men by its brutality. Sailing from Gibraltar nearly six weeks after their arrival at Lisbon, they stepped ashore in Sardinia and in Sicily and had a short stay in Malta. There Byron and the charming Mrs Constance Spencer Smith fascinated each other. Though nothing came of the affair, probably Byron's first with a woman of his own social class, it very nearly caused a duel between him and one of the British officers on the island.

In mid-September the young men left for the nearer parts of the Ottoman Empire. They were very handsomely received by Ali Pasha, who had made himself absolute ruler both of Albania and of what is now western Greece as far south as the Gulf of Corinth. Byron seems not to have guessed that this hospitality was partly motivated by a wish to secure British co-operation against the French in the neighbouring islands. To meet Ali, they had to travel far into the interior, and Byron was deeply impressed by what he saw. The mountains reminded him of the Scottish highlands, and the people won his admiration by their colourfulness and their wildness. The cruel and cunning Ali treated his visitors with dignified amiability. Did this perhaps qualify him to serve in due course as a model for the noble villains of some of Byron's narrative poems?

On Christmas Day 1809, the young men reached Athens, after

journeying through a countryside rich in associations for anyone who had received a classical education. Towards the end of *English Bards, and Scotch Reviewers,* Byron had scoffed at the Elgin marbles. Now that he saw the Parthenon, from which they had been removed, he felt as keenly as could any Greek patriot that a desecration had been committed. He was becoming deeply attached to Greece. Life there was congenial to him, and in Theresa Macri, the 'Maid of Athens' of his poem, he found a new representative of ideal love. He felt a genuine regret when on 5 March 1810 he embarked for Smyrna.

After a month there, during which he visited the site of Ephesus, he sailed for Constantinople. While the ship lay at anchor awaiting a favourable wind for passing the Dardanelles, Byron and one of the naval lieutenants succeeded in swimming the Hellespont. He was inordinately proud of having thus emulated Leander, the lover of Hero, and wrote of the achievement several times, both in prose and in verse. In the previous year, shortly after arriving at Lisbon, he had swum the Tagus; and eight years later he was to triumph in a strenuous swimming contest in Venice. In this particular athletic pursuit, he was not handicapped by the clubbed right foot with which he had been born, which he felt as a bitter humiliation, and with which his mother could not refrain from taunting him when in one of her rages. Nevertheless, swimming was not the only sport he cultivated. He had played cricket for Harrow against Eton in 1805. Both before and after his grand tour, 'Gentleman' John Jackson, the ex-champion, tutored him in boxing. He rode, fenced, and shot – though from 1809 he was reluctant to shoot birds and preferred to restrict his aim to inanimate targets.

At last the wind changed, and on 14 May the young men were able to land in Constantinople. Towards the end of their two months' stay, they were present when the retiring British ambassador had his final audience with the Sultan, Mahmoud II. Byron thus came briefly into the presence of the sovereign against whom at the time of his death he would be planning to take military action.

Back in Greece, Byron and Hobhouse separated. Hobhouse, the more methodical tourist, had been the less ready to adapt himself to the squalor and discomfort that they had often had to endure in the course of their twelve months' travels. Byron, idly absorbing impressions of the picturesque and human aspects of the regions they visited, had put up with the hardships uncomplainingly. Their association had been generally harmonious, however, and their parting was amicable. Hobhouse returned to England, Byron lingered in Greece.

Relieved of Hobhouse's restraining influence, Byron gave himself up more completely to a life of pleasure. As always, he enjoyed the company of young boys – Nicolo Giraud was an especial favourite – and it may well have been during this period that the fondness first took an overtly sexual form. But he had adventures of another kind, too. By threatening or bribing an official, he rescued a Turkish girl who was to have been drowned for a sexual irregularity. Byron already knew the girl but never said how well. The incident was to provide the starting-point for *The Giaour*, the most compelling of his Turkish tales.

After nine months spent mainly in Athens, he sailed for home on 22 April 1811. The city had a firm place in his affections (*Childe Harold's Pilgrimage*, II. lxxiii, *note*):

> Setting aside the magic of the name, and all those associations which it would be pedantic and superfluous to recapitulate, the very situation of Athens would render it the favourite of all who have eyes for art or nature. The climate, to me at least, appeared a perpetual spring; during eight months I never passed a day without being as many hours on horseback: rain is extremely rare, snow never lies in the plains, and a cloudy day is an agreeable rarity.

Ill-health and depression aggravated the inevitable tedium of the voyage. He set foot once more in England on 14 July 1811, having been absent for just over two years.

Fame

Within three weeks of his arrival, and before he had revisited Newstead, Mrs Byron died. Though he can have felt little love or respect for her, he was deeply shocked: she was, after all, his mother, and intimately bound up with his earliest recollections. The shock was augmented by the almost simultaneous news of the accidental death by drowning of one of the liveliest of his Cambridge friends; and before long he learned of the death of one of his Harrow schoolfellows. But a severer blow than any of these was the death of Edleston, whom he had loved deeply ever since first seeing him as a Trinity choirboy. In *Childe Harold's Pilgrimage*, II, and in the 'Thyrza' poems, he voiced his agonized sense of loss.

An unfought duel provides welcome light relief. In 1809, Thomas Moore, the Irish lyrist, had believed himself insulted by a passage in *English Bards, and Scotch Reviewers* and had sent Byron a challenge which arrived after his departure for Portugal and was not forwarded to him. In the autumn of 1811, the two men had to resort to elaborate epistolary manoeuvres in order to extricate themselves from their somewhat stale predicament in accordance with the code of honour. The outcome was happy: Moore and Byron became close friends. Through the Irishman, Byron met two more of the fashionable poets whom he admired, Samuel Rogers and Thomas Campbell.

Meanwhile, John Murray, the publisher, was preparing to issue the long poem, *Childe Harold's Pilgrimage*, I and II, which the grand tour had elicited from Byron. Murray felt uneasy about some of the theological and political attitudes it expressed, and the poet was resisting requests for significant changes. Publication came in March 1812, following closely on Byron's maiden speech in the House of Lords. The poem was an immediate success and made its author a doubly welcome guest of the Whig aristocrats, with whose parliamentary opposition to the Tory government he had associated himself. Within a few weeks, the Duchess of Devonshire was writing to her son in America:

> The subject of conversation, of curiosity, of enthusiasm almost, one might say, of the moment is not Spain or Portugal, Warriors or Patriots, but Lord Byron! . . . [*Childe Harold's Pilgrimage*] is on every table, and himself courted, visited, flattered, and praised whenever he appears. He has a pale, sickly, but handsome countenance, a bad figure, animated and amusing conversation, and, in short, he is really the only topic almost of conversation – the men jealous of him, the women of each other.

The chief of the dandies, Beau Brummell, regarded him with favour. The Prince Regent asked to see him and by his social charm and his feeling for literature temporarily overcame the poet's Whig recalcitrance.

At Holland House, one of the principal Whig mansions, Byron met the sensitive, impulsive, and unstable Lady Caroline Lamb. A stormy love-affair followed. To Caroline Lamb there succeeded, in the autumn of 1812, the mature and worldly Lady Oxford. By this time, Byron's parliamentary enthusiasm was evaporating. Since speaking in April in favour of Catholic Emancipation, he had lost interest. Lady Oxford, a pupil of Horne Tooke, encouraged him to a more frequent attendance early in 1813, but he found the sessions dull. He was happier visiting the Radical Leigh Hunt in the gaol to which he had been sent for libelling the Prince Regent. Nevertheless, Byron made a third and last parliamentary speech in the summer of 1813, perhaps at the renewed prompting of Lady Oxford. This time the subject was, indirectly, the explosive one of Reform.

Shortly after this speech the Oxfords set out on a foreign tour, and Byron began to see a good deal of the half-sister whom he had not met for some years. Their blood-relationship helped them to a relaxed understanding of each other; Augusta was in any case an affectionate and undemanding person. They appear to have become lovers. If so, she may well have acted out of simple amoral fondness for her brother, but his attitude must assuredly have been more complex. He would have been painfully aware of the possible catastrophic social conse-quences of their liaison, and in his more dejected moods he would have seen his actions as proceeding from that innate depravity which Calvinist tutors had taught him long ago to relate to predestined damnation. An inconclusive flirtation with Lady Frances Wedderburn Webster provided a distraction during the autumn of 1813, but he then lapsed, as so often, into boredom, indecision, and gloom. As on previous occasions when his sexual entanglements had seemed intoler-able, he thought of solving his problems by marriage or escaping them foreign travel.

Nevertheless, he and Augusta had a very happy period together early in 1814 at Newstead, which he had reluctantly agreed to sell in order to meet his debts but which was still in his possession. He then sought distraction in general society; in the theatre, where the passion-ate and energetic acting of Edmund Kean had no more fervent admirer; and in the festivities of 'the summer of the sovereigns'. Eventually he decided that he could regularize his life only by marriage.

For some time he had known Annabella Milbanke as a high-minded and demure young woman. He had proposed marriage to her in the early autumn of 1812 when desperately looking for a way out of his 'scrape' with Caroline Lamb. No doubt her refusal had piqued him; and he proposed to her again in September 1814 when looking for a way out of a more serious 'scrape', presumably with Augusta Leigh. This time she accepted him.

Byron was an unlikely candidate for matrimony. He had always thought it an absurd and humiliating state for a man. 'All my coupled

33

contemporaries', he had scoffed, halfway between his two proposals, 'are bald and discontented' ('Journal', 14 November 1813). The opening words of the letter in which he told Moore of his engagement show him very much on the defensive: 'I am going to be married – that is, I am accepted, and one usually hopes the rest will follow' (20 September 1814). Given his settled aversion to the married state, and his dubious motives for entering it, his black and savage moods as a husband can excite little surprise, especially in view of the facts that his financial affairs were in seemingly hopeless confusion and that he was drinking heavily. But they terrified Annabella, and in January 1816, twelve months after their wedding and one month after the birth of their daughter, she left him. Byron, not realizing how intolerable his conduct had been, and no doubt remembering mainly their happier moments together, was genuinely surprised.

A wife with a lighter and more humorous touch than Annabella's, a woman more like Augusta, might have preserved harmony by laughing him out of his dark moods and melodramatic postures. Annabella was incapable of this. The only child of middle-aged parents, she was intellectual, earnest, complacent, and humourless. She saw herself in a missionary rôle when she decided to marry the notorious author of *Childe Harold's Pilgrimage* and the subsequent Turkish tales. A good Victorian ahead of time, she was eager to inspire and reform a reckless eighteenth-century aristocrat who happened to be also a man of genius. Inevitably, she irritated and oppressed him.

Having left him, and having satisfied herself that his conduct had not been caused by mental illness, Annabella insisted upon a total separation. Was this because she had received confirmation of a slowly forming suspicion as to the nature of his relationship with Augusta? Or was it because he had initiated her in sexual practices which she had only recently learned were unlawful? There is strong evidence in support of the first of these explanations, though not enough to establish it conclusively. With regard to the second, it is pertinent to ask how anyone can be very positive about what went on in the Byrons' bed. But even without either explanation we should have no difficulty in accounting for the eventual collapse of this impossible marriage.

Byron's contrasting moods of despondency and cheerfulness seem to have been even more marked than usual during this time. On the one hand, he could reproach his wife for not agreeing to marry him when he first proposed and so helping him to avoid some dreadful undefined offence into which he had subsequently fallen. On the other hand, his acquaintances could think him high-spirited and companionable. He found pleasure in visiting Leigh Hunt, now released from prison, and in meeting Sir Walter Scott, with whom he quickly established a cordial friendship despite their standing at opposite political poles. He became an active member of the Sub-Committee of Management of Drury Lane Theatre.

Having rejoiced at Napoleon's escape from Elba, he regretted the outcome of Waterloo. His reception of the news was characteristic. An uncle of his wife's entered the room where he was receiving a visitor and said abruptly (L. A. Marchand, *Byron: A Biography*, p. 553):

'My lord, my lord, a great battle has been fought in the Low Countries, and Bonaparte is entirely defeated.'

'But is it true?' asked Byron, 'is it true?'

'Yes, my lord, it is certainly true; an aide-de-camp arrived in town last night. . . . He says he thinks Bonaparte is in full retreat towards Paris.'

After an instant's pause, Byron replied, 'I am damned sorry for it.' There was another brief pause. Then he added, 'I didn't know but I might live to see Lord Castlereagh's head on a pole. But I suppose I shan't, now.'

Byron's new writing during these years in England consisted mainly of the five Turkish tales: *The Giaour* (1813), *The Bride of Abydos* (1813), *The Corsair* (1814), *Lara* (1814), and *The Siege of Corinth* (1816). They greatly increased the fame that *Childe Harold's Pilgrimage*, I and II, had brought him in 1812. Six thousand copies of *The Bride of Abydos* were sold within a month of publication, ten thousand copies of *The Corsair* on the day of publication itself.

News of his separation from his wife for reasons apparently discreditable to him naturally provoked a considerable revulsion of public feeling. Hostility towards him was widespread, though less nearly universal than he later chose to believe. At a gathering at Lady Jersey's, he was cold-shouldered by some who would once have sought him out. Moreover, his financial embarrassments remained acute. In April 1816, he left England for the second and last time. Hobhouse, who saw him off at Dover, recorded in his diary:

the bustle kept B in spirits – but he looked affected when the packet glided off. I ran to the end of the wooden pier – and as the vessel toss'd by as through a rough sea & contrary wind saw him again – the dear fellow pulled off his cap & wav'd it to me – I gazed until I could not distinguish him any longer – God bless him for a gallant spirit and a kind one.

Exile

Byron left England by his own choice. His countrymen did not expel him; if he had enemies among them who were glad to see him go, he had also friends among them who regretted his going. Nor did he at first think of his departure as final. When the musician Isaac Nathan asked whether he really meant not to return, he expostulated, 'Good God! I never had it in contemplation to remain in exile – why do you ask that question?' Nevertheless, he was to stay in voluntary exile for the rest of his life.

He had little love for the society which, after fêting him in 1812, treated him so coolly in 1816. He detested what he thought its canting and hypocritical morality. The motive power in England today, he was to write nearly five years later (7 February 1821, *Letters and Journals*, v, p. 542),

> is *cant*; cant political, cant poetical, cant religious, cant moral; but always *cant*, multiplied through all the varieties of life. It is the fashion, and while it lasts will be too powerful for those who can only exist by taking the tone of the time. I say *cant*, because it is a thing of words, without the smallest influence upon human actions; the English being no wiser, no better, and much poorer, and more divided amongst themselves, as well as far less moral, than they were before the prevalence of this verbal decorum.

Byron sailed from Dover to Ostend and journeyed through the Low Countries. He visited the ground over which the battle of Waterloo had been fought less than a year previously. Having travelled up the Rhine to Switzerland, he settled for four months close to the lake of Geneva. Here a meeting with Shelley initiated a friendship that was of great importance to both poets.

Shelley was accompanied by his wife-to-be, Mary, daughter of William Godwin, and by a young woman, Mary Jane or 'Claire' Clairmont, who was the daughter by an earlier marriage of William Godwin's second wife. Without Shelley's knowledge, Claire Clairmont had already forced her acquaintance on Byron in England during the separation crisis. Despite his distaste for her feminism, they had become lovers and she was now pregnant by him. Their daughter

Allegra was to be born early in 1817 and to die at the age of five in the Italian convent where Byron would send her for her education.

With Shelley, Byron sailed on the Lake of Geneva and visited the places associated with Rousseau and Gibbon. Under Shelley's influence, he read Wordsworth more sympathetically than at any other time in his life and presumably found in his doctrine of nature something capable of alleviating the grief and bitterness caused by the breakdown of his marriage. Aided no doubt by what he read, he responded almost ecstatically to the Alpine scenery which he viewed on a short tour with Hobhouse, who had joined him towards the end of his stay in Switzerland. 'I have lately repeopled my mind with Nature', he wrote on 19 September 1816 in the journal which he kept during this tour. The statement is one that Byron can hardly be imagined as making during any other period.

Many of the things he saw turned his thoughts back to his own situation. On 23 September 1816, for example, he recorded: 'Passed *whole woods of withered pines, all withered*; trunks stripped and barkless, branches lifeless; done by a single winter, – their appearance reminded me of me and my family.' He intended this journal for Augusta. But Annabella was successfully urging on Augusta a greater reserve in her correspondence with Byron. The change of tone was to puzzle and distress him.

His recent travels across Europe and in Switzerland supplied much of the material for *Childe Harold's Pilgrimage*, III, and *The Prisoner of Chillon*, both published in 1816; the partial derivation of the dramatic poem, *Manfred* (1817), from his Alpine tour with Hobhouse can be demonstrated by comparison of the poem with the journal. All three publications enjoyed great success.

Before long, Byron and Hobhouse were on the move again. In Milan, during October 1816, Byron had his first opportunity of observing Austrian rule in Italy. He disliked what he saw, and in due course his dislike was noted by the secret police. In November, still accompanied by Hobhouse, he reached Venice. He had expected this fabulous city to please him, and he was not disappointed. Its beauty and decay, its gloom and gaiety, and its rich historical and literary associations, all appealed strongly to him. Early in December, Hobhouse left to continue his tour; but Byron chose to remain behind.

This was in part because he had fallen in love again, this time with Marianna Segati, the wife of the draper over whose shop he lodged.

37

Her charms, the delights of the Carnival, an attack of fever following the Carnival, and an unwillingness to serve as an object of interest for British tourists prevented him from joining Hobhouse in Rome until April 1817. After the two of them had spent three weeks there together, Hobhouse went on to Naples, while Byron returned to Venice and Marianna. Rome had delighted him 'beyond every thing, since Athens and Constantinople' (5 May 1817). *Childe Harold's Pilgrimage*, IV (1818), was to record his impressions of Italy, and especially of Rome.

He was finding life in Italy more and more congenial – and this at a time when Augusta's changed tone was making England seem less attractive than ever. At La Mira, a village near Venice where he decided to spend the summer of 1817, Hobhouse rejoined him. One evening when they were riding together, Byron made the acquaintance of Margarita Cogni, a baker's wife, who became his mistress. Her assurance and ferocity amused and delighted him: for example, when Marianna dared to threaten her, she retorted: '*You* are *not* his *wife*: *I* am *not* his *wife*: *you* are his *Donna*, and *I* am his *Donna*: *your* husband is a cuckold, and *mine* is another. For the rest, what *right* have you to reproach me? if he prefers what is mine to what is yours, is it my fault?' (1 August 1819). A further link with England was severed when his agent succeeded at last in selling Newstead.

Hobhouse left for home in January 1818, and Byron threw himself into the pleasures of that 'drama without the fiction' (6 February 1823, *Letters and Journals*, vi, p. 440), the Carnival. He met the Countess Teresa Guiccioli, married three days earlier to an ageing husband; but this first meeting did not make much impression upon either of them. A little later, he broke with Marianna and left his cramped lodgings over the draper's for the Palazzo Mocenigo on the Grand Canal, where he soon assembled no fewer than fourteen servants and a whole menagerie of animals. Margarita continued a favourite with him for some time, but at the end of the summer he could estimate that she was only one out of at least two hundred women whom he had known since his arrival in Venice. An acquaintance who saw him in November 1818 was shocked by his physical deterioration: 'Lord Byron could not have been more than 30, but he looked 40. His face had become pale, bloated, and sallow. He had grown very fat, his shoulders broad and round, and the knuckles of his hands were lost in fat.' Knowledge of his dissipations disturbed Shelley, who visited Venice several times during this period, and who on his first visit enjoyed with Byron the ride along the sands of the Lido commemorated in his *Julian and Maddalo.*

In 1819, Byron gave himself up once more to the pleasures of the Carnival. But by now he had almost had enough of them. A second meeting with Teresa Guiccioli, more than a year after the first, in-augurated what was to be his last attachment. A dozen years younger than himself, she was a cultivated aristocrat who combined a lively sense of fun with a deep-rooted sentimentalism. Her husband, nearly forty years her senior, was an intelligent and wealthy man whose political adaptability had been fully exercised during the revolutionary and counter-revolutionary periods. Teresa's father and brother, how-ever, were committed liberals and patriots and would before long be active among the Carbonari.

Byron became her *cavalier servente,* or sanctioned lover. A strict code governed his behaviour in this rôle, and the ludicrousness of his situation was not lost on him. 'I double a shawl with considerable alacrity,' he told Hobhouse, 'but have not yet arrived at the perfection of putting it on the right way; and I hand in and out, and know my post in a conversazione and theatre' (*Correspondence,* 3 March 1820). But, even while laughing at himself, he sensed that this would be his last adventure, and he said so. 'As to libertinism, I have sickened myself of that, as was natural in the way I went on, and I have at least derived that advantage from vice, to *love* in the better sense of the word' (2 July 1819).

To be near Teresa, he moved to Ravenna, and from there to Bologna. Her husband being otherwise engaged, he then escorted her to Venice and La Mira. There he was delighted to receive a visit from Moore, whom he always found the most affectionate, as he found Hobhouse the most frank and independent, of his close friends. He entrusted to Moore the prose Memoirs that Hobhouse and John Murray, the publisher, were to override Moore in burning after Byron's death, out of a regard for his reputation.

When Count Guiccioli led a reluctant Teresa back to Ravenna, Byron toyed with the idea of returning to England. But Teresa fell ill, and her father had her husband's support in summoning her lover. He arrived in Ravenna on Christmas Eve, 1819, and before long he had agreed to occupy the upper floor of the Guicciolis' palace. He settled into his favourite daily routine of sleeping until after mid-day, riding during the afternoon, passing the evening with Teresa at home or elsewhere, and writing into the early hours of the morning.

In May 1820, the hitherto complaisant husband became suddenly and unaccountably resentful. His conduct was such that Teresa's father felt entitled to apply to the Pope for a separation. This was granted, and Teresa returned to her father's house. Byron, remaining in the Palazzo Guiccioli, made his visits to her as discreetly as possible. Towards the end of the year, he sent Moore a continuation of his Memoirs.

Politically, too, it had been an eventful year. In England, the sub-sidence of the post-war unrest had begun but was not yet apparent. The authorities were still nervous. The House of Commons in 1820 took fright at a pamphlet by Hobhouse – a believer in Reform, but certainly no incendiary – and committed him to Newgate. Byron's aristocratic disdain for such demagogues among Hobhouse's fellow-reformers as Cobbett and Henry Hunt prevented him from sympathiz-ing fully with his friend's predicament. While he supported popular movements for the overthrow of tyranny and of foreign domination, he always assumed that the natural leaders of these liberal movements would be members of the enlightened gentry or aristocracy: men like George Washington, or Simón Bolívar, or himself. When leaders emerged from the middle or lower classes, he tended to think them blackguards.

His concern for the liberation of Italy began to flourish in the spring of 1820. Already notorious as a liberal and a freethinker, he had naturally attracted the attention of the Austrian and Papal authorities and their spies. But he gave them no serious cause for anxiety until the success of the Neapolitans in forcing their King to accept a constitution encouraged the liberal and patriotic movement throughout Italy. This found expression in the growth of such secret fraternities as the Carboneria. Count Ruggero Gamba and his son Pietro, Teresa's father and brother, were both Carbonari, and Byron, too, became a member.

He doubted whether the Italians had sufficient unity and consistency to achieve their aims. But he believed that they meant to make a fight of it, and he was ready to take up arms with them. Through the later months of 1820 and the first days of 1821, he awaited the summons ('Diary', 9 January 1821):

They mean to *insurrect* here, and are to honour me with a call thereupon. I shall not fall back; though I don't think them in force or heart sufficient to make much of it. But, *onward!* – it is now the time to act, and what signifies *self*, if a single spark of that which would be worthy of the past can be bequeathed unquenchedly to the future? It is not one man, nor a million, but the *spirit* of liberty which must be spread. The waves which dash upon the shore are, one by one, broken, but yet the *ocean* conquers, nevertheless.

But no call came, and the powers of the Holy Alliance – Austria, Prussia, and Russia – began to react. At the Congress of Troppau, they asserted their right to intervene in support of any government congenial to themselves that was threatened by internal revolution. Byron offered his services to the Neapolitan liberals in a letter that apparently went astray. Then, early in 1821, the Austrians crossed the Po and marched south. Byron expected that the Neapolitans would resist them and that the Carbonari would operate in their rear. But the Neapolitans collapsed, and the Carbonari did not move. The Austrians occupied Naples, and the constitution was repudiated.

At the height of the suspense, there occurred an incident that showed Byron in a characteristic light. An unknown assassin shot down the military commandant in the street outside the Palazzo Guiccioli. Byron made his servant and a couple of lookers-on carry the dying man into his apartment. 'Poor fellow!' he reflected, 'he was a brave officer, but had made himself much disliked by the people' (9 December 1820). Byron's susceptibility to humane rather than political considerations in this crisis displeased some of his fellow-Carbonari.

Another incident showed how much the local patriots nevertheless relied upon him. He had supplied them with arms at their request and at his own risk and expense. After the Austrians began their march, the government issued an order, backed by severe penalties, against the possession of concealed weapons. With some alacrity, the patriots restored the encumbrances to Byron.

The outbreak of the Greek War of Independence evoked little comment from him during this period of disappointment, despite the fact that Greek patriots had been in touch with him from time to time during his years in Italy. News of Napoleon's death merely deepened his dejection. Before the news arrived, the authorities had struck against him by exiling Ruggero and Pietro Gamba. Since the terms of the separation decree required Teresa to live with her father, and since Byron would predictably follow her, the government seems to have calculated that the banishment of the Gambas would rid the Papal

States of the subversive Englishman without the embarrassment of direct action.

Though the Gambas quickly found asylum in Tuscany, Byron's habitual dilatoriness caused him to linger in Ravenna. During a short stay there in August 1821, Shelley saw him for the first time for nearly three years and was pleased to note a great improvement in his health. Eventually, three months after Teresa's departure, he broke out of the melancholy that was settling on him in his loneliness and moved to Pisa. There, with the congenial companionship of the Gambas, the Shelleys, and others, he achieved a greater contentment than for some time past.

Though spies continued to watch him, they had little of interest to record. A visitor might briefly rekindle his zeal in the cause of Greek independence, but he was not yet ready to lend the movement his active support. He was giving politics a rest. This middle-aged quiescence was rudely challenged in March 1822 when a party including Shelley and himself, riding back into Pisa after pistol-practice in the neighbouring countryside, became involved in a foolish squabble with a Tuscan dragoon. Blows were exchanged, and the dragoon was seriously injured. Byron naturally felt some concern lest the authorities in Tuscany or the public in England should assume that he had provoked the trouble. Despite his efforts, the Tuscan government grew more suspicious both of him and of his friends, the Gambas.

In May 1822, he moved to a summer house at the seaside. This was near Leghorn, where the Mediterranean squadron of the American navy happened to be at anchor. An invitation to visit the *Constitution*, and a friendly welcome from its officers, pleased him greatly, and he voiced his republican sympathies by assuring Moore that he would rather have 'a nod from an American, than a snuff-box from an emperor' (8 June 1822). Shelley and he had already ordered boats to be built for themselves in Genoa, and during May and June they took possession of these. Byron proclaimed his liberalism by calling his the *Bolivar*.

The Tuscan government then adopted the tactics which had dislodged Byron from the Papal States; and, almost simultaneously with its decision to expel the Gambas, Leigh Hunt arrived from England with his family. He had come at the invitation of Shelley and Byron to join with them in editing a literary periodical. Despite a growing habit of economy, Byron treated the Hunts with some generosity. He had already sent money for their voyage, and he now placed at their disposal the ground floor of his Pisan residence, the Casa Lanfranchi, furnished for them at his own expense.

In July 1822, a few days after the Hunts' arrival, Shelley was drowned while sailing his newly built *Don Juan*. This calamity removed the one person in whose presence Byron and Hunt might have collaborated effectively and who might have given a clearly defined editorial policy to the projected periodical. Byron had long admired Hunt's political courage; he appreciated Hunt's amiability; but Hunt's attitude towards himself, at once fawning and demanding, irritated him. Moreover, Mrs Hunt's stuffy censoriousness, and the unchecked rowdiness of the six children, annoyed him further. Without Shelley to stimulate it, his interest in *The Liberal* flagged. Hunt was to get out only four numbers, the first in October 1822 and the last in July 1823.

In September 1822, Byron and the Hunts left Pisa for Genoa, where the Gambas had settled after their expulsion from Tuscany. Hobhouse spent a few days with Byron immediately before his departure. The spy Torelli noted in his diary:

> Lord Byron has finally decided to leave for Genoa. It is said that he is already sated or tired of his Favourite, the Guiccioli. He has, however, expressed his intention of not remaining in Genoa, but of going on to Athens in order to make himself adored by the Greeks.

Cynicism is part of a spy's stock-in-trade. Byron was still deeply fond of Teresa. But he was beginning to feel cramped in Italy.

His last Italian residence, the Casa Saluzzo, stood on a hill in Albaro overlooking the port of Genoa. Among his visitors during the eight months of his tenancy was 'the most gorgeous Lady Blessington'. She was touring with her husband and the young dandy, Count D'Orsay. During her nine weeks in Genoa she met Byron, by arrangement or by chance, on twenty-one occasions, according to her own reckoning. A result of these meetings was that she became the only woman to report Byron's conversation at great length.

They had certain interests in common. Lady Blessington had recently moved in very much the same masculine society in London as Byron had known seven years previously. Already an ardent admirer of *Childe Harold's Pilgrimage* and *Manfred*, and herself a writer, she shared in some degree the poet's literary tastes. Moreover, their past lives had been such as to subject both of them to hostile comment and ostracism by the exponents of the new respectability. They evidently found each other friendly and sympathetic, and their brief relationship even acquired a slightly romantic tinge.

He talked to her of friends and acquaintances, love and marriage, women, the English, the Italians, the craft of writing, fame, vanity, melancholy, and death. At once sardonic and exuberant, he was far from being the Harold or the Manfred whom she had been expecting. On the contrary, he was conspicuously the author of *Don Juan*.

This was his major literary achievement in the five years that were to conclude with his departure for Greece. *Beppo*, the light-hearted work in which he discovered for himself the possibilities of the *ottava rima* form, appeared in 1818. In the same year, he started *Don Juan*, also in *ottava rima*; sixteen cantos of it were published at various dates between 1819 and 1824. For almost a year from July 1821, he gave up writing *Don Juan* because Teresa objected to its moral tone. During this interval, however, he produced *The Vision of Judgment* in the same metrical form and style. Hunt printed this in the first number of *The Liberal*, which appeared on 15 October 1822.

Though generally regarded nowadays as Byron's masterpieces, these *ottava rima* poems do not by any means constitute the whole of his output from 1818 onwards. He wrote also a number of dramatic poems, *Marino Faliero*, *Sardanapalus*, *The Two Foscari*, and *Cain*, all published in 1821, being the most notable. The first three of these represent a deliberate repudiation of the extravagance of his early work. But they are in the most damaging sense academic. The *ottava rima* poems make the repudiation more effectively because less deliberately. During these years, Byron also completed a final romantic tale in verse, *The Island* (1823).

In April and May 1823, he was making up his mind to go to Greece. He did not at first dare to tell Teresa, and she, noticing his preoccupation, became unreasonably jealous of Lady Blessington. Eventually she learned the truth from her brother Pietro, an ardent youngster whose determination to accompany Byron seems even to have anticipated Byron's determination to go.

As well as his personal services, Byron resolved to make considerable funds available to the Greek insurgents. He was no longer the debtor who had left England in 1816. The sale of Newstead, his earnings as a writer, an inheritance, the low cost of living in Italy, and recently his own stringent economies had raised him to a level of affluence he had never known before. In addition to Pietro and himself, his party was to include the half-genuine and half-bogus adventurer, E. J. Trelawny, who had been a member of his Pisan circle and who had directed the cremation of the drowned Shelley on the sands near Viareggio. Its doctor was to be a rather timid young Italian, Francesco Bruno.

Greece

They embarked on the brig *Hercules* on 13 July 1823 but had to wait three days for weather conditions in which they could get clear of the port. Though Byron had now committed himself, his feelings remained ambivalent. What could be more inspiring than the ideal of a free Greece? What, on the other hand, could be more discouraging than the actual character of the Greeks as shaped by many centuries of servitude? But at the worst even a fool's errand was preferable to a life in Italy that had been leading nowhere.

He had wisely decided to sail in the first instance to one of the Ionian Islands, then under the protection of Great Britain. He would there be in a good position to learn how matters were progressing on the mainland, and so to make a judicious choice between the various parties that were currently contending for the leadership of the independence movement. He chose the island of Cephalonia, where the British Resident, Colonel Charles Napier, was known to sympathize with the Greek insurgents. On 3 August, the *Hercules* anchored near the town of Argostoli on that island. Byron was deeply touched two days later to receive an invitation to dine with the officers of the 8th Regiment of Foot. He really had deluded himself into supposing that his countrymen in general regarded him with aversion.

While awaiting news, he visited Ithaca, the island of Homer's Odysseus. On learning from Greece that the military chieftains, Kolokotrones and Androutsos ('Odysseus'), had challenged the civil party and forced Mavrokordatos, its leader, to take refuge on the island of Hydra, he decided to remain on Cephalonia until the situation became clearer. This refusal to commit himself prematurely to any one of the warring factions was judicious, though Trelawny found it unromantic and pressed on to the mainland. By refusing to act precipitately, Byron also enabled himself to gain strength from Napier's realistic confidence in the Greek cause. In the meantime, he found life on Cephalonia very pleasant.

In November 1823 he was joined by Colonel Stanhope, a zealous and pedantic Benthamite sent by the London Greek Committee. A few weeks later he followed Stanhope to Missolonghi on the mainland.

The sea voyage included an uncomfortably narrow escape from a Turkish frigate, during which Byron felt particularly anxious on account of Loukas Chalandritsanos, a fifteen-year-old Greek page for whom he had an affection such as several previous youthful dependants had aroused in him. It also included an uncomfortably narrow escape from shipwreck. At Missolonghi, he set about the formation of an artillery corps with which, despite his lameness, he was ready to go into action. At the same time, he sought to humanize the war by arranging the return of Turkish captives.

He found the third emissary of the London Greek Committee as congenial as he found Stanhope uncongenial. William Parry, a fire-master, came to superintend the manufacture of explosives; he undertook also to train the artillery corps. His energy and his practical ability recommended him to Byron, who preferred his hard-headed commonsense to Stanhope's doctrinaire progressivism.

No doubt to Byron's relief, Stanhope left for Athens in February 1824. There the unscrupulous military chieftain Odysseus won his support by expressing Radical views and assenting to his establishment of such commendable institutions as a utilitarian society and a Lancastrian school. Trelawny, too, had become a supporter of Odysseus. But Byron continued to stand by the moderate leader, Mavrokordatos.

The subsequent history of the Greek War of Independence was to prove him right. But during the last weeks of his life he must have feared that his mission had failed. He had not reconciled the warring Greek factions; the artillery corps was still not an effective military instrument; the men enlisted under him had been turbulent and unreliable; he could retain little confidence in Trelawny or Stanhope; and he was a sick man. Missolonghi was a notoriously unhealthy place; and Byron was exposing a constitution already weakened by years of persistent but unscientific dieting to constant and heavy strain. On 9 April, he was caught in a rainstorm while riding three miles from the town – the weather was bad during much of his time at Missolonghi – and at once he became seriously ill. Not until 15 April did his doctors appreciate the gravity of his condition. Their treatment failed, and he died on 19 April 1824.

No military success that he might have achieved if he had lived could have been as effective as was the news of his death in uniting Greece and in bringing it the sympathy and support of men in every part of the civilized world. As for Byron himself, there could be no more appropriate conclusion to a biographical account than his own speculations, uttered to Lady Blessington, concerning his future biographers (*Lady Blessington's 'Conversations of Lord Byron'*, pp. 220–1):

People take for gospel all I say, and go away continually with false impressions. *Mais n'importe!* it will render the statements of my future biographers more amusing; as I flatter myself I shall have more than one. Indeed, the more the merrier, say I. One will represent me as a sort of sublime misanthrope, with moments of kind feeling. This, *par exemple*, is my favourite *rôle*. Another will portray me as a modern Don Juan; and a third (as it would be hard if a votary of the Muses had less than the number of the Graces for his biographers) will, it is to be hoped, if only for opposition sake, represent me as an *amiable*, ill-used gentleman, 'more sinned against than sinning.' Now, if I know myself, I should say, that I have no character at all. ... [What] I think of myself is, that I am so changeable, being every thing by turns and nothing long, – I am such a strange *mélange* of good and evil, that it would be difficult to describe me. There are but two sentiments to which I am constant, – a strong love of liberty, and a detestation of cant, and neither is calculated to gain me friends. I am of a wayward, uncertain disposition, more disposed to display the defects than the redeeming points in my nature; this, at least, proves that I understand mankind, for they are always ready to believe the evil, but not the good; and there is no crime of which I could accuse myself, for which they would not give me implicit credit.

3

Byron's Prose

No portrait of Byron can equal that which he himself gives in his letters and journals. Nor is this their only source of interest. They provide glimpses of life in the England of his time and in the foreign countries through which he passed; they record his views on literature and politics and religion. But, in so far as they compose a bold and vivid self-portrait, they claim something of the status of a work of art. For they do not merely inform us; they coerce our imaginations as we read, until we seem almost to be in the presence of the living and speaking man.

Letters

Byron was a voluminous correspondent; and his voluminousness, both in prose and in verse, is no accidental characteristic. When we read his *Don Juan*, our sense of copiousness, of casual, uninhibited improvisation, is an important part of our total experience. The same is true when we turn to the letters. These are evidently the work of a writer who disposes easily and confidently of an abundance of matter and a wealth of words. What he offers us at any one moment is but a particular instance of his continuous, profuse, even careless productivity.

More than the mere bulk of his correspondence, the very texture of its prose draws attention to these qualities. Thomas Moore, who knew him well, informs us that Byron was in the habit of answering letters as soon as he received them; and Moore rightly suggests that this habit gave to his correspondence 'all the aptitude and freshness of replies in conversation' (*Prose and Verse*, London [1878], p. 421). From internal evidence alone, it is clear that, with few exceptions, Byron's are letters thrown off in haste. They are at the furthest remove from planned pronouncements. They give immediate utterance to whatever ideas or observations were suggested by his present circumstances and dominant feelings. So expressive are they of these feelings that they repeatedly come near to dramatic monologue. A good, but by no means exceptional, example is the letter to John Murray dated 14 March 1820.

Murray was Byron's publisher from 1812 to 1822. Byron thought him a gentleman and 'a very good fellow' (29 January 1816), and regarded him as a friend, while never quite forgetting that theirs was after all a relationship between an aristocrat and a tradesman. He opens his letter in a friendly, informal, casual manner with a reference to a new poem, *The Prophecy of Dante*, the first four cantos of which he is sending: 'DEAR MURRAY, – Enclosed is *Dante's Prophecy – Vision* – or what not.' This last phrase is a favourite of Byron's; again and again he cuts short a list with it, or with the similar 'and all that', and by so doing conveys a careless and slightly haughty refusal to specify further. In the present letter he continues with a bantering reference to Murray's 'Utican Senate' of die-hard literary advisers and indulges in a jibe at one of the senators, his friend Hobhouse, whose Radical politics had recently landed him in gaol. He then directs his mockery on to himself. If the first instalment of *The Prophecy* is liked, he says, 'I will go on like Isaiah.' He exhorts Murray to take pains to see that the new volume is correctly printed.

He then turns to give news of himself and devotes the main part of his letter to an account of an accident which had happened to him while driving outside Ravenna. A little premeditation might have led him deliberately to postpone the climax of this story. Instead, he rushes in, tells the worst at once, catalogues the damage, and rounds off the sentence with a humorous comparison:

> Four days ago I was overturned in an open carriage between the river and a steep bank: – wheels dashed to pieces, slight bruises, narrow escape, and all that; but no harm done, though Coachman, footman, horses, and vehicle, were all mixed together like Maccaroni.

It was natural to suppose that Murray would ask what caused the spill.

> It was owing to bad driving, as I say; but the Coachman swears to a start on the part of the horses: we went against a post on the verge of a steep bank, and capsized.

Again, it was natural to suppose a question from Murray: How did you come to be out driving at the place in question?

> I usually go out of the town in a carriage, and meet the saddle horses at the bridge: it was in going there that we boggled; but I got my ride, as usual, after the accident.

Having shown that the accident did not even suffice to deflect him from his normal routine, Byron dismisses the topic with a laughing consideration of a theory favoured by the local people:

> They say here it was all owing to St. Antonio, of Padua (serious, I assure you), who does thirteen miracles a day, that worse did not come of it. I have no objection to this being his fourteenth in the four and twenty hours. He presides over overturns and all escapes therefrom, it seems: and they dedicate pictures, etc., to him, as the Sailors once did to Neptune, after 'the high Roman Fashion'.
>
> Yours, in haste,
>
> B.

Byron's impetuosity here shows itself not only in the unrehearsed sequence of his thoughts but also in his not having paused to avoid such inelegances as 'a start on the part' and 'presides over overturns' and in his abrupt conclusion. His continuous awareness of his correspondent makes the passage read, as I have tried to suggest by interpolating Murray's supposed questions, almost like the utterances of one actually engaged in eager, friendly talk. The parenthesis in which he directly addresses Murray, 'serious, I assure you', is one of several phrases which give to the whole narrative a tone of careless, detached, quizzical humour: 'and all that' and 'it seems' also contribute to this effect. Byron does not wish Murray to take his spill too seriously; and his lightly mocking humour is more evident still in his initial description of the physical confusion and in his final references to St Antonio.

His letters to Murray are not all as cheerful as this. On 20 September 1821, expressing the hope that certain of his papers will be edited for publication after his death, he writes:

> The task will, of course, require delicacy; but that will not be wanting, if Moore and Hobhouse survive me, and, I may add, yourself; and that you may all three do so, is, I assure you, my very sincere wish. I am not sure that long life is desirable for one of my temper and constitutional depression of Spirits, which of

course I suppress in society; but which breaks out when alone, and in my writings, in spite of myself. It has been deepened, perhaps, by some long past events (I do not allude to my marriage, etc. – on the contrary, *that* raised them by the persecution giving a fillip to my Spirits); but I call it constitutional, as I have reason to think it.

Here his gravity is momentarily relieved by the spurt of defiance on the subject of his marriage. Nevertheless, it dominates this passage and the greater part of the letter from which it comes.

Byron is equally in earnest, and much more spirited, when, in his letter of 23 November 1820, he voices his hope that the Italians will not always remain subject to their Austrian oppressors. 'Of the state of things here,' he begins, 'It would be difficult and not very prudent to speak at large, the Huns opening all letters: I wonder if they can read them when they have opened them?' This question serves not only to give forcible expression to his indignation and contempt but also to remind him that Murray, to whom the letter is addressed, will not be its sole reader. The Austrian censor can be counted on to examine carefully anything the notorious English liberal sets down. He is a captive audience; and Byron in effect reduces Murray to eavesdropping as he proceeds to deliver his opinion of Austrian imperialism to the censor himself:

> I wonder if they can read them when they have opened them? if so, they may see, in my most legible hand, that I think them damned scoundrels and barbarians, their emperor a fool, and themselves more fools than he; all which they may send to Vienna, for anything I care. They have got themselves masters of the Papal police, and are bullying away; but some day or other they will pay for it all. It may not be very soon, because these unhappy Italians have no union nor consistency among themselves; but I suppose Providence will get tired of them at last, and show that God is not an Austrian.

Here, his robust and resentful denunciation of the oppressors, his menacing confidence that retribution will be exacted, and his sad acknowledgment of Italian unpreparedness are all serious enough. But they do not exclude the humorous assurance, from a man who knew well that his handwriting was difficult to read, that the unpalatable truths would be set down in his 'most legible hand'.

At other times, his scorn can be more particular, as when he condemns 'Johnny Keats's *piss a bed* poetry' (12 October 1820) or denounces William Sotheby as 'that wretched leper of literature – that Itch of Scribbling personified' (17 April 1818); and a similar, though less violent, anger could be provoked by Murray's dilatoriness during the later years of their correspondence, a dilatoriness which may have been motivated in part by a reluctance to go on publishing the subversive *Don Juan* and which eventually helped to drive Byron to another publisher. But his ferocity is decidedly jocular when he rounds off his letter of 25 May 1821 with the words: 'Yours, in haste and hatred, you scrubby correspondent! B.'

In fact, his anger, his gravity, and his earnestness of every kind keep turning to humour as he writes. We can watch this happen, and then see Byron deliberately reverse the tendency, in his affectionate letter of 8 March 1822 to Moore. In this, he refers to the current attacks on himself for writing and on Murray for publishing the allegedly blasphemous *Cain* and to his resultant decision to continue one of Murray's authors after all. He goes on:

> I really feel ashamed of having bored you so frequently and fully of late. But what could I do? You are a friend – an absent one, alas! – and as I trust no one more, I trouble you in proportion.
>
> This war of 'Church and State' has astonished me more than it disturbs; for I really thought *Cain* a speculative and hardy, but still a harmless, production. As I said before, I am really a great admirer of tangible religion; and am breeding one of my daughters a Catholic, that she may have her hands full. It is by far the most elegant worship, hardly excepting the Greek mythology. What with incense, pictures, statues, altars, shrines, relics, and the real presence, confession, absolution, – there is something sensible to grasp at. Besides, it leaves no possibility of doubt; for those who swallow their Deity, really and truly, in transubstantiation, can hardly find any thing else otherwise than easy of digestion.
>
> I am afraid that this sounds flippant, but I don't mean it to be so; only my turn of mind is so given to taking things in the absurd point of view, that it breaks out in spite of me every now and then. Still, I do assure you that I am a very good Christian. Whether you will believe me in this, I do not know; but I trust you will take my word for being
>
> > Very truly and affectionately yours, etc.

Moore and Byron had a very warm regard for each other. Byron thought Moore 'the best-hearted, the only *hearted* being I ever encountered' ('Journal', 10 December 1813) and got on with him the more easily because he was no mere scribbler but a man of the world. Shortly after Byron's death, Moore composed '"The Living Dog" and "The Dead Lion"', surely our classical protest by an admirer of a great man against the posthumous defilement of his reputation by the issuing of ungenerous and disparaging 'Reminiscences'. For Moore had not only the sentimental vein which yielded 'The Minstrel Boy', ''Tis the Last Rose of Summer', 'The Harp that Once through Tara's Halls', and 'Believe Me, If All those Endearing Young Charms' but also a lively satirical wit. So had Byron, and he gives exuberant expression to it in his letter of 24 December 1816 to Moore. In this, he tells a story he has just heard in Milan about a young British junior officer who had been parted from his Italian mistress by the outbreak of war between England and France in 1793; and who, when the first fall of Napoleon temporarily restored peace in 1814, returned as a colonel to claim her. Byron does not fail to exploit the fact that the officer was, like Moore, an Irishman.

Six-and-twenty years ago, Col. [Fitzgerald], then an ensign, being in Italy, fell in love with the Marchesa [Castiglione], and she with him. The lady must be, at least, twenty years his senior. The war broke out; he returned to England, to serve – not his country, for that's Ireland – but England, which is a different thing; and *she* – heaven knows what she did. In the year 1814, the first annunciation of the Definitive Treaty of Peace (and tyranny) was developed to the astonished Milanese by the arrival of Col. [Fitzgerald], who, flinging himself full length at the feet of Mad. [Castiglione], murmured forth, in half-forgotten Irish Italian, eternal vows of indelible constancy. The lady screamed, and exclaimed, 'Who are you?' The Colonel cried, 'What! don't you know me? I am so and so', etc., etc., etc.; till, at length, the Marchesa, mounting from reminiscence to reminiscence, through the lovers of the intermediate twenty-five years, arrived at last at the recollection of her *povero* sub-lieutenant. She then said, 'Was there ever such virtue?' (that was her very word) and, being now a widow, gave him apartments in her palace, reinstated him in all the rights of wrong, and held him up to the admiring world as a miracle of incontinent fidelity, and the unshaken Abdiel of absence.

Here, as often elsewhere, Byron scoffs at 'sentimental and sensi-bilitous' (29 June 1811) persons. The romantic lover murmurs forth 'eternal vows of indelible constancy'; Byron observes that he does so in 'half-forgotten Irish Italian'. When the Marchesa peers back into her love-life, the structure of Byron's sentence comically reflects the stages by which she mounts to the recollection of her suitor. Her reunion with him terminates the little satirical farce; and it is the irony of a gay and resourceful raconteur which plays upon her praise of his 'virtue', her reinstatement of him 'in all the rights of wrong', her upholding him 'as a miracle of incontinent fidelity', and her final comparison of him with the loyal seraph in *Paradise Lost*. A similarly lightly mocking treatment of the cant of sensibility characterizes Byron's later presentation of Julia's love-affair in Canto I of *Don Juan*.

Moore's cheerful sociability made him a very suitable recipient for Byron's high-spirited description, in his letter of 31 October 1815, of a party at which 'all was hiccup and happiness for the last hour or so'. Byron, who was well aware of the comic possibilities of the catalogue, whether in verse or in prose, here lists the eight stages of conviviality:

> Like other parties of the kind, it was first silent, then talky, then
> argumentative, then disputatious, then unintelligible, then
> altogethery, then inarticulate, and then drunk. When we had
> reached the last step of this glorious ladder, it was difficult to get
> down again without stumbling; and, to crown all, Kinnaird and
> I had to conduct Sheridan down a damned corkscrew staircase,
> which had certainly been constructed before the discovery of
> fermented liquors, and to which no legs, however crooked, could
> possibly accommodate themselves. We deposited him safe at home,
> where his man, evidently used to the business, waited to receive
> him in the hall.

After the polysyllabic labels applied to the five previous stages – 'altogethery' being a particularly apt coinage – the monosyllable 'drunk' ends the list with a conclusive thud. The whole passage is representative in its flexibility, vigour, and raciness of language.

Douglas Kinnaird, who helped to take home the convivial author of *The School for Scandal*, was at this time a regular associate of Byron's and later became his business adviser, his 'trusty and trust-worthy trustee and banker, and crown and sheet-anchor' (13 December 1823). The poet's decision to place his fortune, as well as his life, at the service of the Greek national movement, made him continue in close touch with Kinnaird throughout his last year. In general, correspondents knew a somewhat more sober Byron during this period, and his letters to Kinnaird and others at the time of the Greek enterprise are notably judicious, practical, and resolute.

Another firm friend, an older and more intimate one than Kinnaird, was Hobhouse, with whom Byron had embarked upon his Mediterranean tour in 1809. Hobhouse was a loyal, sensible, and candid ally: 'a cynic after my own heart' (*Correspondence*, 7 May 1813), said Byron. He did not hesitate to tell Byron his faults, and Byron frequently made him the butt of affectionate laughter. While their relationship was not free from friction, each man retained a sincere respect for the other's independence. On this point, the evidence of the letters is clear. 'After all,' wrote Byron, when he and Hobhouse had parted in 1810, before the end of his Mediterranean tour, 'I do love thee, Hobby, thou hast so many good qualities, and so many bad ones, it is impossible to live with thee or without thee' (*Correspondence*, 23 August 1810). The greater part of Byron's liveliest and most intimate correspondence with male friends seems to have been addressed to Hobhouse, Kinnaird, Murray and Moore.

In general, female correspondents came off less well. Byron insisted that 'Lovers ... never can be friends' (10 November 1822), and his letters to his lovers suffered accordingly. No one can say for certain whether his half-sister Augusta was his lover or not; if she was, as seems likely, their congenital relationship must have sustained a friendship which sexual love would otherwise have overthrown. At all events, Augusta was one of the two women who received excellent letters from him during his adult years.

He had no very high opinion of her abilities. But she was good-natured, affectionate, and a Byron. His letters to her tend to be simple, relaxed, gossipy, playful. During the autumn of 1822, there was an extraordinary rainfall in the part of Italy where he was living. On 7 November, he sent Augusta a report of the facts with an embroidery of fanciful and absurd inventions. This account illustrates the remarkable mobility of his temperament. He feels surprise and bewilderment at the violence of the deluge and the devastation caused by it; but his irony asserts itself when he records that his own household, with the 'lower floor afloat', enjoyed a 'comfortable view of the whole landscape under water, and people screaming out of their garret windows'; after noting, with the additional emphasis given by underlining, that there were '*two bridges* swept down', he provides a delightful and ludicrous description of the looting of neighbouring shops by the turbulent elements, 'which marched away with a quantity of shoes, several Perukes, and Gingerbread in all its branches'; finally, he expresses simple astonishment at the suddenness and volume of the flood and at the drowning of a child 'a few yards from its own door'.

An extravagant humour dominates the rest of the letter:

> Well, after all this comes a preaching Friar and says that the day of Judgement will take place positively on the *4th* with all kinds of tempest and what not, in consequence of which the whole City (except some impious Scoffers) sent him presents to avert the wrath of Heaven by his prayers, and even the *public authorities* had warned the Captains of Ships, who, to mend the matter, almost all bought *new Cables* and anchors by way of weathering the Gale.
>
> But the fourth turned out a very fine day. All those who had paid their money are excessively angry, and insist either upon having the day of judgement or their cash again. But the Friar's device seems to be 'no money to be returned,' and he says that he merely made a mistake in the time, for the day of Judgement will certainly come for all that, either here or in some other part of Italy.
>
> This has a little pacified the expectants. You will think this a fiction. Enquire further then. The populace actually used to kiss the fellow's feet in the streets.

Byron's other most-favoured female correspondent was Lady Melbourne, an older woman who was his honorary 'aunt' during his years of fame in England. At the period when he was writing to her regularly, he set down in his 'Journal' under 24 November 1813:

> To Lady Melbourne I write with most pleasure – and her answers, so sensible, so *tactique* – I never met with half her talent. If she had been a few years younger, what a fool she would have made of me, had she thought it worth her while, – and I should have lost a valuable and most agreeable *friend*.

On 16 March 1818, he expressed himself similarly in a letter to Moore: 'She was my greatest *friend*, of the feminine gender: – when I say "friend," I mean *not* mistress, for that's the antipode.' His letters to her, as printed in *Correspondence*. are more sophisticated in tone and characterized by a sharper curiosity regarding human behaviour than are his letters to Augusta. On 5 September 1813, for example, he records an impression of the young woman who later became his wife:

She seems to have been spoiled – not as children usually are – but systematically Clarissa Harlowed into an awkward kind of correctness, with a dependence upon her own infallibility which will or may lead her into some egregious blunder. I don't mean the usual error of young gentlewomen, but she will find exactly what she wants, and then discover that it is much more dignified than entertaining.

The compact phrases 'systematically Clarissa Harlowed' and 'more dignified than entertaining' accurately define the character, and plausibly predict the future, of the precise, formal, and rather complacent Annabella Milbanke. She is also the subject of candid investigation on 4, 6, and 13 November 1814, shortly before their marriage.

While visiting an absurd acquaintance, James Wedderburn Webster, Byron found himself involved in an intrigue reminiscent of Restoration comedy. Before the plot became really complicated, he wrote to Lady Melbourne on 21 September 1813:

W[ebster] don't want sense, nor good nature, but both are occasionally obscured by his suspicions, and absurdities of all descriptions; he is passionately fond of having his wife admired, and at the same time jealous to jaundice of everything and everybody. I have hit upon the medium of praising her to him perpetually behind her back, and never looking at her before his face; as for her, I believe she is disposed to be very faithful, and I don't think anyone now here is inclined to put her to the test. W[ebster] himself is, with all his jealousy and admiration, a little tired; he has been lately at Newstead, and wants to go again. I suspected this sudden *penchant*, and soon discovered that a foolish nymph of the Abbey, about whom fortunately I care not, was the attraction. Now if I wanted to make mischief I could extract much good perplexity from a proper management of such events; but I am grown so good, or so indolent, that I shall not avail myself of so pleasant an opportunity of tormenting mine host, though he deserves it for poaching. I believe he has hitherto been unsuccessful, or rather it is too astonishing to be believed.

Here, asides and afterthoughts – 'about whom fortunately I care not', 'or so indolent', 'though he deserves it for poaching', 'or rather it is too astonishing to be believed' – develop the tone of polite, detached amusement established by the antithetical constructions with which the passage opens. We are reminded of Byron's tellingly qualified praise of the Roman Catholic as 'by far the most elegant worship, *hardly excepting the Greek mythology*'. But he has more to say about the uxorious Webster:

> He proposed to me, with great gravity, to carry him over there [that is, to Newstead and the nymph], and I replied with equal candour, that *he* might set out when he pleased, but that I should remain here to take care of his household in the interim – a proposition which I thought very much to the purpose, but which did not seem at all to his satisfaction. By way of opiate he preached me a sermon on his wife's good qualities, concluding by an assertion that in all moral and mortal qualities, she was very like 'Christ!!!' I think the Virgin Mary would have been a more appropriate typification; but it was the first comparison of the kind I ever heard, and made me laugh till he was angry, and then I got out of humour too, which pacified him, and shortened the panegyric.

This is the narrative of one who knows that he is addressing an alert, experienced, sympathetic, and worldly-wise woman. The egregious Webster emerges very clearly from it.

At a later stage, when it was conceivable that the two men might fight a duel about Webster's wife, Byron took humorous consolation in the thought that his death in such circumstances 'would be so *dramatic* a conclusion; all the sex would be enamoured of my memory, all the wits would have their jests, and the moralists their sermon. C[aroline Lamb] would go wild with *grief* that *it did not happen about her*' (*Correspondence*, 25 November 1813).

Such is the self-portrait which these letters compose. They show Byron as impulsive, even reckless; quick to feel resentment and aggressive in his anger. At times, as he acknowledges, he is subject to feelings of profound despondency. But these afflict him more in solitude than in society; so they are more prominent in his poetry and his journals than in his letters, letter-writing being inevitably in some degree a social activity. It was particularly so with him, his letters being scribbled rapidly and spontaneously with the image of each correspondent vividly present to his mind. Wit and humour are never long absent; and there is no denying the truth of his insistence that such friends as Moore knew him not as a 'misanthropical and gloomy gentleman ... but [as] a facetious companion, well to do with those with whom I am intimate, and as loquacious and laughing as if I were a much cleverer fellow' (10 March 1817). It amuses him to tell Moore of a young American who visited him, expecting 'to meet a misanthropical gentleman, in wolf-skin breeches, and answering in fierce monosyllables' (5 July 1821). He is friendly, exuberant, derisive, voluble, pugnacious, outspoken, and genial. These qualities receive highly colloquial and even dramatic expression in his impatient retort of 6 April 1819 to Murray's suggestion that he should give up seven or eight years to composing a great literary work:

> So you and Mr. Foscolo, etc., want me to undertake what you call a 'great work?' an Epic poem, I suppose, or some such pyramid. I'll try no such thing; I hate tasks. And then 'seven or eight years!' God send us all well this day three months, let alone years. If one's years can't be better employed than in sweating poesy, a man had better be a ditcher. And works, too! – is *Childe Harold* nothing? You have so many '*divine*' poems, is it nothing to have written a *Human* one? without any of your worn-out machinery. Why, man, I could have spun the thoughts of the four cantos of that poem into twenty, had I wanted to book-make, and its passion into as many modern tragedies. Since you want *length*, you shall have enough of *Juan*, for I'll make 50 cantos.

This explosion staggered Murray: 'I never read a more powerful Letter in my life' (*Letters and Journals*, iv, p. 286). Byron always felt some scorn for the sedentary trade to which he devoted so much of his time. He was ill at ease in the company of all but a very few of his fellow-writers: 'I never know what to say to them after I have praised their last publication' ('Detached Thoughts', 53). He preferred men of fashion, and he very much preferred men of action. It was as a man of action, translating his faith in freedom and hatred of despotism into deeds, that he lived his last months in a Greece fighting for independence.

It is a fascinating personality that we meet in these letters, and the letters are intrinsically important mainly because they enable us to meet it. But they have an importance of another kind for those interested in Byron's poetry. Until 1818, this must indeed have seemed to be the work of a 'misanthropical and gloomy gentleman'. Then, in *Beppo*, *Don Juan*, and *The Vision of Judgment*, Byron transcended the childish and theatrical romanticism of so much of his earlier verse and produced the great anti-romantic and disconcertingly truthful serio-comic poetry of his maturity. Dominating this, there stands the literary personality we have been meeting in the letters. The interesting thing is that this personality was present in Byron's letters long before 1818, the date when it began effectively to invade his verse. Of the longer passages that I have quoted, four – the verdict on Annabella Milbanke, the portrait of Wedderburn Webster, the description of the drinking-party, and the narrative of Colonel Fitzgerald's belated reunion with his mistress – were written before 1818; and these offer already a kind of prose that is the equivalent of what we value in *Don Juan*. In short, Byron's letters supply convincing evidence that the powers which he was successfully mobilizing for the first time as a poet during his last half-dozen years were powers which he had long possessed but which romantic inhibitions had hitherto prevented him from exploiting fully in verse.

Among these was his power of alert and shrewd observation of his fellow men and women. To Lady Melbourne, he wrote: 'anything that confirms, or extends one's observations on life and character delights me' (*Correspondence*, 1 October 1813). So we should not be surprised to find him attending a public execution and noting not only the behaviour of the condemned persons but also his own reaction to the spectacle (30 May 1817); or reporting with the keenest interest and in considerable detail the shooting, and the subsequent death after being carried indoors, of the military commandant in Ravenna (9 December 1820). His letters contain many lively portraits of friends and acquaintances. As well as the sharp sketches of Annabella Milbanke and Wedderburn Webster, there are, for example, the passages concerned with his literary relative, R. C. Dallas (3 October 1810); his valet, William Fletcher (14 January 1811); Madame de Staël (*Correspondence*, 8 August 1813 and 8 January 1814); the Italian poet, Pindemonte (4 June 1817); the fantastic Dr Polidori (24 January 1817, 17 June 1817); Richard Porson, the classical scholar (20 February 1818); John Hanson, Byron's solicitor (*Correspondence*, 11 November 1818); Angelina, one of his Venetian mistresses (18 May 1819); Allegra, his illegitimate daughter (31 March 1820); Maria Edgeworth's father (4 November 1820); Byron's dead friend, C. S. Matthews (19 November 1820); and the Hunts and Shelley (*passim*).

But the fullest and most revealing of his epistolary portraits is that of his Venetian mistress, Margarita Cogni, which he wrote on 1 August 1819 in response to a request from Murray. This is a fascinatingly detailed character-study, more than five times as long as the few paragraphs which must suffice to represent it here. Byron speaks of Margarita's ascendancy over him:

The reasons of this were, firstly, her person – very dark, tall, the Venetian face, very fine black eyes – and certain other qualities which need not be mentioned. She was two and twenty years old, and, never having had children, had not spoilt her figure ... She was, besides, a thorough Venetian in her dialect, in her thoughts, in her countenance, in every thing, with all their naïveté and Pantaloon humour. Besides, she could neither read nor write, and could not plague me with letters, – except twice that she paid sixpence to a public scribe, under the piazza, to make a letter for her, upon some occasion, when I was ill and could not see her. In other respects she was somewhat fierce and *prepotente*, that is, overbearing, and used to walk in whenever it suited her, with no very great regard to time, place, nor persons; and if she found any women in her way, she knocked them down. . . .

Madame Benzone . . . took her under her protection, and then her head turned. She was always in extremes, either crying or laughing; and so fierce when angered, that she was the terror of men, women, and children – for she had the strength of an Amazon, with the temper of Medea. She was a fine animal, but quite untameable. *I* was the only person that could at all keep her in any order, and when she saw me really angry (which they tell me is rather a savage sight), she subsided. But she had a thousand fooleries: in her *fazziolo*, the dress of the lower orders, she looked beautiful; but, alas! she longed for a hat and feathers, and all I could say or do (and I said much) could not prevent this travestie. I put the first into the fire; but I got tired of burning them, before she did of buying them, so that she made herself a figure – for they did not at all become her. . . .

In the mean time, she beat the women and stopped my letters. I found her one day pondering over one: she used to try to find out by their shape whether they were feminine or no; and she used to lament her ignorance, and actually studied her Alphabet, on purpose (as she declared) to open all letters addressed to me and read their contents.

I must not omit to do justice to her housekeeping qualities: after she came into my house as *donna di governo*, the expences were reduced to less than half, and every body did their duty better – the apartments were kept in order, and every thing and every body else, except herself. ...

I forgot to mention that she was very devout, and would cross herself if she heard the prayer-time strike – sometimes when that ceremony did not appear to be much in unison with what she was then about.

Animating the whole of this description, and inspiring its author's choice of anecdotes, is something which is evident from the beginning in Byron's work both in prose and in verse: his ready responsiveness to every manifestation of instinctive energy. As he wrote in his 'Journal' on 23 November 1813, 'I like energy – even animal energy – of all kinds'.

But in its lively appreciation of human idiosyncrasy the passage is strikingly different from anything that we should expect to find in the poetry Byron published before 1818. In the letters of those earlier years, we have glimpses of Dallas, Fletcher, Madame de Staël, Annabella Milbanke, Wedderburn Webster, Pindemonte, and Polidori; in the verse of the same period we encounter only such attitudinizing dummies as Childe Harold, Conrad the Corsair, and Manfred – dummies capable of provoking the suspicion that their creator knew about the human race only from hearsay. From 1818 onwards, however, Byron's verse as well as his prose testifies to his eager and perceptive observation of life. He found it possible to admit to *Don Juan* and *The Vision of Judgment* the humour, the satire, and above all the realism, the fidelity to life as he had really experienced it, of which his correspondents had long known him capable but for which he had found little or no place in his rather extensive romantic juvenilia.

These poems in *ottava rima* are his finest achievements as an artist. They express a zest for life which is conditioned but not inhibited by a sober sense of what life really is. In their degree, his letters express the same thing, as do his journals; and they express it, powerfully and unforgettably, by projecting upon our imaginations the living and speaking presence of their author.

Journals

Journals or similar documents survive from six periods in Byron's life. He started the earliest on 14 November 1813, when an unusually troublesome 'scrape', presumably with Augusta, was causing him some anxiety; he ended it on 19 April 1814, shortly after the first fall of Napoleon. His second journal recorded for Augusta his experiences and thoughts during his tour of the Bernese Alps with Hobhouse in September 1816. The third covers the period from 4 January to 27 February 1821, when Byron was living in the Palazzo Guiccioli at Ravenna and awaiting a call to arms with the Carbonari. The fourth, begun later in the same year, is not a diary at all, but 'Detached Thoughts', preceded by a page or two of 'My Dictionary'. The fifth consists of three entries made on Cephalonia, and the sixth of a single entry made at Missolonghi.

Of these, the second is really a long letter to Augusta written at a time of desolation and distress; and the last two, which share the characteristic tone of Byron's letters during his Greek adventure, are quite brief. Our main concern now must be with the 'Journal' of 1813–14, the 'Diary' of early 1821, and the 'Detached Thoughts' of 1821–2.

It might seem natural to assume that, whereas Byron wrote his letters with his particular correspondents vividly in mind, his purpose in his journals would have been simply to put something on record for his own interest. But the first sentence of the first journal alerts us by a regretful 'heigho!' to the fact that the writer is not merely describing or analysing his feelings but acting them out, as if for an audience. As the journal continues, the emphatic 'oons!', the dubitative 'um!' or 'umph!', the dismissive 'psha!', and the indignant ''sdeath!' provide further indications. Repetition and aposiopesis sometimes dramatize his reluctance to give outright expression to painful or dangerous thoughts; in his remark on Madame de Staël, 'she always talks of *myself* or *herself*, and I am not (except in soliloquy, as now,) much enamoured of either subject' ('Journal', 6 December 1813), the parenthesis contains his defence against an anticipated charge of egocentricity; and, when he writes, 'Got up and tore out two leaves of this Journal – I don't know why' ('Journal', 20 February 1814), he must surely be trying to tantalize an imaginary reader.

In this 'Journal' of 1813–14, Byron is clearly writing not for himself, and not for any individual, but for an ideal audience. This would naturally include such close friends as Hobhouse, Kinnaird, and Moore, the last of whom actually became the recipient of the completed manuscript; no doubt Byron envisaged also its extension into a posthumous public. In the 'Diary' of 1821 and the 'Detached Thoughts' of 1821–2, he seems less acutely aware of this audience. Though he never forgets it, he is less self-conscious in its imagined presence, less anxious to justify himself to it. His tone remains dramatic but has become more assured and more composed.

Despite this distinction, the three documents have a great deal in common. What Byron states in the first evidently applies to all of them ('Journal', 6 December 1813):

> This journal is a relief. When I am tired – as I generally am – out comes this, and down goes every thing. But I can't read it over; and God knows what contradictions it may contain. If I am sincere with myself (but I fear one lies more to one's self than to any one else), every page should confute, refute, and utterly abjure its predecessor.

In his steady consciousness of his public, his unchecked spontaneity of utterance, and his veracious disregard of consistency, the Byron of the journals comes near to the commentator whose observations accompany and interrupt the narrative in *Don Juan* (XV. lxxxvii):

> if a writer should be quite consistent,
> How could he possibly show things existent?

The 'Journal' and the 'Diary' belong to two critical periods in Byron's life, and each of them concludes with a serious disappointment. The author of the 'Journal' is unhappy and bored: his personal relationships have become perilously irregular, and, while he has lost his taste for 'parliamentary mummeries' ('Journal', 14 November 1813), he feels that a serious commitment to poetry would degrade him. From the start, he takes note of the European reaction against Napoleon. He does not want the Emperor to subdue England, but he would like him to trounce the 'three stupid, legitimate-old-dynasty boobies of regular-bred sovereigns' ('Journal', 17 November 1813) of Austria, Prussia, and Russia. Three months later, his hero's situation is more critical ('Journal', 18 February 1814):

> Napoleon! – this week will decide his fate. All seems against him; but I believe and hope he will win – at least, beat back the invaders. What right have we to prescribe sovereigns to France? Oh for a Republic! 'Brutus, thou sleepest.'

He rejoices at subsequent minor successes of the French and sends his print of Napoleon to be framed. But disappointment follows ('Journal', 8 April 1814). He finds his poor little pagod, Napoleon, pushed off his pedestal; – the thieves are in Paris. It is his own fault. Like Milo, he would rend the oak; but it closed again, wedged his hands, and now the beasts – lion, bear, down to the dirtiest jackal – may all tear him. That Muscovite winter *wedged* his arms; – ever since, he has fought with his feet and teeth. The last may still leave their marks.

Worse than the defeat, however, is Napoleon's abdication. 'What! wait till they were in his capital, and then talk of his readiness to give up what is already gone!! ... I am utterly bewildered and confounded ... [To] outlive *Lodi* for this!!!' ('Journal', 9 April 1814). In the last words of the 'Journal' the catastrophe is completed by news of the restoration of a Bourbon King to France.

The 'Diary' likewise acquires a degree of unity from the fact that it sets miscellaneous personal deeds and thoughts within a context of public affairs that are of special interest to the diarist. Indeed, the unity is stronger in this instance because the public affairs directly involve the diarist himself. He awaits daily the outbreak of hostilities against the Austrians and their dependants. He learns of the deliberations at Laibach of the representatives of the reactionary powers who had earlier met at Troppau ('Diary', 13 January 1821):

Dined – news come – the *Powers* mean to war with the peoples. The intelligence seems positive – let it be so – they will be beaten in the end. The king-times are fast finishing. There will be blood shed like water, and tears like mist; but the peoples will conquer in the end. I shall not live to see it, but I foresee it.

In the meantime he advises the Carbonari on tactics and supplies them with arms, while doubting whether their strength and determination are yet sufficient for them to achieve their aims. The cause inspires him, however, 'It is a grand object – the very *poetry* of politics. Only think – a free Italy!!!' ('Diary', 18 February 1821). Then the Austrians march, the Neapolitans collapse, and the Carbonari do nothing. Like the 'Journal', the 'Diary' ends in political disappointment.

Within this framework, the 'Diary' contains, again like the 'Journal', reports and recollections and reflections. These find expression in the same clear, natural, and vigorous prose as distinguishes the letters. The same shrewd observation and sardonic wit are also active throughout. These are well exemplified by the remarks on R. L. Edgeworth, whom Byron had met in 1813 ('Diary', 19 January 1821):

65

I thought Edgeworth a fine old fellow, of a clarety, elderly, red complexion, but active, brisk, and endless. He was seventy, but did not look fifty – no, nor forty-eight even. I had seen poor Fitzpatrick not very long before – a man of pleasure, wit, eloquence, all things. He tottered – but still talked like a gentleman, though feebly. Edgeworth bounced about, and talked loud and long; but he seemed neither weakly nor decrepit, and hardly old. . . .

The fact was – every body cared more about *her* [his daughter, Maria, the novelist]. She was a nice little unassuming 'Jeanie Deans-looking body,' as we Scotch say – and, if not handsome, certainly not ill-looking. Her conversation was as quiet as herself. One would never have guessed she could write *her name*; whereas her father talked, *not* as if he could write nothing else, but as if nothing else was worth writing.

Byron could think of those years in England with some tenderness. 'Oh! there is an organ playing in the street – a waltz, too! I must leave off to listen. They are playing a waltz which I have heard ten thousand times at the balls in London, between 1812 and 1815. Music is a strange thing' ('Diary', 2 February 1821). Richly varied reminiscences make up much of the 'Detached Thoughts' which he began writing on 15 October 1821. He recalls his passionate schoolboy friendship with Lord Clare, and before the end of 'Detached Thoughts' he records an unexpected meeting with Clare on the road between Imola and Bologna on 29 October 1821. 'This meeting annihilated for a moment all the years between the present time and the days of *Harrow*. . . . We were but five minutes together, and in the public road; but I hardly recollect an hour of my existence which could be weighed against them' ('Detached Thoughts', 113). He likewise recalls a visit to a flooded cave in Derbyshire with a party that included his early love, Mary Chaworth.

He remembers ludicrous incidents, too ('Detached Thoughts', 9): Sheridan, found drunk in the street and asked by the watchman for his name, once answered, 'Wilberforce'. In 'Detached Thoughts', 16:

['Monk'] Lewis at Oatlands was observed one morning to have his eyes red, and his air sentimental: being asked why? replied, 'that when people said any thing *kind* to him, it affected him deeply;

and just now the Duchess has said something *so* kind to me that ...' here 'tears began to flow' again. 'Never mind, Lewis,' said Col. Armstrong to him, 'never mind, don't cry. *She could not mean it.*'

A coarse parody, too, can delight Byron ('Detached Thoughts', 49):

A beau (*dandies* were not then christened) came into the P. of W.'s and exclaimed, 'Waiter, bring me a glass of Madeira Negus with a Jelly, and rub my plate with a Chalotte.' This in a very soft tone of voice. A Lieutenant of the Navy, who sate in the next box, immediately roared out the following rough parody: 'Waiter, bring me a glass of d—d stiff Grog, and rub ✶ ✶ with a brick-bat.'

Since most of the 'Detached Thoughts' date from Byron's last, lonely days at Ravenna, it is not surprising that serious and even gloomy ponderings should find an important place in the collection. The origin of the universe, the relationship of soul and body, the immortality of the soul, and the doctrine of eternal punishment are among the matters on which Byron speculates. He dwells, too, upon his own temperamental melancholy ('Detached Thoughts', 73, 74, 75, 76):

People have wondered at the Melancholy which runs through my writings. Others have wondered at my personal gaiety; but I recollect once, after an hour, in which I had been sincerely and particularly gay, and rather brilliant, in company, my wife replying to me when I said (upon her remarking my high spirits) 'and yet, Bell, I have been called and mis-called Melancholy – you must have seen how falsely, frequently.' 'No, B.,' (she answered) 'it is not so: at *heart* you are the most melancholy of mankind, and often when apparently gayest.'

If I could explain at length the *real* causes which have contributed to increase this perhaps *natural* temperament of mine, this Melancholy which hath made me a bye-word, nobody would wonder; but this is impossible without doing much mischief. I do not know what other men's lives have been, but I cannot conceive anything more strange than some of the earlier parts of mine. I have written my memoirs, but omitted *all* the really *consequential* and *important* parts, from deference to the dead, to the living, and to those who must be both.

I sometimes think that I should have written the *whole* as a *lesson,* but it might have proved a *lesson* to be *learnt* rather than *avoided*; for passion is a whirlpool, which is not to be viewed nearly without attraction from its Vortex.

I must not go on with these reflections, or I shall be letting out some secret or other to paralyze posterity.

4

Heroes and Rhetoric, 1812–18

Before leaving for the Mediterranean in 1809, Byron had published a collection of derivative, mannered, and sentimental short poems entitled *Hours of Idleness* and a humorous and purposeful satire, *English Bards, and Scotch Reviewers*, provoked in part by the rough handling of *Hours of Idleness* in the *Edinburgh Review*. In *English Bards, and Scotch Reviewers*, he had employed Pope's form, the heroic couplet, with a confidence and a vigour that were quite remarkable in a poet barely twenty-one years of age.

After his return from the Mediterranean in 1811, he made what was in effect a fresh start, and between then and 1818 he published the works that gave him his contemporary reputation. Childe Harold, Manfred, and the heroes of the Turkish tales, often loosely identified with one another and with Byron himself, succeeded in imposing themselves upon the imaginations of a whole generation of young readers throughout Europe and in America. Nineteenth-century literature, music, and painting testify to their deep and lasting influence. Yet these very works seem to many modern readers to exhibit a 'childish and theatrical romanticism' and to be dominated by heroes who are 'attitudinizing dummies capable of provoking the suspicion that their creator knew about the human race only from hearsay' (see above pp. 59–62). What is the secret of the power that these poems had over contemporary readers? And what value do they retain in the fourth half-century after their composition?

It will be convenient to depart from chronology so far as to consider the Turkish tales first and then to turn to *Childe Harold's Pilgrimage*, the first two cantos of which preceded them. *Manfred*, which appeared after the third but before the fourth and final canto of *Childe Harold's Pilgrimage*, will be considered last.

69

The Turkish Tales

The Giaour (1813) owed much of its rapid success with the reading public to the novelty and fascination of its Eastern Mediterranean setting. Byron saw this as a setting juxtaposing natural beauty with human savagery, and he was to achieve his best-known expression of the contrast in the first section of *The Bride of Abydos* (1813). In the meantime, he opens *The Giaour* by progressing from this to another contrast that was a favourite with him: that between Greece's past freedom and glory and her present servitude and shame. These reflections occupy a full eighth of his poem, although, as he admits, they have no direct relevance to its characters and action. Relinquishing them, he focuses upon a particular fisherman.

Without warning, he hands over the narrative to this fisherman, who provides a glimpse through Moslem eyes of the remorseful, vengeful young Venetian, the Giaour or infidel. The new narrator then leaps forward in time to an account of the desolation of the Turkish Hassan's hall, eventually disclosing that the Giaour has slain its owner. As soon as he has made this revelation, he moves back to a killing which occurred about the time of his first glimpse of the Giaour. Gradually he lets us know that on this occasion the killer had been Hassan, the victim one of his women who had loved the Giaour. He describes this woman, Leila, before again leaping forward to his narrative of the Giaour's violent revenge.

Early in the second half of the poem, the fisherman introduces a third narrator, a member of a religious community to which the successful revenger has retired. A long impenitent confession makes the Giaour himself a fourth narrator.

Written from so many different points of view, and following no straightforward chronological line of development, *The Giaour* is conspicuously fragmentary in form. No doubt, Samuel Rogers's *Voyage of Columbus* (1810; revised edition, 1812) had suggested to Byron some of the advantages of the method. 'These scattered fragments', Rogers had written, 'may be compared to shreds of old arras, or reflections from a river broken and confused by the oar; and now and then perhaps the imagination of the reader may supply more than is lost. Si qua latent, meliora putat' ('Additional Notes' to Canto III). Rogers's fragments provide intermittent glimpses of Columbus's voyage in strictly chronological order and from a single point of view;

his verse invests the whole action with a genteel epic decorum. Byron, preferring tumult to decorum, more successfully holds our interest; and he heightens it by so disposing his fragments and so employing his narrators as to excite curiosity, raise suspense, and suggest mystery, while tantalizingly deferring the looked-for explanations and resolutions. His deviousness is that of a born story-teller.

But his success in 1813 was due above all to his hero. According to Peter L. Thorslev, whose *Byronic Hero: Types and Prototypes* has forced us to recognize the considerable differences between Byron's various heroes, the Giaour is a remorseful and sympathetic Gothic Villain. He has many of the distinctive features of the type. He has the pale and gloomy brow, the evil eye, and the bitter smile. His air is that of a fallen angel, and his habitual attitude is one of 'mixed defiance and despair' (l. 908). He feels no guilt for having slain Hassan, though he suffers an agonizing remorse for having been the occasion of Leila's death. To these characteristics which affiliate him to the traditional Gothic Villain, we may add one that is more particularly Byronic. This is the craving for sensation – 'I loathed the languor of repose' (l. 987) – that he shares with characters in *The Corsair* (ll. 7–22) and *Lara* (ll. 115–30).

Byron's next hero, Selim in *The Bride of Abydos* (1813), has very little of the Gothic about him. Thorslev describes him as almost pure Hero of Sensibility. He enjoys tales and songs, he responds to natural beauty, he has humanitarian sympathies, and his love for Zuleika is as tender as it is passionate. But the gentleness and even softness of manner at which Giaffir sneers have not prevented Selim from becoming, during his occasional absences from Giaffir's palace, the successful leader of a 'lawless brood' (l. 845) of pirates. In this rôle, he exhibits something of the nature of a third type of hero, the Noble Outlaw. Whereas the Gothic Villain was a pre-Romantic eighteenth-century type, the Noble Outlaw, like the Hero of Sensibility, is a Romantic type. Sir Walter Scott's Border outlaws in his tales in verse represent it at the stage at which Byron took it over and transferred it to the Mediterranean. The Giaour, leading his band to ambush Hassan, anticipates Selim in coming near to it. But it receives its fullest Byronic development in *The Corsair* (1814) and *Lara* (1814).

The Corsair was initially the most popular of all Byron's Turkish tales. Its hero, Conrad, resembles Selim in being a pirate. But this Noble Outlaw has the physical traits of the Gothic Villain: the pale and gloomy forehead, the 'searching eye' (l. 216) which few dare to meet, and the proud and bitter expression about the mouth. Conrad is Gothic also in his mysterious past, his present misanthropy, and his air of a fallen angel. On the other hand, just as the Giaour suffered an agonizing remorse for having been the occasion of Leila's death, so Conrad reveals a tender sensibility in his chivalrous rescue of the women of his Moslem enemy's harem, in his shrinking from Gulnare after she has rescued him by murdering that enemy, and above all in his 'love – unchangeable – unchanged' (l. 287) for Medora. Like the other heroes of Byron's Turkish tales, though much less so than Selim, Conrad is something of a Hero of Sensibility.

But primarily this 'man of loneliness and mystery' (l. 173) is a Noble Outlaw. His command over his men is imperious and unquestioned; his loyalty to them, and theirs to him and to one another, is entire and unshakeable. In *Lara*, a sequel to *The Corsair*, he reappears, bearing the name which gives the poem its title. Having 'changed the scene' (l. 892), he returns to his vocation, but he is now a distinctly darker, more Gothic, and less sympathetic outlaw than he was while known as Conrad. He nurses a guilty secret, and his attitude towards the world is one of proud and ferocious defiance. His leadership of a peasants' revolt links him with Goethe's Götz von Berlichingen, perhaps the earliest major presentation of the Romantic type to which he chiefly approximates. It also permits him to be an expression of Byron's liberalism.

Alp, the hero of *The Siege of Corinth* (1816), the last of the Turkish tales, is less fully characterized than any of his predecessors. He is a renegade, proud and vindictive, but deeply in love with Francesca. Both the Noble Outlaw and the Hero of Sensibility seem to have contributed to his composition.

In none of the Turkish tales subsequent to *The Giaour* did Byron follow up his initial experiments in narrative technique. *The Bride of Abydos*, *The Corsair*, *Lara*, and *The Siege of Corinth* are all told quite straightforwardly. In them, the poet evidently means his reader's attention to be held by the enigmatic heroes, the exotic settings, and the declamatory verse.

The last of these constitutes probably the most serious impediment to the modern reader's sympathetic enjoyment of the poems. Here, for example, are the lines in which he learns how Giaffir, the murderer of Selim's father, Abdallah, prevents the rescue of Selim by shooting him (*The Bride of Abydos*, ll. 1051–8):

His [Selim's] back was to the dashing spray;
Behind, but close, his comrades lay,
When, at the instant, hissed the ball –
'So may the foes of Giaffir fall!'
Whose voice is heard? whose carbine rang?
Whose bullet through the night-air sang,
Too nearly, deadly aimed to err?
'Tis thine – Abdallah's Murderer!

Byron can be declamatory enough when, as here, he is using the metre of Scott, but he achieves an even more stilted rhetoric when he turns to the heroic couplet. He does this in *The Corsair* and *Lara* and evidently has in mind the eighteenth-century masters of the form. There is a ludicrous incompatibility, however, between the self-conscious dignity which their influence fosters and the preposterous characters, relationships, and deeds which Byron's imagination bodies forth under the influence of current literary fashions. When Conrad has routed his Moslem enemies and burned their fleet, he gives the order to fire their city (*The Corsair*, ll. 802–12):

Quick at the word they seized him each a torch,
And fire the dome from minaret to porch.
A stern delight was fixed in Conrad's eye,
But sudden sunk – for on his ear the cry
Of women struck, and like a deadly knell
Knocked at that heart unmoved by Battle's yell.
'Oh! burst the Haram – wrong not on your lives
One female form – remember – *we* have wives.
On them such outrage Vengeance will repay;
Man is our foe, and such 'tis ours to slay:
But still we spared – must spare the weaker prey.'

This abrupt diversion of his men's effort into a fire rescue service brings about their defeat and his capture. The idea of a ruthless Mediterranean pirate who behaves in this chivalrous and altruistic fashion, and who exhorts his followers as married men to treat their protégées with decent restraint, is absurd enough in itself; but, when Byron invests it in formal and elevated eighteenth-century couplets, the incongruity provokes irrepressible laughter.

Gulnare murders her master and frees his prisoner, Conrad. She accompanies Conrad on his return voyage (*The Corsair*, ll. 1620–31):

Embarked – the sail unfurled – the light breeze blew –
How much had Conrad's memory to review!
Sunk he in contemplation, till the Cape
Where last he anchored reared its giant shape.
Ah! – since that fatal night, though brief the time,
Had swept an age of terror, grief, and crime.
As its far shadow frowned above the mast,
He veiled his face, and sorrowed as he passed;
He thought of all – Gonsalvo and his band,
His fleeting triumph and his failing hand;
He thought on her afar, his lonely bride:
He turned and saw – Gulnare, the Homicide!

Resonant cliché, sombre exclamation, portentous antithesis, swelling climax, and grim anticlimax make this a highly theatrical presentation; and we note the careful posing of the dominant figure of Conrad himself. The whole incident is melodramatically staged. Thorslev picks out *The Corsair* as a Byronic romance that 'can still be read for enjoyment' (p. 197). But for what kind of enjoyment, and by whom? To some readers, the poem offers only the trivial pleasure of ridiculing its author's foolishnesses and extravagances.

Two later verse tales are notably free from the characteristic faults of the Turkish series. In *The Prisoner of Chillon* (1816), Bonivard's simple account of his sufferings amounts to an indictment of injustice more forcible than any explicit polemic could have been. In *Mazeppa* (1819), Byron realizes sufferings of a more sensational kind and, as in parts of *Don Juan*, employs a few ironical touches to throw his vigorous narrative of the ride into high relief.

A number of distinguished poets and critics have taken a more favourable view of the Turkish tales than has been taken here. During the nineteenth century these tales achieved great popularity both at home and abroad. In France alone, Alfred de Vigny considered *The Giaour* astonishing poetry, Lamartine described it as brilliant, and Villemain, while rating *Mazeppa* even higher, went along with them in their judgment of it. In late Victorian England, J. A. Symonds singled it out as the Turkish tale that was still worth reading. But T. S. Eliot half a century later found all of them surprisingly readable and, however absurd their view of life, 'very well told'; he went so far as to rank *Childe Harold's Pilgrimage* below them.

Nor is Thorslev the only recent scholar to have praised them. In

Byron and the Ruins of Paradise, R. F. Gleckner sees as Byron's constant theme 'the misery and lostness of man, the eternal death of love, and the repetitive ruination of paradise' (p. 251). He concentrates upon the early poems as the works in which Byron was seeking the most effective form in which to embody this vision of the world and of the human condition. Admitting that 'torrential rhetoric, simple plot, melodramatic single-dimensional characterization, and obvious emotion' (p. 92) are characteristic of the Turkish tales, he restores a favourable balance by insisting upon Byron's bold and sustained experiments with the handling of point of view, speaker, and divergent attitudes in them, in the successive cantos of *Childe Harold's Pilgrimage*, and in the other works of the same period.

The Giaour, in his opinion, 'cheers no heroes, advances no cause (private or public), asserts no values. It is a completely depressing, pessimistic, even nihilistic view of man and the world' (p. 106). He sees *The Bride of Abydos* as Byron's *Hamlet*, and he regards *The Corsair* as a kind of summing-up of the view of the human predicament that Byron had presented in its predecessors. Gleckner sometimes forces his argument, and he is prone to dejected existentialist moralizing. But his moralizing genuinely illuminates the despondency of Byron's early writings, and we must feel gratitude for a sympathetic appreciation of the Turkish tales as learned and as intelligent as his.

Childe Harold's Pilgrimage

Since the heroes of the Turkish tales are primarily Noble Outlaws, they are men of action; but Childe Harold is passive, a meditative observer. Byron seems to have been in two minds about the best way of telling the story of his pilgrimage. At first he entrusts it to a narrator with a taste for archaic, Spenserian language and for conventional moralizing:

> Whilome in Albion's isle there dwelt a youth,
> Who ne in Virtue's ways did take delight;
> But spent his days in riot most uncouth,
> And vexed with mirth the drowsy ear of Night.
> Ah me! in sooth he was a shameless wight,
> Sore given to revel and ungodly glee.
>
> (I. ii)

But elsewhere we find ourselves listening to a narrator with a more modern, though still highly literary, style and with strongly marked, personal opinions. Of the Spaniards killed resisting the Napoleonic invaders, he asks:

> And must they fall? the young, the proud, the brave,
> To swell one bloated Chief's unwholesome reign?
> No step between submission and a grave?

(I. liii)

Mourning a friend who had died from natural causes while serving in the British army in the Peninsula, he demands:

> thus unlaurelled to descend in vain,
> By all forgotten, save the lonely breast,
> And mix unbleeding with the boasted slain,
> While Glory crowns so many a meaner crest!
> What hadst thou done to sink so peacefully to rest?

(I. xci)

It is tempting to identify this second narrator with Byron, but it would be more accurate to describe him as that version of himself that Byron was then able and willing to project in verse. Throughout Cantos I and II, he breaks in from time to time with personal protests and personal elegies. His intrusions become increasingly important as time goes on, and by the end of the first canto his Spenserian rival has been almost completely silenced.

Childe Harold changes in the course of the poem. In Cantos I and II, he is a somewhat incongruous agglomeration of current hero types: 'the Child of Nature; the Gothic Villain (unregenerate, as in the novel, or remorseful, as in the drama or in Scott's romances); the accursed Wanderer; the Gloomy Egoist, meditating on ruins, death, or the vanity of life; and the Man of Feeling, suffering from a lost love, or philanthropically concerned with the suffering caused by war or oppression' (Thorslev, pp. 138–9). In Cantos III and IV, the Gothic element has declined, and the Gloomy Egoist and the Man of Feeling, both of them eighteenth-century types, have merged to form the Hero of Sensibility, a Romantic type of which Childe Harold is the earliest major English specimen. As a Hero of Sensibility, Harold is 'passive, intensely self-analytic, and given to projecting his peculiar ennui and suffering on the whole world of his vision.' Moreover, he is 'the first great English victim of the Romantic malady of *Weltschmerz*' (Thorslev, p. 142). This fact goes far to account for the extraordinary popularity of *Childe Harold's Pilgrimage* on the Continent, where the

Classical and Romantic schools were more sharply distinguished than in Britain.

The later Childe Harold is a much more coherent character than his predecessor. He is also less easily distinguishable from the narrator. Even in Cantos I and II we can sometimes be puzzled to know where the one ends and the other begins. Nor is our bewilderment dispelled when the narrator, after having apparently held the stage himself for some time, offers the tardy and implausible assurance that 'So deemed the Childe' (I. xxvii) or 'Thus Harold deemed' (II. xxxi). Early in Canto II, the narrator implicitly acknowledges his tendency to squeeze the hero out of the poem. After fifteen stanzas in which he deplores the woes of Greece, he turns and asks, 'But where is Harold?' (II. xvi). This is a question that the reader of the later cantos finds himself re-iterating with growing insistence. It leads to the discovery that Harold has disappeared in the middle of Canto III. Perhaps it would be more accurate to say that he has been transformed. He has been absorbed into the narrator, who by now is himself the Hero of Sensibility dominating the poem.

So Harold starts as a composite hero, high-born, proud, restless, solitary, sinful, sated, loving, and sad. The main narrator starts as a humane liberal, keenly aware of the impermanence of all that men prize in this world. As the poem proceeds, they come together. By Canto III. lxii, they have combined to form the sensitive, meditative, melancholy observer who is thenceforth the first-person recorder of his own pilgrimage.

The pilgrim of the earlier cantos seems unlikely ever to excite again the interest he aroused in 1812. The record of sights seen and things encountered by Harold concerns us now more than does Harold himself, or the narrator who is sometimes difficult to distinguish from him. Among the more powerfully reported items are several manifesta-tions of natural or instinctive energy. There is the doomed but defiant beast in the bull-ring, for example:

> Bounds with one lashing spring the mighty brute,
> And, wildly staring, spurns, with sounding foot,
> The sand, nor blindly rushes on his foe:
> Here, there, he points his threatening front, to suit
> His first attack, wide-waving to and fro
> His angry tail; red rolls his eye's dilated glow,
>
> (I. lxxv)

and there is the savage life observed in Albania:

> Here roams the wolf – the eagle whets his beak –
> Birds – beasts of prey – and wilder men appear,
> And gathering storms around convulse the closing year.

(II. xlii)

In Canto I, travel in Spain naturally provokes laments for the sufferings caused by war, even if it leads also to applause for the determination of the Spaniards in fighting their just war against Napoleonic imperialism. In Canto II, travel in Greece equally naturally provokes laments for the woes of Greece, enslaved by the Turks and pillaged by collectors such as Lord Elgin. Though Byron's contemporaries detected an element of misanthropy in his poetry, his attitudes are not simply those of one who detests his fellow-men. The prevailing feeling towards humanity is one not of hatred but of sadness – sadness that the things which men delight in and revere are so transient, 'Swept into wrecks anon by Time's ungentle tide' (I. xxiii) and 'All, all forgotten – and shall Man repine . . . ?' (II. liii).

The character of the pilgrim-narrator gives to the later cantos, and more especially to III, a higher degree of unity than is to be found in the earlier ones. In Canto III, this 'wandering outlaw of his own dark mind' (III. iii) crosses the Netherlands and travels up the Rhine to Switzerland. Seeking solitude and forgetfulness, he flies to Nature – to be more specific, to the Alps. Some of the lines recording this impulse are surprisingly, if not quite convincingly, Wordsworthian, as when he assures us that 'to me/High mountains are a feeling, but the hum/Of human cities torture' (III. lxxii). But the other main themes of Canto III link it with the previous instalment of the poem. The sight of the field of Waterloo stimulates reflections upon the 'antithetically mixed' (III. xxxvi) character of Napoleon, and admiration for his energy recalls the admiration expressed in Canto II for the same quality in the men of Albania. The memory of Waterloo and of other battles leads the pilgrim-narrator to voice his detestation of war, except when fought in defence of freedom (III. xvii–xx, lxiii–lxiv). This had been his reaction in Canto I to the fighting in Spain and Portugal. His sympathy with popular movements of resistance to despotism extends to the French Revolution itself (III. lxxxi–lxxxiv).

The Revolution had been followed in 1815 by the re-establishment of the old régimes throughout the Continent; and in Canto IV he goes on to ask whether men are now hopelessly subject to their newly restored tyrants. He decides that they are not. The banner of freedom, 'torn, but flying,/Streams like the thunder-storm *against* the wind' (IV. xcviii). The main thought of Canto IV, however, is the transiency of empires, exemplified especially by the decline of Venice (IV. i–iv, xi–xvii) and the fall of Rome. Rome, indeed, supplies the greater part of the subject-matter. The pilgrim-narrator has its 'buried greatness' (IV. xxv) in mind almost from the beginning, he reaches the city itself before we are half-way through the canto, and he is still in its vicinity at the close. His prevailing feeling is that expressed when he describes the Palatine Hill:

> Cypress and ivy, weed and wallflower grown
> Matted and massed together – hillocks heaped
> On what were chambers – arch crushed, column strown
> In fragments – choked up vaults, and frescos steeped
> In subterranean damps, where the owl peeped,
> Deeming it midnight: – Temples – Baths – or Halls?
> Pronounce who can: for all that Learning reaped
> From her research hath been, that these are walls –
> Behold the Imperial Mount! 'tis thus the Mighty falls.
>
> (IV. cvii)

'A ruin amidst ruins' (IV. xxv), the Hero of Sensibility passes easily from such scenes to his own pains and sorrows. In the Coliseum, he bitterly proclaims his unforgiving 'Forgiveness' (IV. cxxxv) of those who have wronged him and calls on Nemesis to take the vengeance which he forgoes.

Bravura passages provide one of the chief attractions of *Childe Harold's Pilgrimage*. In the earlier cantos we have, for example, that describing the bull-fight (I. lxviii, lxxi–lxxix) and that celebrating the beauty and mourning the decay of Greece (II. lxxxv–xc); in the later cantos, in addition to the prayer to Nemesis just mentioned, we have the stanzas on Napoleon (III. xxxvi–xliv) and the splendid concluding address to the ocean (IV. clxxix–clxxxiv). Such purple patches occur more frequently in the latter part of the poem, where both they and the passages which link them testify to the more practised hand of their author. Byron no longer essays Spenserian pastiche; he has become boldly resourceful in adapting the stanza to his own kind of rhetoric; and, while careless and wordy formulations still sometimes disfigure his writing, they have become distinctly rare.

The strength of his writing remains a rhetorical strength. Almost

79

any of the set pieces would illustrate this fact. Two will suffice for present purposes. The first, an exercise in historical painting, is the passage of sombre eloquence that takes its start from the ball given by the Duchess of Richmond in Brussels on 15 June 1815, immediately before the opening hostilities of the Waterloo campaign. The second, an exercise in landscape painting, is the passage recording the ferocity of the falls at Terni.

The Waterloo passage is well-known, though no longer as hackneyed as it used to be:

> There was a sound of revelry by night,
> And Belgium's Capital had gathered then
> Her Beauty and her Chivalry – and bright
> The lamps shone o'er fair women and brave men;
> A thousand hearts beat happily; and when
> Music arose with its voluptuous swell,
> Soft eyes looked love to eyes which spake again,
> And all went merry as a marriage bell;
> But hush! hark! a deep sound strikes like a rising knell!

> Did ye not hear it? – No – 'twas but the Wind,
> Or the car rattling o'er the stony street;
> On with the dance! let joy be unconfined;
> No sleep till morn, when Youth and Pleasure meet
> To chase the glowing Hours with flying feet –
> But hark! – that heavy sound breaks in once more,
> As if the clouds its echo would repeat;
> And nearer – clearer – deadlier than before!
> Arm! Arm! it is – it is – the cannon's opening roar! . . .

> Ah! then and there was hurrying to and fro –
> And gathering tears, and tremblings of distress,
> And cheeks all pale, which but an hour ago
> Blushed at the praise of their own loveliness –
> And there were sudden partings, such as press
> The life from out young hearts, and choking sighs
> Which ne'er might be repeated; who could guess
> If ever more should meet those mutual eyes,
> Since upon night so sweet such awful morn could rise!

> And there was mounting in hot haste – the steed,
> The mustering squadron, and the clattering car,

Went pouring forward with impetuous speed,
And swiftly forming in the ranks of war –
And the deep thunder peal on peal afar;
And near, the beat of the alarming drum
Roused up the soldier ere the Morning Star;
While thronged the citizens with terror dumb,
Or whispering, with white lips – 'The foe! They come! They come!'

And wild and high the 'Cameron's Gathering' rose!
The war-note of Lochiel, which Albyn's hills
Have heard, and heard, too, have her Saxon foes: –
How in the noon of night that pibroch thrills,
Savage and shrill! But with the breath which fills
Their mountain-pipe, so fill the mountaineers
With the fierce native daring which instils
The stirring memory of a thousand years,
And Evan's – Donald's fame rings in each clansman's ears!

And Ardennes waves above them her green leaves,
Dewy with Nature's tear-drops, as they pass –
Grieving, if aught inanimate e'er grieves,
Over the unreturning brave, – alas!
Ere evening to be trodden like the grass
Which now beneath them, but above shall grow
In its next verdure, when this fiery mass
Of living Valour, rolling on the foe
And burning with high Hope, shall moulder cold and low.

Last noon beheld them full of lusty life; –
Last eve in Beauty's circle proudly gay;
The Midnight brought the signal-sound of strife,
The Morn the marshalling in arms, – the Day
Battle's magnificently-stern array!
The thunder-clouds close o'er it, which when rent
The earth is covered thick with other clay
Which her own clay shall cover, heaped and pent,
Rider and horse, – friend, – foe, – in one red burial blent!

(III. xxi–xxii, xxiv–xxviii)

This is a powerful piece of unashamedly rhetorical writing. Byron elevates the officers and their ladies at the Duchess's ball into the 'Chivalry' and 'Beauty' of 'Belgium's Capital', and then reminds us that these personifications stand for 'fair women and brave men'. He elevates the young people enjoying themselves into 'Youth and Pleasure' meeting 'To chase the glowing Hours with flying feet', and then renders their distress on parting in the more literal terms of, for example, 'gathering tears' and 'choking sighs'.

He presents the gradual interruption of their festivity semi-dramatically. There are interjections, 'But hush! hark!'; a tense question, 'Did ye not hear it?'; an exhortation to let the dance continue, 'let joy be unconfined;/No sleep till morn'; a fresh interjection, 'But hark!'; and finally urgent commands, 'Arm! Arm! it is – it is – the cannon's opening roar!' The disturbance at the ball and the bustle of the soldiers' departure are conveyed hurriedly and impressionistically: for instance, 'the steed,/The mustering squadron, and the clattering car.' A series of present participles gives a lively sense of feverish activity: 'mounting', 'mustering', 'clattering', 'pouring', 'forming', and 'alarming'. In apt contrast, the slowest and most halting alexandrine in the passage communicates the terror of the demoralized citizens.

Opposed to this in its turn, the fifth stanza celebrates the 'fierce native daring' of the Highland troops. This modulates into a quiet lament for the 'unreturning brave', in the course of which Byron exceptionally allows himself to toy with the pathetic fallacy. A solemn recapitulation in one powerful periodic sentence opens the last stanza:

Last noon beheld them full of lusty life; –
Last eve in Beauty's circle proudly gay;
The Midnight brought the signal-sound of strife,
The Morn the marshalling in arms, – the Day
Battle's magnificently-stern array!

In the previous lines, the comparison of the dead with grass recalled the burial service; in this stanza, the metaphor 'clay' evokes similar associations. When the battle is over, we perceive that the clay which is flesh covers the clay which is earth: 'heaped and pent,/Rider and horse, friend, – foe, – in one red burial blent.'

This is public speech. Byron does not seem, like T. S. Eliot for example, to be admitting us individually to his confidence; he seems to be addressing us collectively. He has something to say that he needs urgently to communicate, and he is prepared to use all the methods of the orator, as well as those of the poet, in order to communicate it. The result is a wonderfully persuasive piece of writing.

The description of the falls at Terni has attracted much less attention:

The roar of waters! – from the headlong height
Velino cleaves the wave-worn precipice;
The fall of waters! rapid as the light
The flashing mass foams shaking the abyss;
The Hell of Waters! where they howl and hiss,
And boil in endless torture; while the sweat
Of their great agony, wrung out from this
Their Phlegethon, curls round the rocks of jet
That gird the gulf around, in pitiless horror set,

And mounts in spray the skies, and thence again
Returns in an unceasing shower, which round,
With its unemptied cloud of gentle rain,
Is an eternal April to the ground,
Making it all one emerald: – how profound
The gulf! and how the Giant Element
From rock to rock leaps with delirious bound,
Crushing the cliffs, which, downward worn and rent
With his fierce footsteps, yield in chasms a fearful vent

To the broad column which rolls on, and shows
More like the fountain of an infant sea
Torn from the womb of mountains by the throes
Of a new world, than only thus to be
Parent of rivers, which flow gushingly,
With many windings, through the vale: – Look back!
Lo! where it comes like an Eternity,
As if to sweep down all things in its track,
Charming the eye with dread, – a matchless cataract,

Horribly beautiful! but on the verge,
From side to side, beneath the glittering morn,
An Iris sits, amidst the infernal surge,
Like Hope upon a death-bed, and, unworn
Its steady dyes, while all around is torn
By the distracted waters, bears serene
Its brilliant hues with all their beams unshorn:
Resembling, 'mid the torture of the scene,
Love watching Madness with unalterable mien.

(IV. lxix–lxxii)

In Cantos I and II of *Childe Harold's Pilgrimage* almost every stanza-ending coincides with a sentence-ending; but here a single sentence pours tumultuously through four successive stanzas. The climax is reached quickly. The three stages of the waters' approach to the edge, their fall, and their turmoil in the depths are marked by the repetitive phrases which open the first, third, and fifth lines. The last of these phrases, 'The Hell of Waters', introduces a metaphor which the rest of the stanza elaborates. The waters 'howl and hiss,/And boil in endless torture'. The cloud of spray above their 'great agony' is their 'sweat . . . wrung out from this/Their Phlegethon'. The next stanza develops this into a poignant contrast. From the cloud of 'sweat', there falls an 'unceasing shower' of 'gentle rain' which is 'an eternal April to the ground,/Making it all one emerald'. A second contrast follows, between 'the broad column which rolls on' through the 'fearful vent' and its eventual offspring, the 'rivers, which flow gushingly,/With many windings, through the vale'. The eye then returns to the cataract and perceives a third contrast, between the 'infernal surge' – the epithet reminding us that it is a 'Hell' – and the serenity of the rainbow that overarches it. Nor do the contrasts stop there. The rainbow over the cataract suggests 'Hope upon a death-bed', or – an analogy for which we are prepared by the phrase, 'the distracted waters' – 'Love watching Madness with unalterable mien.'

No doubt this passage, with its 'pitiless horror', 'Horribly beautiful', and the rest, does call a little too insistently for the required response. No doubt its rhetoric is a shade too assertive. But such admissions should not prevent us from recognizing in it a skilful and confident, eloquent and powerful piece of descriptive writing. The later cantos of *Childe Harold's Pilgrimage* consist very largely of such descriptions. In these cantos, Byron's Hero of Sensibility provides the single point of view from which we look upon a whole series of impressive panoramas. Admittedly, panoramic poetry is not today the most highly esteemed kind of poetry. But it is the kind in which Byron at this period most certainly excelled.

Manfred

In a letter to Murray, Byron described *Manfred* with defensive humour as a dramatic poem 'of a very wild, metaphysical, and inexplicable kind' (15 February 1817). The description is apt. Manfred, who lives alone in the Alps, suffers from remorse for some unforgivable and unmentionable crime or sin. He invokes the Spirits of the Universe in his search for forgetfulness, but he cannot obtain it from them. Feeling himself accursed, he attempts suicide, and a Chamois Hunter rescues him. He then summons the Witch of the Alps, but such help as she may be able to supply is offered only on the unacceptable condition that he swear obedience to her. Penetrating to the hall of Arimanes, the spirit of evil, where Nemesis and the Destinies have assembled, Manfred refuses to prostrate himself before Arimanes and eventually obtains speech with the phantom of Astarte, the woman who was the victim of his unnameable offence. She predicts that on the following day he will die. On the evening of that day, an Abbot exhorts him to repent his 'converse with the things/Which are forbidden to the search of man' (III. i. 34–5). Manfred replies that no pardon can dispel his self-accusations. Nevertheless, the Abbot perseveres. As a result, he witnesses Manfred's death and, immediately prior to it, his resolute defiance of the Spirits who come to claim him:

> What I have done is done; I bear within
> A torture which could nothing gain from thine:
> The Mind which is immortal makes itself
> Requital for its good or evil thoughts, –
> Is its own origin of ill and end –
> And its own place and time.
>
> (III. iv. 127–32)

By refusing to submit himself to any supernatural authority, and by asserting the independence and self-sufficiency of the human mind, Manfred attracted the awed curiosity of believers and the eager approval of unbelievers through much of the nineteenth century. No doubt his mysterious sin – presumably incest – gave the poem an additional, vaguely scandalous interest. But a twentieth-century reader with a more matter-of-fact attitude towards belief and unbelief, and with less readiness to contemplate unspecified sins with fascinated horror, can only see *Manfred* as a confused and confusing phantasmagoria. There appears to be no necessary connection between its 'metaphysical' theme of defiant humanism and its psychological theme of remorse for an unmentionable sin. Some of the writing is stilted and turgid: for instance, the Chamois Hunter protests to Manfred, 'Why on thy brow the seal of middle age/Hath scarce been set' (II. i. 49–50), and the First Destiny praises Manfred by saying, 'This

85

man/Is of no common order, as his port/And presence here denote'
(II. iv. 51–3). These pompous phrases give local expression to the unguarded solemnity with which Manfred himself, like his contemporary,
the later Childe Harold, is presented throughout. At the same time, it
is only fair to acknowledge that Manfred's own utterances are notably
less stilted than are those of the other speakers. Some of his descriptive
passages – that on the Coliseum by moonlight (III. iv. 8–41), for example, and those on Alpine landscapes (*passim*) – have much in common
with passages on similar subjects in the later cantos of *Childe Harold's
Pilgrimage*.

As Thorslev points out (pp. 165–76), Manfred represents a development of the Byronic hero beyond Childe Harold. Admittedly, he
resembles the Giaour, Conrad, and the earlier Childe Harold in that he
conceals behind a Gothic exterior the tender heart of a Hero of Sensibility. But other Romantic hero types have also contributed to his
make-up. He has the desire for self-oblivion of such accursed Wander-
ers as Cain or Ahasuerus, he has the limitless aspiration of a Faust, and
he has the defiant Titanism of a Satan or a Prometheus. Byron's later
'metaphysical' drama, *Cain* (1821), shows the completion of this development in the characters of Lucifer and of the first murderer himself.
These, writes Thorslev, 'are true Romantic rebels, and free as they are
from the taint of Gothic melodrama, they show this heroic tradition
for what it was: a metaphysical rebellion in the cause of Romantic
self-assertion' (p. 178). Each of them embodies the Titanic impulse, but
Cain 'is also a Hero of Sensibility, capable of strong and impassioned
love, and he has none of Manfred's Gothic misanthropy' (p. 180).

Cain makes its protest more lucidly than does *Manfred*. Its dialogue
is less high-pitched; and its metaphysical theme is not entangled with a
distracting psychological theme such as leads the reader of *Manfred* to
divine unruly subjective pressures on the author's part. But its clarity
and consistency are achieved at some cost. It remains an altogether
more prosaic and arid work than the confused and turbulent but inter-
mittently moving *Manfred*.

Readers who incline to a more favourable assessment of *Manfred*
than that taken here may find some interesting hints in a final quotation
from R. F. Gleckner (p. 258). He describes the poem as:

> the tragedy of the infinite human mind and the finite human
> heart, eternally in unresolved conflict, the one destructive of the
> other, each destructive of itself. The guilt involved in such

destruction is not the moral guilt of committed sin, but rather, as M. K. Joseph so aptly put it, the guilt of being 'a member of the human race.' As such, Manfred is gifted with both the capacity for knowledge and the capacity for love. His signal success in the achieving of both should have made him a god; as it is, he can only die as a man.

Conclusion

There is nothing novel about my claim that Cantos III and IV of *Childe Harold's Pilgrimage* constitute the most enduring of the longer works of Byron's earlier period. Nor are many readers likely to disagree with my description of much of his poetry of the period as excessively stilted and declamatory. His rhetorical presentation of impressive scenes and important general themes in *Childe Harold's Pilgrimage* achieves its own distinctive kind of success. But his heroes are simply incapable of standing up to such treatment. Presented with what, while discussing Manfred, I called 'unguarded solemnity', they are almost embarrassingly exposed to the irony and mirth of those who cannot share Byron's surely rather immature admiration for them.

Yet these preposterous creatures enjoyed an extraordinary vogue during Byron's lifetime and for some years after. Thorslev rightly insists that we should distinguish them from one another. This is precisely what was not done during the period of their greatest popularity. A composite 'Byronic Hero' came to dominate the imaginations of readers and even of many who knew Byron's writings only from hearsay. Thomas Babington Macaulay, reviewing Moore's *Life of Byron* (1830), described this hero as 'a man proud, moody, cynical, with defiance on his brow, and misery in his heart, a scorner of his kind, implacable in revenge, yet capable of deep and strong affection'. This sounds more like Conrad, *alias* Lara, than any of the others. But the assumption prevailed that all Byron's heroes were of this kind and, what was more, that they were identifiable with Byron himself. The resultant legend, favoured by its independence of particular verbal formulations, was more readily exportable than any poetry could ever be; hence, in part, the speed with which Byron's fame crossed linguistic frontiers.

Yet in 1818 a gloomy, passionate, and somewhat misanthropic Byron would have been a reasonable inference from the poetry available to the public. Even then, however, a closer scrutiny of the poetry might have led to the perception that other possibilities existed in it. A reading of Byron's letters, had this been permissible, could have led to a perception of what some of these other possibilities were.

5

Beppo and the Octave Stanza

A Pleasant Place

For much of the summer of 1817, Byron was living at La Mira, a village a few miles from Venice. His mistress, Marianna Segati, was with him, and her complaisant husband, Piero Segati, used to visit her each weekend with a view to courting another lady in the neighbourhood. At dinner on 29 August, Piero told them an odd story. Hobhouse was present and recorded it in his diary (L. A. Marchand, *Byron: A Biography*, p. 708):

> A Turk arrived at the Regina di Ungheria inn at Venice and lodged there – he asked to speak to the mistress of the inn a buxom lady of 40 in keeping with certain children & who had lost her husband many years before at sea – after some preliminaries my hostess went to the Turk who immediately shut the door & began questioning her about her family & her late husband – She told her loss – when the Turk asked if her husband had any particular mark about him she said – yes he had a scar on his shoulder. Something like this said the Turk pulling down his robe – I am your husband – I have been to Turkey – I have made a large fortune and I make you three offers – either to quit your amoroso and come with me – or to stay with your amoroso or to accept a pension and live alone. . . . The lady has not yet given an answer, but M[adam]e Zagati [i.e., Segati] said I'm sure I would not leave my amoroso for any husband – looking at B. this is too gross even for me.

This story appealed strongly to Byron, who had become a connoisseur of Italian life and morals. A similar anecdote which he had heard in Milan had stimulated the exuberantly comic report in his letter to

89

Moore dated 24 December 1816. This time, he was to provide his exuberantly comic report in verse.

He started to write *Beppo* in September 1817, and on 12 October he could inform Murray, 'I have ... written a poem (of 84 octave stanzas), humourous, in or after the excellent manner of Mr. Whistlecraft (whom I take to be Frere), on a Venetian anecdote which amused me'. On 23 October he added, 'Mr. Whistlecraft has no greater admirer than myself. I have written a story in 89 stanzas, in imitation of him, called *Beppo* (the short name for Giuseppe, that is, the *Joe* of the Italian Joseph)'. There were 95 stanzas when Murray first published the poem on 28 February 1818, and before long there were 99.

It was thanks to 'Mr. Whistlecraft' that Byron was able to write *Beppo* at all. Admittedly, there are early poems in which he momentarily anticipates its casual and lightly mocking tone: for example, 'To a Lady who Presented to the Author a Lock of Hair Braided with his Own, and Appointed a Night in December to Meet Him in the Garden', in which he asks,

> Then wherefore should we sigh and whine,
> With groundless jealousy repine;
> With silly whims, and fancies frantic,
> Merely to make our love romantic?
>
> (ll. 7–10)

In the main, however, his representative poems of the years before 1818 are *Childe Harold's Pilgrimage*, the Turkish tales, and *Manfred*. Though the gloomy rhetoric of the first of these – especially in its later cantos – is preferable to the strained theatricality of the rest, none of them gives any promise of the brilliant comic poet who was to emerge. Even his energetic satire, *English Bards, and Scotch Reviewers*, is too heavy-handed to have encouraged expectations of the kind.

Yet Byron was unwilling to acquiesce in this limitation. His friends knew him to be a humorist, and his letters confirm their judgment. He even tried to make *Childe Harold's Pilgrimage*, I and II, a medley poem embracing a wide variety of moods, from the 'tender' and 'sentimental' to the 'satirical' and 'droll'. He explains in his 'Preface' that he chose to write in the Spenserian stanza because he believed it well suited for this purpose. Perhaps he was mistaken in this belief, or perhaps he was not yet mature enough to write the poem he wanted to write. Whatever the explanation, *Childe Harold's Pilgrimage*, I and II, fails completely as a medley poem. Byron presumably meant to be 'satirical' in his stanzas on the Convention of Cintra (I. xxiv–xxvi) and to be 'droll' in his stanzas on the London Sunday (I. lxix–lxx). In each instance, he succeeds only in being laboriously and tiresomely quaint.

But by the summer of 1817 he had reached what men of his time and place thought the verge of middle age. Italy suited him, and he had settled into a congenial way of life. He felt more at his ease than for many years past. The full realization of his comic gifts in poetry was becoming possible. This was the moment at which 'Mr. Whistlecraft' placed a superb instrument in his hands.

The pseudonym belonged to John Hookham Frere, a Tory politician, diplomat, and man of letters whom Byron had known in London. Frere started to write a mock-romantic Arthurian poem about 1813, and he published his first two cantos in 1817 under the facetious title, *Prospectus and Specimen of an Intended National Work, by William and Robert Whistlecraft, of Stow-market, in Suffolk, Harness and Collar-Makers. Intended to Comprise the Most Interesting Particulars Relating to King Arthur and his Round Table*. For convenience, readers usually refer to this work either as *Whistlecraft*, after its supposed author, or as *The Monks and the Giants*, this being the title given in 1821 to the four cantos which were all that Frere ever completed.

Frere writes as a disciple of the fifteenth and sixteenth-century Italian medley poets, and in particular of Luigi Pulci, who rehandled the old story of Charlemagne with irreverent humour, though without satirical purpose, in the twenty-eight cantos of his *Morgante Maggiore*. As Frere sees it, these masters 'never laid a plan' (II. i); so he proceeds with a deliberate disregard of structure. Still following their example, he claims the right to switch abruptly between gaiety and gravity – though he exercises this right only to a limited extent in what is almost entirely a burlesque poem – and he digresses as much as he pleases. Like Pulci, he turns to medieval romance for his story – though to King Arthur instead of Charlemagne; and he brings romance down to earth by entrusting the narrative to William Whistlecraft, harness-maker of Stowmarket. In carrying out this design, he naturally employs language as racy and idiomatic as Pulci's. Moreover, he owes particular debts to the *Morgante Maggiore* for the idea of the feud between the monks and the giants and for the character of the clumsy young giant Ascopart. But his most important obligation to Pulci is for his stanza-form. Admittedly, this was also the stanza-form favoured by other and better-known Italian poets – above all, by Ariosto and Tasso; but in *Whistlecraft* Frere is using the octave stanza (*ottava rima*) under Pulci's influence and on the whole in Pulci's way. Like Pulci, he revels in his own virtuosity: for example, he writes three successive stanzas in what purports to be monkish Latin (III. xxiv–xxvi), and he repeatedly surprises us with his ingenious rhymes.

R. D. Waller, in his edition of *The Monks and the Giants*, provides an authoritative account – which the present account summarizes – of this literary relationship; and he adds a judicious assessment of Frere's achievement when he states that *Whistlecraft* 'is little more than a *jeu d'esprit*; it lacks the warmth of real life' (p. 42). The poem has in fact the liveliness and the insignificance of harmless schoolboy tomfoolery. To be sure, it can be read with mild enjoyment; Frere entertains us by his agility as a metrist and rhymer. But we should find the agility more impressive if it were serving something that seemed urgently to require utterance, if, that is, we could sense an insistent pressure of experience.

A copy of *Whistlecraft*, I and II, must have reached Byron in Italy about the time of the dinner-party at which Piero Segati told his 'Venetian anecdote'. Byron had read some of the Italian poets of the octave stanza, but he had no acquaintance with Pulci prior to this encounter with Pulci's English disciple. In due course, he was to supply the omission and to produce a verse translation of the opening canto of the *Morgante Maggiore*. Immediately, however, he recognized in Frere's Italianate verse form and manner the perfect medium for such a retelling of Piero Segati's story as would express his own delight in his Italian existence.

Whereas *Whistlecraft* burlesques medieval romance, *Beppo* tells a modern tale. Admittedly, Byron sets it back slightly in time. It all happened, he tells us, 'some years ago,/It may be thirty, forty, more or less' (xxi). In the same way, he sets the action of *Don Juan* in the generation between Beppo's and his own. But in neither instance does he think of himself as writing historical fiction. He views his characters exactly as if they were his contemporaries and makes no attempt to hang the fashions and manners of the seventeen-eighties upon them. No doubt he found it easy to do this in an age in which the rate of social change was very much lower than in the twentieth century. For an artist there are advantages in a relatively stable society.

But, if Byron does not conceive himself as describing the past for his contemporaries, he clearly does conceive himself as describing Italy for the English. He contrasts the country he has adopted with that he has abandoned, and he gives it the advantage in respect of its climate, its language, and its women:

With all its sinful doings, I must say,
　　That Italy's a pleasant place to me,
Who love to see the Sun shine every day,
　　And vines (not nailed to walls) from tree to tree
Festooned, much like the back scene of a play,
　　Or melodrame, which people flock to see,
When the first act is ended by a dance
In vineyards copied from the South of France.

I like on Autumn evenings to ride out,
　　Without being forced to bid my groom be sure
My cloak is round his middle strapped about,
　　Because the skies are not the most secure;
I know too that, if stopped upon my route,
　　Where the green alleys windingly allure,
Reeling with *grapes* red wagons choke the way, –
In England 'twould be dung, dust, or a dray.

I also like to dine on becaficas,
　　To see the Sun set, sure he'll rise to-morrow,
Not through a misty morning twinkling weak as
　　A drunken man's dead eye in maudlin sorrow,
But with all Heaven t'himself; the day will break as
　　Beauteous as cloudless, nor be forced to borrow
That sort of farthing candlelight which glimmers
Where reeking London's smoky cauldron simmers.

I love the language, that soft bastard Latin,
　　Which melts like kisses from a female mouth,
And sounds as if it should be writ on satin,
　　With syllables which breathe of the sweet South,
And gentle liquids gliding all so pat in,
　　That not a single accent seems uncouth,
Like our harsh northern whistling, grunting guttural,
Which we're obliged to hiss, and spit, and sputter all.

I like the women too (forgive my folly!),
　　From the rich peasant cheek of ruddy bronze,
And large black eyes that flash on you a volley
　　Of rays that say a thousand things at once,
To the high Dama's brow, more melancholy,
　　But clear, and with a wild and liquid glance,

Heart on her lips, and soul within her eyes,
Soft as her clime, and sunny as her skies.

(xli–xlv)

Byron balances this with an ironical tribute to his own country. He introduces the tribute with the much-quoted opening line of William Cowper's patriotic praise of England as against France and Italy (*The Task*, II. 206–21).

'England! with all thy faults I love thee still,'
  I said at Calais, and have not forgot it;
I like to speak and lucubrate my fill;
  I like the government (but that is not it);
I like the freedom of the press and quill;
  I like the Habeas Corpus (when we've got it);
I like a Parliamentary debate,
Particularly when 'tis not too late;

I like the taxes, when they're not too many;
  I like a seacoal fire, when not too dear;
I like a beef-steak, too, as well as any;
  Have no objection to a pot of beer;
I like the weather, – when it is not rainy,
  That is, I like two months of every year.
And so God save the Regent, Church, and King!
Which means that I like all and every thing.

Our standing army, and disbanded seamen,
  Poor's rate, Reform, my own, the nation's debt,
Our little riots just to show we're free men,
  Our trifling bankruptcies in the Gazette,
Our cloudy climate, and our chilly women,
  All these I can forgive, and those forget,
And greatly venerate our recent glories,
And wish they were not owing to the Tories.

(xlvii–xlix)

Beppo, then, is Byron's celebration of life in Italy. The first fifth of the poem consists of a discussion of the Carnival, with incidental comments on marital jealousy, or the lack of it, in Italy, on the Venetian gondola, and on the travelling Englishman's need for such sauces as 'Ketchup, Soy, Chili-vinegar, and Harvey' (viii) if he is to face the fish-dishes of a Roman Catholic Lent. The introduction of the Count whom Laura takes as her lover during her husband's long absence leads to a description of his behaviour at the opera and to a digression on *cavalieri serventi*. Laura first sees her returned husband, though without recognizing him, at the Ridotto, 'a hall/Where People dance, and sup, and dance again' (lviii); and Byron takes the opportunity of supplying some account of a Venetian social assembly. A year had elapsed since his arrival in Italy, and during that time he had got to know the country well. He found that it suited him. But he had not learned to take the Italian way of life for granted. It could liberate and delight him, and it could surprise and even shock him. *Beppo* is an appreciation of Italian life written with both sets of responses fully active. It expresses an eager love of Italy that co-exists with a very clear and dispassionate vision of the loved object.

With such a subject, *Beppo* is one of the most cheerful poems in the English language. Its three characters are sharply defined. Laura is pretty, vain, and foolish, Beppo is 'a person both of sense and vigour' (xxvi), and the Count is a wealthy dilettante and a coxcomb. The two men distinguish themselves by what they say when the husband, still disguised as a Turk, confronts the lovers. The Count's stiff and elaborate delivery of his protest is underlined by the breezy directness of Beppo's retort:

> 'Sir,' said the Count, with brow exceeding grave,
>   'Your unexpected presence here will make
> It necessary for myself to crave
>   Its import? But perhaps 'tis a mistake;
> I hope it is so; and, at once to waive
>   All compliment, I hope so for *your* sake;
> You understand my meaning, or you *shall*.'
> 'Sir,' (quoth the Turk) ''tis no mistake at all:
>
> 'That Lady is *my wife!*'
>
> (lxxxviii–lxxxix)

But the most comically revealing speech of all is that uttered by Laura when they all go indoors to make their explanations over coffee. Twenty headlong lines of verse suffice to render perfectly her babbling inconsequentiality and blithe self-centredness:

> 'Beppo! what's your pagan name?
> Bless me! your beard is of amazing growth!

And how came you to keep away so long?
Are you not sensible 'twas very wrong?

'And are you *really*, *truly*, now a Turk?
  With any other women did you wive?
Is't true they use their fingers for a fork?
  Well, that's the prettiest Shawl – as I'm alive!
You'll give it me? They say you eat no pork.
  And how so many years did you contrive
To – Bless me! did I ever? No, I never
Saw a man grown so yellow! How's your liver?

'Beppo! that beard of yours becomes you not;
  It shall be shaved before you're a day older:
Why do you wear it? Oh! I had forgot –
  Pray, don't you think the weather here is colder?
How do I look? You shan't stir from this spot
  In that queer dress, for fear that some beholder
Should find you out, and make the story known.
How short your hair is! Lord! how grey it's grown!'

(xci–xciii)

Piero Segati's story ended with the woman obliged to choose between her husband, her lover, and a retirement pension. But from Laura a deliberate choice is unimaginable. Naturally and apparently without thought, she goes back to the husband we have just heard her nagging; and equally naturally, in the cheerful and easy-going world of this poem, though in the course of their subsequent lives she 'sometimes put him [Beppo] in a rage,/I've heard the Count and he were always friends' (xcix).

Like Frere, Byron makes little or no attempt to produce what might generally be thought a well-constructed poem. He claims the right to digress as often as he pleases, and he exercises this right much more boldly than does Frere in the two cantos of *Whistlecraft* published in 1817, in which the digressions are seldom more than brief asides. Encouraged perhaps by his own intimacy with *Tristram Shandy*, Byron explores the possibility of a work which will consist mainly of digressions. Only 41 of his 99 stanzas contribute to telling the story, and even within these 41 stanzas further brief digressions occur. In his major excursions, he discusses the Carnival at Venice, he contrasts Italian and English life, he compares sexual manners and morals in Italy, Turkey, and England, and he comments upon women and fortune and poetry.

These digressions constitute an important means by which he compels us to imagine the narrator as we read. For, just as Frere entrusts his tale of Arthurian chivalry to a tradesman of Stowmarket who is in imperfect sympathy with the ideals it embodies, so Byron entrusts his story of sexual entanglement to a gay, mocking, worldly-wise narrator who has a sharp eye for pretences and deceptions. This narrator – 'A broken Dandy lately on my travels' (lii), he calls himself – so closely resembles Byron that we shall not go far wrong in identifying the two. At the same time he does dissociate himself from at least the younger Byron when he ridicules such works as the Turkish tales of 1813–16 by declaring that, if he had 'the art of easy writing', he would sell us, 'mixed with western Sentimentalism,/Some samples of the *finest Orientalism*' (li).

In general, the digressions are as humorous as the story itself. But, just as Frere claimed the right to switch abruptly between gaiety and gravity, so Byron, or his narrator, from time to time intercalates a more tender or a more passionate utterance among his passages of frivolous and disabused mockery. Such utterances include the evocation of a real but irrecoverable love in stanzas xiii–xiv and the passing thoughts on youth in stanza lv. Byron is evidently coming near to writing the kind of medley poem that he intended *Childe Harold's Pilgrimage*, I and II, to be. In this respect, *Beppo* points forward to *Don Juan*.

The Octave Stanza

But Frere's greatest service to Byron was to suggest to him the verse form and the literary manner that he would exploit in his major poems. Though by no means the first English writer to use the octave stanza – Byron had himself used it in his 'Epistle to Augusta' – Frere was the first to handle it in anything like the way in which it was to be handled in *Don Juan*.

He saw clearly how its concluding couplet might be exploited. Coming as it does after six lines linked by alternate rhyming, it tends to make a forcible impact. Spenser softened this, in the stanza known by his name, by using the final couplet rhyme to link lines which differ in length. But in the octave stanza all eight lines are iambic pentameters. Moreover, its final couplet rhyme is not picked up from earlier in the stanza, as with Spenser. So the final couplet, composed of lines of equal length, and introducing a fresh rhyme, tends to stand out as the couplet that it is and to separate itself slightly from the rest of the stanza. This is no more than a tendency, and writers are quite able to resist and to overcome it when they choose to do so. But, if they let things take their course, the octave stanza tends to fall into a group of six lines with alternate rhyming and a group of two lines rhymed as a couplet, much as the Petrarchan sonnet tends to split into an octet and a sestet.

In many of his most successful stanzas, Frere goes along with this tendency. In the last of seven on the nature and accomplishments of Sir Tristram, his couplet conveys a bathetic reminder of the primitive reality which romantic sentiment veils:

> Strange instruments and engines he contrived
>   For sieges, and constructions for defence,
> Inventions some of them that have surviv'd,
>   Others were deem'd too cumbrous and immense:
> Minstrels he lov'd, and cherish'd while he liv'd,
>   And patronized them both with praise and pence;
> Somewhat more learned than became a Knight,
> It was reported he could read and write.
>
> (I. xxii)

Emphatic couplets serve a variety of purposes for Frere. One of them – that in II. xliii, for example – will disclose a surprising new development in the action or argument. Another will embody the telling formulation to which a whole stanza directly leads:

> We must take care in our poetic cruize,
>   And never hold a single tack too long;
> Therefore my versatile ingenious Muse
>   Takes leave of this illiterate, low-bred throng,
> Intending to present superior views,
>   Which to genteeler company belong,
> And show the higher orders of society
> Behaving with politeness and propriety.
>
> (I. ix)

The rhyme of three syllables, *society/propriety*, here gives memorable form to the stated intention.

Such rhymes of more than a single syllable are frequent in *Whistlecraft*. In the two cantos available to Byron in 1817, they amount to 28 per cent of the whole. Most of them occur in the couplets. Frere presumably used as many as he did because he found them in Pulci and the other Italians. But their effect in Italian poetry is very different from their effect in English poetry. In Italian, rhymes of two syllables (*rime piane*) are the normal rhymes; but in English such rhymes are relatively difficult to achieve and, when achieved, are liable to appear something of a *tour de force*. Triple rhymes (*rime sdruccioli*) and quadruple rhymes (*rime bisdruccioli*) tend to have in English even more of this air of virtuosity about them. As a result, our comic poetry seems to accommodate multiple rhymes more readily than does our serious poetry. Conversely, when a poet who exploits them for comic effect wishes to be taken as speaking a little more in earnest, he is likely to confine himself for the time being to the single-syllable or masculine rhymes that are normal in English. This is what Frere does when he alludes to Sir Launcelot's sin (I. xv).

Like puns, multiple rhymes provoke laughter in direct proportion to their ingenuity; and the ingenuity becomes particularly striking when more than one word contributes to the rhyming sound. Hence our special enjoyment of such rhymes of Frere's as *commodities/oddities/body 'tis* (Proem, ii); *succeeded/He did* (I. xxvi); *Parnassus/surpass us* (II. i); *aided/they did/palisaded* (II. xx); and *of it/profit* (II. lvii).

Frere's manipulation of the octave stanza and his exploitation of humorous rhymes contribute much towards establishing the tone and feeling characteristic of his work. Addressing his readers familiarly and colloquially, he gently ridicules his romantic tale even as he is telling it. Disregarding the claims of strict relevance and decorum, he holds forth at his ease, relaxedly, chattily, genially.

Byron pushes things much further. He swoops triumphantly through his stanzas to couplets which are unpredictable, hilarious, explosive. He uses many more multiple rhymes than does Frere: 44 per cent as against his predecessor's 28 per cent. Well over half of his couplets have them. The rhymes themselves are more ingenious, more extravagant, more absurd: for example, we learn that the 'last parting' of Beppo and Laura was 'pathetic',

> When kneeling on the shore upon her sad knee
> He left this Adriatic Ariadne.
>
> (xxviii)

Sometimes a line-ending seems to leave him with little prospect of finding a rhyme. He states, for instance, that no jealous husband of a Venetian would nowadays, like Othello, 'suffocate a wife no more than twenty . . .' What, we ask, can he do with 'twenty'? Can he possibly find a way of using 'plenty'? As several times elsewhere, however, a foreign word helps him out, and the ingenuity of its introduction surprises and delights us: ' . . . Because she had a "Cavalier Servente"' (xvii). Conversely, he sometimes leaves us with a line-ending which enables us to predict the word that will rhyme with it. After reviewing the condition of England, and especially its political and economic condition, he remarks with some irony that he can 'greatly venerate our recent glories'. Clearly, the word 'Tories' must arrive ten syllables later. Our enjoyment springs from the neatness and precision with which he introduces it and the humorously grudging note he sounds in doing so: ' . . . And wish they were not owing to the Tories' (xlix).

At the end of one of his digressions, he grumbles,

> This story slips for ever through my fingers,
> Because, just as the stanza likes to make it,
> It needs must be – and so it rather lingers.

> (lxiii)

It does linger, but who would wish it to hasten? His pretence that he is at the mercy of the verse form which he has chosen is richly ironical. The stanzas of the competent Frere seem sedate, even prim, beside those in which Byron takes masterful liberties with the form while unfailingly respecting its essential requirements. Since he uses rather more enjambement than does Frere, his sentences can more readily achieve an impetus that carries them through entire stanzas as it were in a single breath:

> However, I still think, with all due deference
>> To the fair *single* part of the creation,
> That married ladies should preserve the preference
>> In *tête à tête* or general conversation –
> And this I say without peculiar reference
>> To England, France, or any other nation –
> Because they know the world, and are at ease,
> And being natural, naturally please.

> (xxxviii)

The next stanza, commenting on the social awkwardness of 'your budding Miss', flows less evenly. Pauses separate the particular observations that compose it. The fourth line has something of an eighteenth-century balance, with alliteration picking out two of its key terms; the sixth line ludicrously catalogues the possible sources of the girl's total embarrassment; and the eighth line intrudes impatiently on its predecessor with a finally dismissive, absurd allegation:

'Tis true, your budding Miss is very charming,
  But shy and awkward at first coming out,
So much alarmed, that she is quite alarming,
  All Giggle, Blush; half Pertness, and half Pout;
And glancing at *Mamma*, for fear there's harm in
  What you, she, it, or they, may be about:
The Nursery still lisps out in all they utter –
Besides, they always smell of bread and butter.

                                                          (xxxix)

Again and again Byron's octave stanzas close with couplets as emphatic and memorable as this.

In another of his digressions, he reflects that 'the older that one grows/Inclines us more to laugh than scold' (lxxix). He had scolded in *English Bards, and Scotch Reviewers*; in *Beppo*, while still a satirist, he is more inclined to laugh. His laughter is that of a somewhat cynical, good-humoured, worldly-wise observer. Describing Laura's self-conscious carriage at the Ridotto, he begins by indicating the social discriminations expressed by her demeanour; he goes on to report her bitchy comments on her friends' appearance – the rhymes *turban/suburban/her bane* marking the stages by which she reaches the point at which he breaks off in mock-terror; and he finishes by contrasting the men's 'half-whispered' admiration for her with the women's indignant condemnation of male taste:

Now Laura moves along the joyous crowd,
  Smiles in her eyes, and simpers on her lips;
To some she whispers, others speaks aloud;
  To some she curtsies, and to some she dips,
Complains of warmth, and this complaint avowed,
  Her lover brings the lemonade, she sips,
She then surveys, condemns, but pities still
Her dearest friends for being dressed so ill.

One has false curls, another too much paint,
  A third – where did she buy that frightful turban?
A fourth's so pale she fears she's going to faint,
  A fifth's look's vulgar, dowdyish, and suburban,

A sixth's white silk has got a yellow taint,
  A seventh's thin muslin surely will be her bane,
And lo! an eighth appears, – 'I'll see no more!'
For fear, like Banquo's kings, they reach a score.

Meantime, while she was thus at others gazing,
  Others were levelling their looks at her;
She heard the men's half-whispered mode of praising
  And, till 'twas done, determined not to stir;
The women only thought it quite amazing
  That, at her time of life, so many were
Admirers still, – but 'Men are so debased,
Those brazen Creatures always suit their taste.'

(lxv–lxvii)

What we have here is a conversational ease and a witty penetration far in excess of anything that Frere can show. What is more, we have a closeness of observation, an experience of life as it is, that Frere nowhere exhibits. *Whistlecraft* is a high-spirited and talented literary prank. *Beppo* is the work of a brilliant, energetic, and uninhibited humorist and satirist. Even while keeping up his air of impatient improvisation, Byron never lets us forget that in his eyes the value of his poem resides in its truth, in its fidelity to life, in its closeness to the reality known to him as a man of the world.

His discipleship gratified Frere. 'Lord Byron has paid me a great compliment indeed', he wrote in a letter dated 4 May 1818 (Samuel Smiles, *Memoir of John Murray*, 1891, ii, p. 24).

6
Don Juan

Composition

Like *Beppo*, *Don Juan* grew from a scandalous story that Byron had heard in Venice. He assured Hobhouse that Juan's adventure with Donna Julia, the subject of Canto I, did not reflect an adventure of his own, 'but one of an acquaintance of mine (*Parolini* by name), which happened some years ago at Bassano, with the Prefect's wife when he was a boy; and was the subject of a long case, ending in a divorce or separation of the parties during the Italian Viceroyalty' (*Correspondence*, 25 January 1819). Byron began *Don Juan* on 3 July 1818, clearly conceiving it as a second poem in the style and manner of *Beppo*.

The dates when he completed the successive first drafts give some indication of his progress: Canto I in September 1818, Canto II in January 1819, Cantos III and IV in November 1819, and Canto V in November 1820. A month before the publication of Cantos III–V in August 1821, Teresa Guiccioli acquired, with the help of a French translation, some knowledge of the cantos published two years earlier. She pronounced *Don Juan* detestable and urged Byron to give it up.

Perhaps the reception of his poem in England had made him ready to do so. Hobhouse, Moore, Kinnaird and others had advised against the publication of Canto I on the grounds that its blasphemy, its bawdry, and its personal satire would wantonly offend his readers. The publication of Cantos I and II, somewhat nervously undertaken by Murray, had enlarged the circle of protest. Sales were disappointing. If, as Byron believed, Cantos III and IV lack some of the sparkle of their predecessors, the resistance to the work may have been partly to blame. More of the original enthusiasm went into the writing of

Canto V, and sales of the volume containing Cantos III–V were good. Nevertheless, Byron obeyed Teresa.

He laid *Don Juan* aside for a year, during which his main literary effort went into the writing of poetic dramas and of another work in octave stanzas, *The Vision of Judgment*. Then, around April 1822, he returned to *Don Juan*. No doubt the discouraging reception of his plays mainly accounts for his doing so, but the story he told Murray on 8 July 1822 emphasized Teresa's authority in the matter:

> It is not impossible that I may have three or four cantos of *D. Juan* ready by autumn, or a little later, as I obtained a permission from my Dictatress to continue it, – *provided always* it was to be more guarded and decorous and sentimental in the continuation than in the commencement. How far these Conditions have been fulfilled may be seen, perhaps, by and bye; but the Embargo was only taken off upon these stipulations.

Moore heard a similar tale. 'I have nearly (*quite three*) four new cantos of *Don Juan* ready', Byron informed him. 'I obtained permission from the female Censor Morum of *my* morals to continue it, provided it were immaculate; so I have been as decent as need be' (27 August 1822). The tone of all this warns us not to take it too seriously.

Between the spring of 1822 and the end of the year he finished Cantos VI–XII; during the opening months of 1823 he added Cantos XIII–XVI; and on 8 May 1823 he wrote the fourteen stanzas of Canto XVII which conclude the poem as we have it. Murray's fear of Tory reviewers and Tory customers making him dilatory, Byron terminated their professional relationship in the latter half of 1822. He entrusted *Don Juan* to Leigh Hunt's brother, John, who published Cantos VI–XVI at various dates between July 1823 and March 1824.

The troubled fortunes of *Don Juan* during the years of its composition elicited a number of defences from Byron. These varied with the nature of the attack and the stage he had reached in the poem. On 12 August 1819, he defended it to Murray as a playful improvisation:

> You ask me for the plan of Donny Johnny: I *have* no plan – I *had* no plan; but I had or have materials; though if, like Tony Lumpkin, I am 'to be snubbed so when I am in spirits,' the poem will be naught, and the poet turn serious again. If it don't take, I will leave it off where it is, with all due respect to the Public; but

if continued, it must be in my own way. You might as well make Hamlet (or Diggory) 'act mad' in a strait waistcoat as trammel my buffoonery, if I am to be a buffoon: their gestures and my thoughts would only be pitiably absurd and ludicrously constrained. Why, Man, the Soul of such writing is its licence . . .

. . . You are too earnest and eager about a work never intended to be serious. Do you suppose that I could have any intention but to giggle and make giggle? – a playful satire, with as little poetry as could be helped, was what I meant: and as to the indecency, do, pray, read in Boswell what *Johnson*, the sullen moralist, says of *Prior* and Paulo Purgante.

On 16 February 1821, shortly before laying the work aside for a year, he assured Murray that he seriously intended a vast comic epic:

The 5th. is so far from being the last of *D.J.*, that it is hardly the beginning. I meant to take him the tour of Europe, with a proper mixture of siege, battle, and adventure, and to make him finish as *Anacharsis Cloots* in the French revolution. To how many cantos this may extend, I know not, nor whether (even if I live) I shall complete it; but this was my notion: I meant to have made him a *Cavalier Servente* in Italy, and a cause for a divorce in England, and a Sentimental 'Werther-faced man' in Germany, so as to show the different ridicules of the society in each of those countries, and to have displayed him gradually *gâté* and *blasé* as he grew older, as is natural. But I had not quite fixed whether to make him end in Hell, or in an unhappy marriage, not knowing which would be the severest. The Spanish tradition says Hell: but it is probably only an Allegory of the other state. You are now in possession of my notions on the subject.

On 25 December 1822, having finished twelve cantos, he gave Murray a sober and cogent statement of his purpose and again resisted the charge of indecency:

Don Juan will be known by and bye, for what it is intended, – a *Satire* on *abuses* of the present states of Society, and not an eulogy of vice: it may be now and then voluptuous: I can't help that. Ariosto is worse; Smollett (see Lord Strutwell in vol. 2d. of R[oderick] R[andom]) ten times worse; and Fielding no better. No Girl will ever be seduced by reading *D.J.*:– no, no; she will go to

Little's poems and Rousseau's *romans* for that, or even to the immaculate De Stael: they will encourage her, and not the Don, who laughs at that, and – and – most other things. But never mind – Ça ira!

Byron normally wrote fast. He finished *The Bride of Abydos* inside a week, needed only a month for *The Two Foscari*, a full-length tragedy, and spent on the average a mere two-and-a-half weeks on each of the last five cantos of *Don Juan*. But the manuscripts of Canto I, as described by T. G. Steffan in the volume introducing the standard edition of *Don Juan*, show that he lavished upon it an amount of verbal and verse revision that was unusual for him. Naturally enough, he paid particular attention to the final couplets of the stanzas. Moreover, he inserted many additional passages into the completed first draft. These include exuberant elaborations, excursions with ideas, autobiographical utterances, and supports for the general structure of the poem. Many of them are less accurately described as insertions than as eruptions.

The manuscripts of Canto II exhibit similar signs of unusual care in composition. Byron was already getting into his stride, however, and in Canto III there is a marked shrinkage of revision. Cantos IV and V to some extent reverse this tendency. But in Canto VI, following the year-long break, Byron began to write with a remarkable facility. By the time he reached Cantos XII–XVI, the octave stanza seems to have become second nature to him.

The Improvvisatore

Don Juan is a vast monologue, in the course of which a story gets told. From the first line of Canto I, the monologist claims to be speaking extempore. 'I want a hero', he starts, as if his hero were still unknown to him.

So far does he seem to be from having rehearsed or even planned his narrative that before long he has to recall himself from a wrong track: 'Jóse, who begot our hero, who/Begot – but that's to come – Well, to renew:' (I. ix). Nor is this the only occasion on which he decides at the last moment to withhold information that is on the tip of his tongue. Four times in a single stanza, he stops himself from stating exactly what it was that Juan might have learned at a public school but did not learn from his private tutors (I. liii). Embarrassment

silences him when Julia and Juan are about to consummate their love
(I. cxv), when the searchers in Julia's room find something other than
what they sought under her bed (I. cxliv), and when the pregnancy of a
country girl reminds him of a particular event in his own early life
(XVI. lxi). Another painful personal recollection cuts short his account
of Haidée's reaction to her father's return (IV. xxxvi), while his interest
in the turncoat poet on Lambro's island causes him to forget where he
is in his story, so that he has deliberately to remind himself of his place
(III. lxxxi). On two other occasions, he offers no excuse for forgetting
what he meant to say (IX. xxxvi, XV. i).[1]

His manner of expression appears to be equally unpremeditated. He
admits his uncertainty about spelling (VIII. lxxiv) and grammar
(VII. xlii) and several times confesses that the words he uses are dic-
tated by the exigencies of rhyming and versifying (I. lxxxiv, I. clxxviii,
V. lxxvii, VI. xvii–xviii, XIII. lxxxiii). His suspicion of fine writing
causes him to protest,

> I won't describe; description is my forte,
>   But every fool describes in these bright days,
>
> (V. lii)

and even to deride his own similes (I. lv, VI. lxviii, XIII. xxxvi). He
emends one simile before he has finished the stanza that introduces it
(VI. xxxiii). We are clearly meant to believe him when he says,

> I ne'er decide what I shall say, and this I call
>   Much too poetical. Men should know why
> They write, and for what end; but, note or text,
> I never know the word which will come next,
>
> (IX. xli)

and when he issues his personal manifesto:

>   speculating as I cast mine eye
> On what may suit or may not suit my story,
>   And never straining hard to versify,
> I rattle on exactly as I'd talk
> With any body in a ride or walk.

[1] In I.xcviii, he professes to have forgotten the serial number of the
commandment against adultery. The manuscript shows that Byron, having
begun to write 'the seventh', decided to make the narrator interrupt himself
with a confession of ignorance.

I don't know that there may be much ability
  Shown in this sort of desultory rhyme;
But there's a conversational facility,
  Which may round off an hour upon a time.
Of this I'm sure at least, there's no servility
  In mine irregularity of chime,
Which rings what's uppermost of new or hoary,
Just as I feel the 'Improvvisatore.'

(XV. xix–xx)

Exploiting his liberty as an improviser, he decides upon radical
changes in the structure of his poem while still engaged in writing it.
He thought at first that 'about two dozen/Cantos would do' – as in the
Iliad and the *Odyssey* – but he decides by Canto XII that he will 'canter
gently through a hundred' (XII. lv). Finding the original Canto III too
long, he informs us that he will make two cantos, III and IV, out of it.
Again he has classical examples in mind, for he describes his 'tedious-
ness' as *'too* epic' (III. cxi).

These and other allusions to the epic draw attention to the casualness
of *Don Juan*. Sometimes they do this directly by advertising the writer's
conscious neglect of the demands of the epic form: for example, he
points out that he is not plunging *in medias res*, but beginning 'with
the beginning' (I. vi–vii). More frequently, they take the form of
ironical claims that he is conforming with the most rigid requirements.
Such a claim is implicit in the perfunctory invocation that opens
Canto III: 'Hail, Muse! *et cetera*'; and before this it has been spelt out
at length:

My poem's epic, and is meant to be
  Divided in twelve books; each book containing,
With love, and war, a heavy gale at sea,
  A list of ships, and captains, and kings reigning,
New characters; the episodes are three:
  A panorama view of hell's in training,
After the style of Virgil and of Homer,
So that my name of Epic's no misnomer.

All these things will be specified in time,
  With strict regard to Aristotle's rules,
The *vade mecum* of the true sublime,
  Which makes so many poets, and some fools;

Prose poets like blank-verse, I'm fond of rhyme,
　　Good workmen never quarrel with their tools;
I've got new mythological machinery,
And very handsome supernatural scenery.

(I. cc–cci)

Here he briskly catalogues the traditional features of the epic and
dutifully appeals to the examples of Virgil and Homer and the precepts
of Aristotle. To be sure, his poem contains 'love, and war, a heavy gale
at sea' and is to that extent in conformity with the rules; but in the
passage as a whole he is exploiting the ludicrous contrast between a
particularly stringent set of requirements, which he professes to respect,
and a poem in which he does not even consistently disobey them, but
proceeds in complete indifference to them. He gives another turn to
his satire in the next stanza when he admits that in one direction he does
deviate from classical example:

There's only one slight difference between
　　Me and my epic brethren gone before . . . ;
　　They so embellish, that 'tis quite a bore
Their labyrinth of fables to thread through,
Whereas this story's actually true.

(I. ccii)

Seven cantos later, he is still insisting upon the veracity which
distinguishes him from his forerunners. But he assures us of his ortho-
doxy in other respects; he has supplied what he promised in Canto I:
'love, tempest, travel, war –/All very . . . *Epic*' (VIII. cxxxviii). He
brings Canto V to a conclusion in accordance with 'the ancient epic
laws' (V. clix), he recognizes in 'conquest and its consequences' the
material which makes 'Epic poesy so rare and rich' (VIII. xc), and he
asks the reader who finds the later cantos less violent than the earlier
to remember that

　　　　you have had before
The worst of tempests and the best of battles
　　That e'er were brewed from elements or gore,
Besides the most sublime of – Heaven knows what else.

(XII. lxxxviii)

By the latest cantos, the mere use of the term in passing – 'mine epic',
'this Epic Satire', 'this Epic' – suffices to convey his mocking pretence

109

that all that he does is in accordance with the rules governing the great classical form (XIV. lxviii, XIV. xcix, XVI. iii). The pretence reflects ironically upon epic poetry itself and at the same time sharpens our awareness of the monologist's casual and improvisational manner.

This achieves its most extravagant manifestation at the end of Canto XII, when he announces to us, after we have read more than 12,000 lines of verse, that

> Here the twelfth Canto of our introduction
> Ends. When the body of the book's begun,
> You'll find it of a different construction
> From what some people say 'twill be when done:
> The plan at present's simply in concoction.
>
> (XII. lxxxvii)

We should be foolish to dismiss this as merely facetious. Canto XII has settled Don Juan in London. In Canto XIII, he first meets Lord Henry and Lady Adeline Amundeville and the Duchess of FitzFulke; two cantos later, he first meets Aurora Raby. These are the important personages in the social comedy that is unfolding at Norman Abbey, also first described in Canto XIII, when the poem breaks off early in Canto XVII.

Farce and satire, adventure and romance, characterize the earlier cantos; ludicrous, horrifying, and tender scenes develop in a wide variety of exotic settings. On the whole, the action moves fairly briskly. After the attempted highway robbery at the beginning of Canto XI, however, it slows down until it almost comes to a halt in Canto XII, the most digressive in the entire poem. It seems then to make a fresh start with its scenes of aristocratic British life before a background that its author knew intimately. Digressions became fewer. Even so, the narrative does not recover its original pace. Nor apparently does the narrator wish it to do so. Greater rapidity would be incompatible with his relaxed, quizzical, ironical contemplation of the familiar social comedy. If the first ten cantos of *Don Juan* show us an innocent and mainly passive hero getting into a series of scrapes rather in the manner of Voltaire's *Candide*, the last six seem to anticipate much that is typical of the novels of Thackeray.

To say this is not to take literally the mocking declaration that the first dozen cantos are merely the 'introduction' to 'the body of the book'. But, if it is unwise to read Byron too soberly, it is also unwise to neglect the element of truth, as he saw it, in even his most high-spirited and outrageous statements. His dismissal of his first dozen cantos as a mere 'introduction' evidently expresses his own sense of the fresh start which we have discerned in Canto XIII. His cheerful readiness to make such a fresh start so late in the poem exemplifies once more his casual and improvisational manner.

To refer at last not to 'the monologist' or 'the narrator' but to Byron himself brings a considerable feeling of relief. Critical theorists rightly discourage us from simply assuming the identity of poet with imagined narrator, but in this particular instance the scrupulous dissociation of the two brings great inconveniences and no advantages. As a matter of biographical fact, Byron evidently thought of himself as speaking with his own voice in *Don Juan*. His account of the assassination of the military commandant in Ravenna (V. xxxiii–xxxix) corresponds so closely with the accounts in his letters dated 9 December 1820 that it is impossible to suppose otherwise; and this is only one instance out of many. As a matter of literary fact, nothing in *Don Juan* encourages us to discern an authorial point of view differing from that of the narrator, or digresser. Perhaps we are getting somewhere near doing so when the story-teller professes to have been a friend of Juan's parents (I. xxiii–xxiv). But very little more is made of this claim than of his claims, implied in passing by his use of the first person, to have been present on the *Trinidada* (II. xlii, xcv) and at the siege of Ismail (VIII. xlvii). Against our doing so, moreover, is the voice in which the narrator and digresser speaks from beginning to end. This is a voice that defines him sharply and leaves him in sole command of the poem; and it is surely the voice of Byron himself as we know it in his letters and journals and in the copious records of his conversation.

It is the voice of a spirited and versatile talker; its tone is normally gay and sociable, but it can easily compass gravity and pathos. The English it employs is clear, vigorous, and racy, sometimes careless, always extraordinarily flexible, and never hardening into mannerism or preciosity. While it remains recognizably the voice heard in Byron's letters and journals, the challenge of utterance in *ottava rima* has elicited from it an even more brilliant virtuosity. In English poetry generally, the intricate rhymes of the octave stanza seem to invite verbal acrobatics; in *Don Juan* they are used to point wit, to release surprises, to clinch arguments, and to fix the most pungent satirical observations permanently in the memory.

Addresses from the Throne

The digressions supply many of the illustrations that come immediately to mind. Following Frere and the Italian medley poets, Byron claims the right to interrupt his story as often as he pleases and to hold forth as long as he likes on any matter that he chooses. 'I must own,' he confesses ironically,

> If I have any fault, it is digression;
> Leaving my people to proceed alone,
>   While I soliloquize beyond expression;
> But these are my addresses from the throne,
>   Which put off business to the ensuing session.
>
>   (III. xcvi)

None of his poetic predecessors exercises this right as freely as he does. In the extreme case, Canto XII, his digressions nearly squeeze out the story altogether.

They range widely in subject-matter. As we have seen, Byron uses many of them to discuss his purposes and methods in the poem actually under way, *Don Juan* itself. He uses others to recall the literary fame he once enjoyed but has now, he believes, lost:

> Even I – albeit I'm sure I did not know it,
>   Nor sought of foolscap subjects to be king, –
> Was reckoned, a considerable time,
> The grand Napoleon of the realms of rhyme.
>
> But Juan was my Moscow, and Faliero
>   My Leipsic, and my Mont Saint Jean seems Cain.
>
>   (XI. lv–lvi)

In still others, he comments on the transiency of all kinds of glory:

> Where is Napoleon the Grand? God knows:
>   Where little Castlereagh? The devil can tell:
> Where Grattan, Curran, Sheridan, all those
>   Who bound the bar or senate in their spell?
> Where is the unhappy Queen, with all her woes?
>   And where the Daughter, whom the Isles loved well?
> Where are those martyred Saints the Five per Cents?
> And where – oh where the devil are the Rents?
>
>   (XI. lxxvii)

Elsewhere, he writes of love: tenderly of 'first and passionate love' (I. cxxvii, V. iv, VI. v), ironically of three distinct varieties of the passion:

> The noblest kind of Love is Love Platonical,
>   To end or to begin with; the next grand
> Is that which may be christened Love Canonical,
>   Because the clergy take the thing in hand;
> The third sort to be noted in our Chronicle
>   As flourishing in every Christian land,
> Is, when chaste Matrons to their other ties
> Add what may be called *Marriage in Disguise*,
>
> (IX. lxxvi)

and satirically of the 'Canonical' kind:

> 'Tis melancholy, and a fearful sign
>   Of human frailty, folly, also crime,
> That love and marriage rarely can combine,
>   Although they both are born in the same clime;
> Marriage from love, like vinegar from wine –
>   A sad, sour, sober beverage – by time
> Is sharpen'd from its high celestial flavour
> Down to a very homely household savour.
>
> (III. v)

Feeling that he is no longer young, he decides to relinquish women and wine and to gratify a more 'old-gentlemanly' appetite:

> My days of love are over, me no more
>   The charms of maid, wife, and still less of widow,
> Can make the fool of which they made before,
>   In short, I must not lead the life I did do;
> The credulous hope of mutual minds is o'er,
>   The copious use of claret is forbid too,
> So for a good old-gentlemanly vice,
> I think I must take up with avarice.
>
> (I. ccxvi)

Throughout the digressions, he exhibits an acute sense of the passage of time, of the impermanence of the things that men value, of the vanity of human wishes. He expresses this sardonically and yet hilariously in a stanza on a Pharaoh's folly:

> What are the hopes of man? old Egypt's King
>   Cheops erected the first pyramid
> And largest, thinking it was just the thing
>   To keep his memory whole, and mummy hid;
> But somebody or other rummaging,
>   Burglariously broke his coffin's lid:
> Let not a monument give you or me hopes,
> Since not a pinch of dust remains of Cheops.
>
> (I. ccxix)

Different subjects tend to engage the digressive Byron at different stages in his poem. Reflections on love, on sexual jealousy, and on marriage are especially common in the earlier cantos; the denunciation of unjust wars, by which he means wars not fought in defence 'of freedom, country, or of laws' (VII. xl), and the praise of political liberty are recurrent topics in Cantos VII, VIII, and IX; and satirical observations on British social life, and on the hypocrisy which he sees as inextricably woven into it, inspire many digressions in the final cantos. Another preoccupation which grows in importance as the poem proceeds is that with philosophical and theological doubt. It can result equally in an incisive critical formulation:

> Nothing more true than *not* to trust your senses;
> And yet what are your other evidences?
>
> (XIV. ii)

or in a sombrely ruminative conclusion to a whole canto:

> Between two worlds life hovers like a star,
>   'Twixt night and morn, upon the horizon's verge:
> How little do we know that which we are!
>   How less what we may be! The eternal surge
> Of time and tide rolls on, and bears afar
>   Our bubbles; as the old burst, new emerge,
> Lash'd from the foam of ages; while the graves
> Of Empires heave but like some passing waves.
>
> (XV. xcix)

The voice that delivers these digressions is the voice of the spirited and versatile talker already described. The cheerful irreverence of Byron's distinction between three kinds of love contrasts with his melancholy gravity in the passage quoted last. The *Ubi sunt?* stanza and that on Cheops convey poignant reflections in boisterously humorous terms. The colloquialism of the opening and closing lines of the *Ubi sunt?* stanza, and of the statement that in 'Love Canonical . . . the clergy take the thing in hand', contrasts with the elegiac formality with which he opens the stanza recording his decision to 'take up with avarice'. Even in these few selected passages, there is some carelessness: for example, the six words 'to be noted in our Chronicle' fail to earn their place in the text; they do nothing more than supply a rhyme to 'Platonical' and 'Canonical'. In general, however, the language is succinct as well as vigorous, and the comic rhymes – those to 'widow' and 'Cheops', for instance – brilliantly point Byron's wit and bring out his flexible conversational tones.

This highly recognizable voice helps to project upon our minds a clear image of the man who speaks to us throughout the digressions, despite their extraordinary variety in subject-matter. He is a man whose youth is behind him and who has developed into a sardonic observer of human folly and an angrily scornful opponent of hypocrisy and tyranny. At the same time, his worldly wisdom does not inhibit his sympathies or deter him from cherishing such ideals as his experience allows him to suppose attainable; and his maturity does not prevent him from giving free expression to an exceptionally lively sense of humour. This can be playful or satirical, teasing or savage. A gay mockery is its most characteristic manifestation and is never long absent from his utterances. No matter what the topic, he speaks his mind fully, spontaneously, even recklessly.

Plain Narration

This strongly individualized and compelling monologist does not appear only in the digressions. He tells the story, too, and so deep is the impression of his personality upon it that we can easily think of the whole of *Don Juan*, digressions and story, as a single monologue long enough to fill half-a-dozen of Shakespeare's plays. With remarkable candour and copiousness, Byron has created the monologist in his own image. Reading the poem, we not only hear his voice but recognize the man himself as we know him from the letters, the reported conversations, and the other biographical documents.

While engaged in 'plain narration' (VI. lvii), he records principally six major adventures of his hero. He starts by describing Juan's childhood and the extraordinary educational system employed by his priggish mother, Donna Inez, to keep him sexually pure. Despite this, Donna Julia, a friend of his mother's, seduces the susceptible sixteen-year-old. But her husband, Don Alfonso, discovers the liaison, and Juan is bundled out of Spain on his second adventure. He suffers shipwreck, followed by prolonged exposure and starvation in an open boat. Eventually he struggles ashore in the Cyclades, and Haidée, the only daughter of Lambro, a successful Greek pirate and slave-trader, inaugurates his third adventure by discovering him unconscious on a beach of the island which is her father's home and base. The two young people become lovers. Lambro's unexpected return shatters the idyll. Haideé dies, and Juan's fourth adventure opens with his being offered for sale as a slave in Constantinople. Gulbeyaz, a wife of the Sultan, purchases him and tries imperiously to seduce him. But Juan resists her and, after a passing encounter with Dudù, one of the women of the seraglio, escapes from the Turks and joins the army of their enemies, the Russians. His fifth adventure follows. He contributes to the capture of the city of Ismail, and Suwarrow (Suvarov), the Russian commander-in-chief, sends him to St Petersburg with a dispatch announcing the success. There he becomes the lover of the notorious Empress Catherine II. His health beginning to deteriorate, she initiates his last adventure by sending him on a diplomatic mission to England. While mixing in English social life, he attracts the attention of three women: Aurora Raby, a young heiress; Lady Adeline Amundeville, a politician's wife; and the lax and lavish Duchess of FitzFulke. The last of these, by masquerading as a ghost, makes herself his lover just before the poem breaks off.

Juan's five lovers are clearly distinguished one from another. Julia is sentimental and self-deluding, Haidée simple and affectionate, Dudù shy and accommodating, Catherine insatiable, and the Duchess frolicsome. The unsuccessful lover, Gulbeyaz, is domineering before, and vindictive after, her frustration. But the story of *Don Juan* is more than a love-story. A shipwreck, a period of slavery, a battle, an attempted highway-robbery, various social occasions in London and in the country, and an apparently supernatural haunting add further variety to Juan's experiences. As a result, his five, or six, lovers are by no means the only important characters with whom he has dealings. Others include his mother, the self-righteous bluestocking Donna Inez; his father, the errant and harassed Don Jóse; Julia's husband, the bewildered and irascible Don Alfonso; Haidée's father, a displaced 'Byronic' hero; Johnson, the downright and fatalistic English soldier of fortune;

Suwarrow, the boorish Russian general; Lord Henry Amundeville, the polished and imperturbable aristocratic politician; and two young women who do not become Juan's lovers, the virtuous Aurora Raby, who is the civilized counterpart of the natural Haidée, and the intense and restless Lady Adeline. Characters who play minor parts are also sharply individualized: for example, Antonia, Pedrillo, Zoe, Raucocanti, Baba, Lolah, Katinka, Leila, and Lady Pinchbeck. Even such anonymous characters as Don Alfonso's attorney, with his 'prying snub-nose, and small eyes' (I. clx), and the turncoat poet who entertains Juan and Haidée have their independent existences.

They have their distinctive voices, too. In *The Corsair*, Conrad, Medora, Gulnare, and Seyd all spoke Byronese; and the same was true of the characters in the other early tales in verse. But in *Beppo* Byron successfully contrasted the grave, formal speech of the Count (lxxxviii, xc) with the effervescent, frivolous chatter of Laura (xci–xciii); and in *Don Juan* he exhibits in a more highly developed form this power of creating characters who seem to speak from independent centres of vitality. Thus, when Don Alfonso doubts his wife's fidelity and ransacks her bedroom, Julia, whom we have previously seen as a charming romantic self-deceiver, reacts as a scornfully self-righteous termagant:

> 'Yes, search and search,' she cried,
> 'Insult on insult heap, and wrong on wrong!
> It was for this that I became a bride!
> For this in silence I have suffer'd long
> A husband like Alfonso at my side;
> But now I'll bear no more, nor here remain,
> If there be law, or lawyers, in all Spain.
>
> 'Yes, Don Alfonso! husband now no more,
> If ever you indeed deserved the name,
> Is't worthy of your years? – you have threescore,
> Fifty, or sixty – it is all the same –
> Is't wise or fitting causeless to explore
> For facts against a virtuous woman's fame?
> Ungrateful, perjured, barbarous Don Alfonso,
> How dare you think your lady would go on so?'
>
> (I. cxlv–cxlvi)

The verbal assault continues with equal energy and verve for another eleven overwhelming stanzas. Lending Julia his own rhetorical gifts,

Byron enables her to utter an indignant protest that is, at the same time, unmistakably factitious.

In the Turkish slave-market, the dialogue between Juan and Johnson contrasts the voice of the impressionable young bereaved lover with that of the humorous and hard-boiled English adventurer:

> 'My boy!' – said he [Johnson], 'amidst this motley crew
>> Of Georgians, Russians, Nubians, and what not,
> All ragamuffins differing but in hue,
>> With whom it is our luck to cast our lot,
> The only gentlemen seem I and you;
>> So let us be acquainted, as we ought:
> If I could yield you any consolation,
> 'Twould give me pleasure. – Pray, what is your nation?'
>
> When Juan answered 'Spanish!' he replied,
>> 'I thought, in fact, you could not be a Greek;
> Those servile dogs are not so proudly eyed:
>> Fortune has played you here a pretty freak,
> But that's her way with all men till they're tried;
>> But never mind, – she'll turn, perhaps, next week;
> She has served me also much the same as you,
> Except that I have found it nothing new.'
>
> 'Pray, Sir,' said Juan, 'if I may presume,
>> *What* brought you here?' – 'Oh! nothing very rare –
> Six Tartars and a drag-chain – '

(V. xiii–xv)

Having alluded to Haidée's death, Juan

> stopped again, and turned away his face.
> 'Ay,' quoth his friend, 'I thought it would appear
>> That there had been a lady in the case;
> And these are things which ask a tender tear,
>> Such as I too would shed if in your place:
> I cried upon my first wife's dying day,
> And also when my second ran away:
>
> 'My third –' – 'Your third!' quoth Juan, turning round;
>> 'You scarcely can be thirty: have you three?'
> 'No – only two at present above ground:
>> Surely 'tis nothing wonderful to see

One person thrice in holy wedlock bound!'
   'Well, then, your third,' said Juan; 'what did she?
She did not run away, too, did she, sir?'
   'No, faith.' – 'What then?' – 'I ran away from her.'

'You take things coolly, sir,' said Juan. 'Why,'
   Replied the other, 'what can a man do?
There still are many rainbows in your sky,
   But mine have vanished. All, when life is new,
Commence with feelings warm and prospects high;
   But time strips our illusions of their hue,
And one by one in turn, some grand mistake
Casts off its bright skin yearly like the snake.'

(V. xix–xxi)

The rhetorical and metrical skill necessary to achieve the furious emphasis upon 'dare' in the last line quoted from Julia's tirade is evident also throughout these stanzas. A careless assumption of racial and social superiority to the 'ragamuffins', 'servile dogs', 'and what not' accompanies the courteous assurance with which Johnson invites Juan's acquaintance. Fatalistic in his acceptance of the whims of fortune, he is facetiously blunt in his explanation of what brought him to Constantinople. Juan's grief provokes an expression of waggish knowingness ('a lady in the case') and, up to a point, of sympathy. But Johnson quickly shifts to an account of his marital misadventures. The exchanges in the stanza devoted to his third wife are easy, rapid, natural, and dramatically pointed by metre and rhyme. Before he comes to the last stanza quoted, he has successfully indicated to us a number of the experiences which justify its sardonic pessimism.

The contrast between the two men grows even more marked in their subsequent debates on Juan's rash proposal to overpower Baba and escape (V. xliii–xlvii) and on Baba's benevolent suggestion that they should both 'condescend to circumcision' (V. lxix–lxxii). The proud impulsiveness of the younger and the worldly-wise prudence of the older determine their conduct, in Canto VIII, at the siege of Ismail.

A less commendable worldly wisdom inspires Donna Inez's complacent advice to her son on learning that he has become the current favourite of Catherine II. She notes that he is drawing less on his banker and is living more economically. She writes

> that she was glad to see him through
>   Those pleasures after which wild youth will hanker;
> As the sole sign of man's being in his senses
> Is, learning to reduce his past expenses.
>
> She also recommended him to God,
>   And no less to God's Son, as well as Mother;
> Warned him against Greek-worship, which looks odd
>   In Catholic eyes; but told him too to smother
> *Outward* dislike, which don't look well abroad:
>   Informed him that he had a little brother
> Born in a second wedlock; and above
> All, praised the Empress's *maternal* love.
>
> She could not too much give her approbation
>   Unto an Empress, who preferred young men
> Whose age, and, what was better still, whose nation
>   And climate, stopped all scandal (now and then):–
> At home it might have given her some vexation;
>   But where thermometers sunk down to ten,
> Or five, or one, or zero, she could never
> Believe that virtue thawed before the river.
>
> > (X. xxxi–xxxiii)

These unctuous and evasive rationalizations make Byron exclaim, 'Oh for a *forty-parson-power* to chaunt/Thy praise, Hypocrisy!' (X. xxxiv). His employment of indirect speech helps him to keep the words of the character under a steady ironical scrutiny.

Indirect speech is several times used in this fashion in *Don Juan*. Another striking example is the report of the arguments advanced by Lord Henry Amundeville, who 'was all things to all men', to justify his continued placid enjoyment of the profits of government sinecures. Both sense and syntax reveal him as a time-server and trimmer, and Byron underscores the irony by commenting parenthetically.

> A friend to freedom and freeholders – yet
>   No less a friend to government – he held,
> That he exactly the just medium hit
>   'Twixt place and patriotism – albeit compelled,
> Such was his Sovereign's pleasure (though unfit,
>   He added modestly, when rebels railed)
> To hold some sinecures he wished abolished,
> But that with them all law would be demolished.

He was 'free to confess' – (whence comes this phrase?
  Is't English? No – 'tis only parliamentary)
That innovation's spirit now-a-days
  Had made more progress than for the last century.
He would not tread a factious path to praise,
  Though for the public weal disposed to venture high;
As for his place, he could but say this of it,
That the fatigue was greater than the profit.

Heaven, and his friends, knew that a private life
  Had ever been his sole and whole ambition;
But could he quit his king in times of strife
  Which threatened the whole country with perdition?
When demagogues would with a butcher's knife
  Cut through and through (oh! damnable incision!)
The Gordian or the *Geo*rdi-an knot, whose strings
Have tied together Commons, Lords, and Kings.
                        (XVI. lxxi–lxxiv)

It hardly needs saying that Byron does not always record the spoken or written words of his characters as successfully as in the instances so far examined. Gulbeyaz's extravagant development of old Baba's astronomical metaphors in V. cxliv–cxlv seems implausible in such a woman on being told that her husband is about to make her a singularly unwelcome visit; and Juan's opening words in his rejection of Gulbeyaz would fit better into one of the Turkish tales than into *Don Juan*: 'The prisoned eagle will not pair, nor I/Serve a sultana's sensual phantasy' (V. cxxvi). But such lapses are exceptional. In addition to the major characters whose speeches have already been cited, Byron allows his minor characters their own distinctive voices: Antonia, for example, whose sharp tones are beautifully caught in Canto I, and Raucocanti, who diverts Juan and us with a brisk and spiteful review of the other members of the operatic company with which he has been sold into slavery (IV. lxxxii–lxxxix).

Juan himself is less clearly individualized than are some of those whom we see over his shoulder. He is very young, being still in his teens when we last set eyes on him (though Byron does forgetfully make him twenty-one in XIV. li–liv). He also differs from the Don Juans of popular imagination in that there is nothing of the predatory seducer about him. While he responds to the active approaches of various women, and does not let slip the opportunity that is forced upon him in the seraglio, he makes no attempt to create opportunities for himself. In a storm at sea, and in battle, he is enterprising and intrepid; but as a lover he is decidedly passive.

Byron evidently intended Juan's amatory and other exploits progressively to disillusion and mature him. The process is that described by Johnson in the slave-market in Constantinople. Accordingly, shortly after his arrival in England, Juan is said to be

> A little '*blâsé*' – 'tis not to be wondered
>   At, that his heart had got a tougher rind:
> And though not vainer from his past success,
> No doubt his sensibilities were less.
>
> (XII. lxxxi)

A few months later, it can be added that

>   his conduct, since in England, grew more
>   Strict, and his mind assumed a manlier vigour;
> Because he had, like Alcibiades,
> The art of living in all climes with ease.
>
> (XV. xi)

These changes are more evident in the narrator's account than in the deeds and words of Juan himself. Admittedly, residence at the Russian court gives his demeanour a higher polish, and his adventures generally help to mature him. But, despite what we are told, he remains very much the same cheerful, modest, amiable paragon from the beginning to the end of the story.

In the poem as Byron left it, Juan's adventures occur successively, during a period of slightly over two years, in Spain, at sea, on a Greek island, again at sea, in Turkey, in Russia, and in England; and Byron on one occasion, as we have noted, expressed the intention of taking him in due course to Italy, Germany, and France. The great length of *Don Juan* – more than 16,000 lines – is no more than is appropriate in view of the wide variety of its settings, incidents, and characters.

Almost without exception, these are credible incidents, involving credible characters in credible settings. No Conrad the Corsair could safely stalk through *Don Juan*; Lambro, his nearest equivalent, would by his mere presence show him up as the posturing dummy that he is. Even the most acceptable parts of the Turkish tales, their settings, were thoroughly romanticized. But those of *Don Juan* testify to an evident concern on Byron's part to be as completely truthful as he was in

presenting the Venetian setting of *Beppo*, the poem in which he first
achieved the style of his full maturity.

Scorching and Drenching

The incidents that make up the story of *Don Juan* vary widely in tone
and feeling, and the order of their occurrence is such as to provide a
series of striking and suggestive contrasts. Juan's adventures at sea,
unmasking the savagery of nature and of man, are sandwiched between
a bedroom farce and a sometimes sentimental idyll; his libertarian
defiance of the predatory Gulbeyaz introduces the frivolous harem
incident, which is itself followed by the bloody storming of Ismail;
having visited the court of one of the monarchs responsible for the war
immediately before himself engaging in it, Juan visits the court of the
other immediately afterwards; and his experience of the open tyranny
and lust of Catherine precedes his experience of the same vices in
disguised forms among the hypocritical English. Similar contrasts
characterize the digressions, both among themselves and in relation to
the narrative.

In all this, Byron is acting on his long-felt desire to write a medley
poem embracing a wide variety of moods, from the 'tender' and
'sentimental' to the 'satirical' and 'droll'. In *Beppo*, a more sympathetic
or more passionate utterance occasionally finds a place amid the frivolous and disabused mockery that normally prevails. In *Don Juan*, such
contrasts become more frequent and more pronounced. They occur
within single incidents and digressions, as well as between them. Juan's
relationship with Julia involves not only bedroom farce but also a
sincere romantic love; Juan's noble defiance of Gulbeyaz, 'Love is for
the free!' (V. cxxvii), starts to weaken when she weeps, and she seems
to be on the verge of having her way with him when a sudden warning
of the Sultan's approach opens up a short cut to absurdity; and the
harrowing account of the storming of Ismail begins with some joking –
pretty feeble joking, it must be admitted – about Russian proper names.

Perhaps the most alarming of all Byron's emotional switchbacks
occurs in Canto II when he tells how the dying men in the open boat
resort to cannibalism:

> At length one whisper'd his companion, who
>   Whisper'd another, and thus it went round,
> And then into a hoarser murmur grew,
>   An ominous, and wild, and desperate sound,

And when his comrade's thought each sufferer knew,
  'Twas but his own, suppress'd till now, he found:
And out they spoke of lots for flesh and blood,
And who should die to be his fellow's food.

But ere they came to this, they that day shared
  Some leathern caps, and what remain'd of shoes;
And then they look'd around them, and despair'd,
  And none to be the sacrifice would choose;
At length the lots were torn up, and prepared,
  But of materials that much shock the Muse –
Having no paper, for the want of better,
They took by force from Juan Julia's letter.

The lots were made, and mark'd, and mix'd, and handed,
  In silent horror, and their distribution
Lull'd even the savage hunger which demanded,
  Like the Promethean vulture, this pollution;
None in particular had sought or plann'd it,
  'Twas nature gnaw'd them to this resolution,
By which none were permitted to be neuter –
And the lot fell on Juan's luckless tutor.

He but requested to be bled to death:
  The surgeon had his instruments, and bled
Pedrillo, and so gently ebb'd his breath,
  You hardly could perceive when he was dead.
He died as born, a Catholic in faith,
  Like most in the belief in which they're bred,
And first a little crucifix he kiss'd,
And then held out his jugular and wrist.

The surgeon, as there was no other fee,
  Had his first choice of morsels for his pains;
But being thirstiest at the moment, he
  Preferr'd a draught from the fast-flowing veins:
Part was divided, part thrown in the sea,
  And such things as the entrails and the brains
Regaled two sharks, who follow'd o'er the billow –
The sailors ate the rest of poor Pedrillo.

The sailors ate him, all save three or four,
  Who were not quite so fond of animal food;
To these was added Juan, who, before
  Refusing his own spaniel, hardly could
Feel now his appetite increased much more;
  'Twas not to be expected that he should,
Even in extremity of their disaster,
Dine with them on his pastor and his master.

'Twas better that he did not; for, in fact,
  The consequence was awful in the extreme:
For they, who were most ravenous in the act,
  Went raging mad – Lord! how they did blaspheme!
And foam and roll, with strange convulsions rack'd,
  Drinking salt-water like a mountain-stream,
Tearing, and grinning, howling, screeching, swearing,
And, with hyaena laughter, died despairing.

Their numbers were much thinn'd by this infliction,
  And all the rest were thin enough, heaven knows;
And some of them had lost their recollection,
  Happier than they who still perceived their woes;
But others ponder'd on a new dissection,
  As if not warn'd sufficiently by those
Who had already perish'd, suffering madly,
For having used their appetites so sadly.

And next they thought upon the master's mate,
  As fattest; but he saved himself, because,
Besides being much averse from such a fate,
  There were some other reasons; the first was,
He had been rather indisposed of late,
  And that which chiefly proved his saving clause,
Was a small present made to him at Cadiz,
By general subscription of the ladies.

(II. lxxiii–lxxxi)

A sinister suggestion swells through 'whisper'd', 'hoarser', 'ominous', and 'wild', to a climax in 'desperate'. As each man learns its import, he recognizes it as a thought which he has been keeping to himself; and the couplet appropriately makes its appalling nature explicit. At first the sufferers shrink from its enactment, trying in vain to appease their

125

hunger by other means. Then they prepare to draw lots. The first feminine rhyme in the passage, introducing a note of flippancy, points the incongruity between Julia's elegant and sentimental letter of fare-well and the grim business which it is now serving. After a sequence of verbs has marked the stages of the hushed ritual, a resumption of the gloomy Byronic rhetoric with which the passage opened enforces the recognition that not any particular man but Nature herself is respon-sible for the crime. By now the lots have been drawn. Since 'neuter' concludes the first line of the couplet, we read the second with a secure foreknowledge of its ending, and poor Pedrillo appears the ludicrous victim of an inevitable process.

The fourth stanza dwells upon the pathos of his end, though the generalization in its sixth line has ironical implications. In contrast with the agitated feminine rhyming throughout the third stanza, rhyming which emphasizes both the gloomy rhetoric and the bathos which terminates it, the fourth has only monosyllabic rhymes. The fifth, despite the traditional joke at the start, continues for a time as earnestly as its predecessor, explaining how the carcass was distributed. But again we feel able to predict the final rhyming word, and when it comes, 'Pedrillo', it both excites a laugh and reminds us that the carcass was once a person. After a stanza which broadly repeats this pattern, Byron resumes his gloomy, even melodramatic, rhetoric and exploits a series of present participles to convey vividly the unremittingness of the turmoil resulting from the offence. The horror of this stanza, the seventh, contrasts both with the immediately preceding jocularity of 'his pastor and his master' and with the subsequent glib facetiousness about the seamen's thinness.

Untaught by calamity, some of them begin to look around for a fresh victim. When they settle upon the master's mate, Byron produces one of his most outrageous stanzas, allowing this fattest and therefore potentially most nourishing member of the crew to escape because his flesh is tainted by venereal disease. The phrase by which he alludes to the mate's sickness, 'a small present made to him at Cadiz,/By general subscription of the ladies', is one of several witty and skilfully-placed euphemisms in the passage. Others include the declarations that the offal 'Regaled two sharks', that the sailors 'ponder'd on a new dis-section', and that the intended victim was 'much averse from such a fate'. These contrast with the barer and more direct statements that the sailors 'ate him', and that they 'Went raging mad' and 'died despairing'. Byron at one and the same time compels us to watch events as from a distance, sardonically, and as from within the boat, sympathetically. The effect is bewildering, unsettling, subversive.

This astonishing mobility of temperament shocked contemporary readers of *Don Juan*. They objected to the poem's numerous abrupt changes of tone and feeling, its switches from gaiety to gravity and back to gaiety. One reader, Francis Cohen, complained to Murray, alleging that in life 'we are never scorched and drenched at the same time'. 'Blessings on his experience!' retorted Byron and supplied a long list of assorted occasions on which a man might expect to be simultaneously 'scorched and drenched' (12 August 1819[1]):

> Did he never play at Cricket, or walk a mile in hot weather?
> Did he never spill a dish of tea over his testicles in handing a cup to his charmer, to the great shame of his nankeen breeches? Did he never swim in the sea at Noonday with the Sun in his eyes and on his head, which all the foam of Ocean could not cool? Did he never draw his foot out of a tub of too hot water, damning his eyes and his valet's? Did he never inject for a Gonorrhea? or make water through an ulcerated Urethra? Was he ever in a Turkish bath, that marble paradise of sherbet and Sodomy?

The appeal to experience is characteristic. Byron feels certain that poetry is, or can be, a direct transcript of life, and that responses which can co-exist in life will not be incompatible in art.

He feels much the same about opinions. When his experience seems to him to validate two contradictory views, he is ready to sponsor both. If this makes him illogical, so much the worse for logic. All that matters is that any doctrine that he adopts should be soundly based upon known facts. Its discrepancy with other doctrines that he adopts does not seriously worry him. For, 'if a writer should be quite consistent,/How could he possibly show things existent?' (XV. lxxxvii). So in *Don Juan* we find that nature is beneficent enough to show up the corruptions of civilization, and at the same time so pitiless as itself to require correction and control; that man is simultaneously the slave of his appetites and a being capable of restraint, fortitude, and nobility; and that love is genuine only if it is free, but, if free, is probably guilty. Believing that experience gives some support to each of these views, the author of *Don Juan* accepts all of them, confident apparently that they will settle down to peaceful co-existence in his poem.

[1] Quoted here from L. A. Marchand, *Byron: A Biography*, 1957, p. 807. See Notes on Chapter III.

Love of Liberty, and Detestation of Cant

Byron, then, goes to some pains to persuade us that *Don Juan* is a vast impromptu; and he really does seem to have improvised freely within the broad limits of a flexible master-plan. What, if anything, holds together the remarkably heterogeneous elements that make up the poem? Its amiable and somewhat passive hero provides a focus of interest but is quite incapable of dominating even the story, as Tom Jones dominates an earlier picaresque narrative; and Juan has naturally no place in the digressions that open and close many cantos and are liable to occur anywhere. A stronger and more pervasive personality is that of the monologist, Byron himself, who tells the story and digresses from it at will. His shrewd and humorous observation of persons and places, his mobility of response to what he records, his constant reliance upon the facts of experience, his laughing distrust of systematic ideologies, and his exuberant manner of speech make his presence one that imposes itself on every reader. He seems to be the sole effective unifying factor in *Don Juan*. He helps to yoke together the miscellaneous items that compose the story, the irregular digressions that are tangential to that story, the fluctuating emotional attitudes, and the conflicting opinions. If he does not successfully relate all of these elements to one another, at least he relates all of them to himself.

It may be remarked that to claim for *Don Juan* the unity of a vast monologue by one who is an idiosyncratic observer and a highly entertaining talker is not to claim for it any very strict unity. But are we content to leave things there? Is it not possible that the political and social attitudes, and the moral and philosophical preoccupations, of the talker have resulted in the evolution of specific thematic patterns within the narrative and the digressions for which he is responsible? Even the demonstration of such patterns will not prove *Don Juan* an economical and closely integrated work of art. But it will add to our understanding of a rich and varied poem.

'There are but two sentiments to which I am constant', remarked Byron, in the conversation with Lady Blessington quoted at the end of Chapter II, ' – a strong love of liberty, and a detestation of cant'. By 'cant', he meant something very similar to what George Orwell diagnoses in his essay, 'Politics and the English Language'. Orwell contends that in the twentieth century 'political speech and writing are largely the defence of the indefensible' and that political language has consequently 'to consist largely of euphemism, question-begging and sheer cloudy vagueness'. Writing over a century earlier, Byron sees cant, 'a thing of words, without the smallest influence upon human actions' (7 February 1821; *Letters and Journals*, v, p. 542), as the hypocritical resource of those who wish to conceal from others, and perhaps even from themselves, the true nature of their deeds and lives. Thus, Lord Henry Amundeville, speaking of political innovation, declares himself 'free to confess' to its spread. Scenting a formula designed to make Lord Henry's hedging acceptable, Byron demands, 'whence comes this phrase?/Is't English? No – 'tis only parliamentary' (XVI. lxxiii). His denunciation of Castlereagh's 'set trash of phrase' (Dedication, xiii) springs from a similar resentment, and in this case his 'detestation of cant' is clearly bound up with his 'love of liberty'.

He recognizes that this 'verbal decorum' can prevail in many areas; he distinguishes 'cant political, cant poetical, cant religious, cant moral' (7 February 1821; *Letters and Journals*, v. p. 542). The last of these receives attention early in *Don Juan*. Donna Inez, a fictional version of Lady Byron, is an intellectual and a moralist with a 'great opinion of her own good qualities' (I. xx). She gives her son an education combining a heavy emphasis upon religion with a deliberate exclusion of 'any thing that's loose,/Or hints continuation of the species' (I. xl). Surprisingly, she befriends the charming young Julia. The rumoured explanation is that Julia's husband, Alfonso, had once been Inez's lover and that Inez hoped to baffle scandal-mongers by keeping on good terms with Julia. But why did she not realize that by this relationship she was exposing her son to temptation? Perhaps she meant to finish his education, conjectures the poet, or to open Alfonso's eyes, 'In case he thought his wife too great a prize' (I. ci). The most richly comic expression in *Don Juan* of the moral cant of respectability comes from Inez nine cantos later when her letter to St Petersburg gives us our last glimpse of her.

Julia exemplifies the moral cant of sensibility. She has 'honour, virtue, truth, and love,/For Don Alfonso' (I. cix). Nevertheless, she seduces Juan. With malicious irony, Byron recounts her decisive action in the passive voice, as if to hint that she was not responsible for it:

> One hand on Juan's carelessly was thrown,
> Quite by mistake – she thought it was her own.

> (I. cix)

When Alfonso suspects her fidelity, she denounces him and defends herself in what sound like the authentic tones of outraged innocence.

But we already know that she is guilty; and her delight in recalling the suitors she has loyally repulsed, together with her frivolous listing of the social activities to which she admits while asserting, 'I scarce went any where,/Except to bull-fights, mass, play, rout, and revel' (I. cxlviii), remind us of the shakiness of her defence.

In the end, her exposure compels her to discard the pretence of respectability, and sensibility dominates the six stanzas of her farewell letter to Juan:

> I have no further claim on your young heart,
>   Mine is the victim, and would be again;
> To love too much has been the only art
>   I used.
>   (I. cxcii)

But, just in case we are responding too simply to the sentiment of her words, Byron follows them with a corrective stanza describing how

> This note was written upon gilt-edged paper
>   With a neat little crow-quill, slight and new ...
>   (I. cxcviii)

This scrap of self-conscious elegance and sentimentalism later serves as the means for choosing a victim of cannibalism.

Byron concludes Canto I by quoting a piece of 'cant poetical' from Robert Southey. A few stanzas earlier, he has formulated a poetical decalogue which offended many contemporary readers by its parody of Scripture: 'Thou shalt believe in Milton, Dryden, Pope;/Thou shalt not set up Wordsworth, Coleridge, Southey ...' (I. ccv). In his main attacks on the Lake Poets, he charges them with 'loyal treason, renegado rigour' (III. xciv) because, after having professed their democratic sympathy with the French Revolution, they had become Tories. A digression, prompted naturally enough by his account of the turncoat poet on Lambro's island, contains his most scornful assault upon Wordsworth's 'cant poetical'. He alludes in this to Wordsworth's poem, 'The Waggoner', and quotes from his 'Peter Bell', which opens with the lines:

> There's something in a flying horse,
> There's something in a huge balloon;
> But through the clouds I'll never float
> Until I have a little Boat,
> Shaped like a crescent-moon.

Here is Byron's passage:

> We learn from Horace, Homer sometimes sleeps;
>   We feel without him: Wordsworth sometimes wakes,
> To show with what complacency he creeps,
>   With his dear '*Waggoners*,' around his lakes;
> He wishes for 'a boat' to sail the deeps –
>   Of ocean? – No, of air; and then he makes
> Another outcry for a 'little boat,'
> And drivels seas to set it well afloat.
>
> If he must fain sweep o'er the etherial plain,
>   And Pegasus runs restive in his 'waggon,'
> Could he not beg the loan of Charles's Wain?
>   Or pray Medea for a single dragon?
> Or if too classic for his vulgar brain,
>   He fear'd his neck to venture such a nag on,
> And he must needs mount nearer to the moon,
> Could not the blockhead ask for a balloon?
>
> 'Pedlars,' and 'boats,' and 'waggons'! Oh! ye shades
>   Of Pope and Dryden, are we come to this?
> That trash of such sort not alone evades
>   Contempt, but from the bathos' vast abyss
> Floats scumlike uppermost, and these Jack Cades
>   Of sense and song above your graves may hiss –
> The 'little boatman' and his 'Peter Bell'
> Can sneer at him who drew 'Achitophel'!

(III. xcviii–c)

This torrent of scorn begins with a sneer, moves through a mounting series of rhetorical questions, brings *The Dunciad* to our thoughts by employing a favourite metaphor of Pope's, and concludes with the withering contempt of the final, clinching couplet. The mention of Jack Cade reminds us that Byron's liberalism did not commit him to sympathizing with demagogues.

This passage occurs shortly before Lambro banishes Juan from Haidée. Despite a few lapses into sentimentalism in his treatment of the love between the two, Byron writes of the death of Haidée, 'Nature's bride, and ... Passion's child' (II. ccii), with unforced tenderness. As so often when avoiding humour, he avoids feminine rhymes:

Thus lived – thus died she; never more on her
    Shall sorrow light, or shame. She was not made
Through years or moons the inner weight to bear,
    Which colder hearts endure till they are laid
By age in earth; her days and pleasures were
    Brief, but delightful – such as had not staid
Long with her destiny; but she sleeps well
By the sea shore, whereon she loved to dwell.

That isle is now all desolate and bare,
    Its dwellings down, its tenants past away;
None but her own and father's grave is there,
    And nothing outward tells of human clay;
Ye could not know where lies a thing so fair,
    No stone is there to show, no tongue to say
What was; no dirge, except the hollow sea's,
Mourns o'er the beauty of the Cyclades.

(IV. lxxi–lxxii)

Haidée's naturalness and innocence contrast with the hypocrisies of Inez and the pretences of Julia. They contrast equally with the arrogance of Gulbeyaz:

Something imperial, or imperious, threw
    A chain o'er all she did; that is, a chain
Was thrown as 'twere about the neck of you, –
    And rapture's self will seem almost a pain
With aught that looks like despotism in view.

(V. cx)

Though Gulbeyaz is the poem's first despot, Byron's attitude towards her can surprise no one who has read the earlier cantos. In III. lxviii, III. cx, and IV. vi, he has pilloried sycophantic 'ministers and favourites' and the 'sovereign buffoons' or 'kings despotic' in whose service they degrade themselves. Gulbeyaz, he now writes, 'deemed her least command must yield delight,/Earth being only made for queens and kings' (V. cxxviii). Who can expect otherwise of the 'born votaries' of the principle of 'Legitimacy' (V. cxxviii)?

Of course, Byron does not wish us to regard Juan's defiance of Gulbeyaz as earnestly as he wished us to regard the idyll in the Cyclades. Scorching and drenching characterize the encounter, and Gulbeyaz's intrusive husband, the Sultan, introduces a note of farce:

His highness was a man of solemn port,
    Shawled to the nose, and bearded to the eyes . . .

He saw with his own eyes the moon was round,
    Was also certain that the earth was square,
Because he had journeyed fifty miles and found
    No sign that it was circular any where;
His empire also was without a bound.

(V. cxlvii, cl)

But this ludicrous creature is dangerous. He and Catherine II of Russia have committed their respective countries to the destructive war that provides the material for Cantos VII and VIII. Derisively, Byron suggests 'a way to end their strife':

She to dismiss her guards and he his harem,
And for their other matters, meet and share 'em.

(VI. xcv)

Byron does not denounce all warfare. 'Defence of freedom, country, or of laws' (VII. xl) can justify a resort to arms under a Leonidas or a Washington, and in VII. lxxxii he alludes sympathetically to the Greek struggle for independence. But Catherine and the Sultan act from mere 'lust of power' (VII. xl). The Russian commander-in-chief, Suwarrow, 'who but saw things in the gross,/Being much too gross to see them in detail' (VII. lxxvii), is the grotesquely appropriate instrument of his monarch's purpose:

Suwarrow chiefly was on the alert,
    Surveying, drilling, ordering, jesting, pondering;
For the man was, we safely may assert,
    A thing to wonder at beyond most wondering;
Hero, buffoon, half-demon and half-dirt,
    Praying, instructing, desolating, plundering;
Now Mars, now Momus; and when bent to storm
A fortress, Harlequin in uniform.

(VII. lv)

Military leaders are merely butchers 'in great business,/Afflicting young folks with a sort of dizziness' (VII. lxxxiii). Byron wishes to give these young folks and others 'the true portrait of one battle-field', where

133

The groan, the roll in dust, the all-white eye
   Turned back within its socket, – these reward
Your rank and file by thousands, while the rest
May win perhaps a ribbon at the breast!

                                   (VIII. xii–xiii)

Though prompt enough in his praise of valour, he blames the savage slaughter upon the 'sovereigns, who employ/All arts to teach their subjects to destroy' (VIII. xcii).

Clearly, men must overthrow their kings. As already in *The Vision of Judgment*, Byron quotes the loyal prayer ironically:

      'God save the king!' and kings!
   For if *he* don't, I doubt if *men* will longer –
I think I hear a little bird, who sings
   The people by and bye will be the stronger:
The veriest jade will wince whose harness wrings
   So much into the raw as quite to wrong her
Beyond the rules of posting, – and the Mob
At last fall sick of imitating Job:

At first it grumbles, then it swears, and then,
   Like David, flings smooth pebbles 'gainst a giant;
At last it takes to weapons such as men
   Snatch when despair makes human hearts less pliant.
Then comes 'the tug of war'; – 'twill come again,
   I rather doubt; and I would fain say 'fie on't,'
If I had not perceived that Revolution
Alone can save the Earth from Hell's pollution.

                                      (VIII. l–li)

He solemnly asserts that he will work to bring about this change,

   For I will teach, if possible, the stones
To rise against Earth's tyrants. Never let it
   Be said that we still truckle unto thrones,

                                     (VIII. cxxxv)

and he opens Canto IX with a ferocious rebuke to Wellington for having 'repaired Legitimacy's crutch'. He reminds the Duke that 'War's a brain-spattering, windpipe-slitting art,/Unless her cause by Right be sanctified', asks him who, 'Save you and yours, have gained by Waterloo?' and proclaims, 'Never had mortal Man such opportunity,

/Except Napoleon, or abused it more' (IX. i–x). But his most comprehensive statement of his political faith in this poem occurs a few stanzas later:

> And I will war, at least in words (and – should
>   My chance so happen – deeds) with all who war
> With Thought; – and of Thought's foes by far most rude,
>   Tyrants and Sycophants have been and are.
> I know not who may conquer: if I could
>   Have such a prescience, it should be no bar
> To this my plain, sworn, downright detestation
> Of every despotism in every nation.
>
> It is not that I adulate the people:
>   Without *me*, there are Demagogues enough . . .
>   I wish men to be free
> As much from mobs as kings – from you as me.
>
> (IX. xxiv–xxv)

These are the views of a left-wing Whig aristocrat writing at a time when the American and French Revolutions, and the Napoleonic Wars and the legitimist restorations which followed them, were salient facts of recent history; and when the movements for Greek and Italian independence were growing in strength. Byron's is a representative voice of this age of revolutions.

His hero goes to Russia and to Catherine II. 'In royalty's vast arms he sighed for beauty' (X. xxxvii), but before long he proceeds to England. In Byron's opinion, the English had 'butchered half the earth, and bullied t'other' (X. lxxxi); they had helped 'to turn the key' (X. lxviii) upon the nations of Europe and by so doing had compromised the very freedom of which they boasted. But in the English cantos of *Don Juan* political satire is on the whole less prominent than is comedy of manners. 'I am sick of politics', Byron declares in XII. xxv.

Lord Henry and Lady Adeline Amundeville show a special interest in Juan, who becomes a welcome guest at their London home and joins the party at Norman Abbey, their country seat. Newstead supplied much of the material for Norman Abbey. Byron delights in recreating and satirizing the life of the aristocratic society which he had known in both town and country as a young man and which was to serve as a setting for his hero's English adventures. No one can say for certain how these adventures would have developed if Byron had finished the poem. The Duchess of FitzFulke has become Juan's lover before it breaks off. The emphasis upon Adeline's repressed emotionalism early in Canto XIII, together with her concern at the Duchess's flirting with Juan in Canto XIV, and her dismissal of Aurora Raby in Canto XV as unsuited to be his wife, suggests that Byron was preparing to carry out the intention formulated in a letter quoted early in this chapter, to make Juan 'a cause for a divorce in England'. Was Juan perhaps to lose Aurora because of a suspected entanglement with Adeline that was to lead Henry to sue for a divorce? and was his actual entanglement with the Duchess in some way to promote this suspicion, or even to provoke Adeline into displacing the Duchess in his affections? Such guesses may be wide of the mark, but they do indicate the kind of intrigue that the English cantos lead us to expect.

Less than ever in them do we lose our consciousness of Byron himself as narrator and commentator. This follows naturally from the fact that Juan's experiences are closer than at any earlier stage to Byron's own. In London, he spends his mornings in business, his afternoons 'in visits, luncheons,/Lounging, and boxing' (XI. lxvi), and his evenings in riding. 'Then dress, then dinner, then awakes the world!' (XI. lxvii). Receptions and balls await the privileged 'twice two thousand' (XI. xlv):

> There stands the noble Hostess, nor shall sink
>   With the three-thousandth curtsey; there the Waltz,
> The only dance which teaches girls to think,
>   Makes one in love even with its very faults.
> Saloon, room, hall o'erflow beyond their brink,
>   And long the latest of arrivals halts,
> 'Midst royal dukes and dames condemned to climb,
> And gain an inch of staircase at a time.
>
> Thrice happy he, who, after a survey
>   Of the good company, can win a corner,
> A door that's *in*, or boudoir *out* of the way,
>   Where he may fix himself, like small 'Jack Horner,'
> And let the Babel round run as it may,
>   And look on as a mourner, or a scorner,
> Or an approver, or a mere spectator,
> Yawning a little as the night grows later.
>
> (XI. lxviii–lxix)

In the second of these stanzas, the catalogue of lookers-on, nicely graduated in order of decreasing interest in the proceedings, with the 'mere spectator' giving the final signal of tedium, recalls the humorous catalogues in Byron's prose. But the chief reason for quoting the passage now is that the poet has, perhaps unconsciously, moved from his account of Juan's day to his own reminiscences of social life in Regency London. He virtually admits as much when, in the stanza immediately following those quoted, he states that Juan was not a looker-on at all, but a dancer.

Pointed, but genial, mockery prevails in these later cantos, and Byron's almost effortless mastery of the octave stanza enables him to convey it in a wide variety of tones. It can be high-spirited, as in the lines just quoted; it can be ironically elegiac:

> When we have made our love, and gamed our gaming,
>   Drest, voted, shone, and, may be, something more;
> With dandies dined; heard senators declaiming;
>   Seen beauties brought to market by the score;
> Sad rakes to sadder husbands chastely taming;
>   There's little left but to be bored or bore;
>
> (XIV. xviii)

and it can switch in a single stanza from the elegant to the downright:

> But Juan was a bachelor – of arts,
>   And parts, and hearts: he danced and sung, and had
> An air as sentimental as Mozart's
>   Softest of melodies; and could be sad
> Or cheerful, without any 'flaws or starts,'
>   Just at the proper time; and though a lad,
> Had seen the world – which is a curious sight,
> And very much unlike what people write.
>
> (XI. xlvii)

Here a graceful and lilting rhythm, emphasized at first by internal rhymes, then sustained by enjambements and marked caesuras, almost subdues the expected metrical pattern while Byron is speaking of Juan's charm. When that pattern eventually reasserts itself, it serves to accentuate the sardonic, knowing chuckle with which the final couplet is delivered. This effect of spontaneous, varied, and expressive talk is wonderfully sustained throughout *Don Juan*.

As always, affectations and pretences invite Byron's satire. The 'public day' at Norman Abbey, during the sixth year of a seven-year Parliament's life, is naturally an occasion for Henry to consolidate his hold on the votes of the local men of substance in readiness for the forthcoming general election. Adeline assists him by charming these squires and their womenfolk,

> watching, witching, condescending
> To the consumers of fish, fowl and game,
>   And dignity with courtesy so blending,
> As all must blend whose part it is to aim
>   (Especially as the sixth year is ending)
> At their lord's, son's, or similar connection's
> Safe conduct through the rocks of re-elections.
>
> (XVI. xcv)

But after the guests have left she assists

> In a most edifying conversation,
> Which turned upon their late guests' miens and faces,
>   And families, even to the last relation;
> Their hideous wives, their horrid selves and dresses,
> And truculent distortion of their tresses.
>
> (XVI. ciii)

Less deliberate pretences can be equally dangerous. Though Juan never becomes involved with a 'cold coquette', Byron devotes a digressive stanza to the type:

> Such is your cold coquette, who can't say 'No,'
>   And won't say 'Yes,' and keeps you on and off-ing,
> On a lee shore, till it begins to blow –
>   Then sees your heart wrecked with an inward scoffing.
> This works a world of sentimental woe,
>   And sends new Werters yearly to their coffin;
> But yet is merely innocent flirtation,
> Not quite adultery, but adulteration.
>
> (XII. lxiii)

To feel 'sentimental woe' on account of such creatures is as ridiculous in Byron's eyes as to sentimentalize the sort of 'sweet Friendship' that he later treats with blighting sarcasm:

There's nought in this bad world like sympathy:
  'Tis so becoming to the soul and face;
Sets to soft music the harmonious sigh,
  And robes sweet Friendship in a Brussels lace.
Without a friend, what were humanity,
  To hunt our errors up with a good grace?
Consoling us with – 'Would you had thought twice!
Ah! if you had but follow'd my advice!'

(XIV. xlvii)

Mockery of the 'sentimental and sensibilitous' (29 June 1811) is as prominent in *Don Juan* as is mockery of the respectable and censorious. Early instances occur in the presentation of Julia, and Byron is still expressing the same aversion at the end of the poem, when he praises a distressed woman because 'she was not a sentimental mourner,/ Parading all her sensibility' (XVI. lxv).

His preference for sense as against sensibility marks him as an anti-romantic; and *Don Juan* is, in its total effect, a great anti-romantic poem. Byron never tires of insisting that its virtue is that it is truthful:

And the sad truth which hovers o'er my desk
Turns what was once romantic to burlesque.

(IV. iii)

Like his hero, he has seen the world and knows that it is 'very much unlike what people write' (XI. xlvii). Informed by experience,

  I mean to show things really as they are,
Not as they ought to be: for I avow,
  That till we see what's what in fact, we're far
From much improvement.

(XII. xl)

Whatever his outraged critics might assert, he was serious in his use of that last word. For he believed that by fastening upon the truth, or, in Pope's phrase, by stooping to it, he was moralizing his song (*Letters and Journals*, vi, pp. 429–30).

He was quite astonished, he said [to a friend six months before his death], to hear people talk in the manner they did about the book. *He* thought he was writing a most moral book. That women did not like it he was not surprised; he knew they could

not bear it because it *took off the veil*; it showed that all their
d——d sentiment was only an excuse to cover passions of grosser
nature; that all platonism only tended to *that*, and they hated it
because it showed and exposed their hypocrisy.

As we saw in the matter of 'scorching and drenching', the truth to
which Byron stoops is a matter of fidelity to what he believes to be
observable facts. Accordingly, he more than once expresses a sceptic's
impatience with metaphysical and theological speculation (XI. v–vi,
XV. lxxxviii–xcii). In so doing, he aligns himself rather with his
Augustan predecessors than with his Romantic contemporaries.

Nevertheless, he differs sharply from these predecessors. Pope and
Dryden seem characteristically to write as the spokesmen of a coherent
and civilized social group. The members of this may not hold identical
religious, political, and other beliefs; but they do share, and their poets
share, a deep respect for the fundamental Augustan virtues of good
sense, reasonableness, and moderation. Byron writes with an equally
keen awareness of his public; and he writes likewise as an exponent of
good sense. But, so far from seeming to feel his public sustaining him,
he evidently draws very much more exclusively on his own resources
and even at times has to defy what he supposes to be a canting, a
moralistic and sensibilitous world. He speaks with the insolence of an
aristocrat and the irresponsibility of an exile. He speaks, in short, for
himself.

His presentation of a comedy of manners in these English cantos
does not prevent him from continuing to voice his political attitudes.
His blood boils when he sees men letting 'these scoundrel Sovereigns
break law' (XV. xcii). He calls for a restraint to be imposed upon
Alexander I of Russia and the other despots who head the Holy
Alliance; on their generals; and, if not on George IV's person, at all
events on his squandering of wealth on Brighton Pavilion:

> Shut up the bald-coot bully Alexander;
>   Ship off the Holy Three to Senegal;
> Teach them that 'sauce for goose is sauce for gander,'
>   And ask them how *they* like to be in thrall?
> Shut up each high heroic Salamander,
>   Who eats fire gratis (since the pay's but small);
> Shut up – no, *not* the King, but the Pavilion,
> Or else 'twill cost us all another million.
>
> (XIV. lxxxiii)

He was 'born for opposition' (XV. xxii). So much so, indeed, that, if the kings were to be dethroned,

> Though at the first I might perchance deride
>   Their tumble, I should turn the other way,
> And wax an Ultra-royalist in loyalty,
> Because I hate even democratic royalty.
>
> (XV. xxiii)

The Human Condition

Byron's concern with social and political matters tends to strengthen such unity as *Don Juan* possesses. What may be broadly termed philosophical preoccupations exert a similar influence. We must be careful not to exaggerate; *Don Juan* remains a somewhat casually assembled work. But two of these preoccupations deserve some attention now. One is Byron's recurrent speculation about the relationship of soul and body; the other is his brooding upon the impermanence of the things men prize.

Uncomprehendingly attracted by Julia, the youthful Juan wanders off alone, thinking 'unutterable things' (I. xc). The poet indicates their nature, making some reference to Wordsworth and Coleridge, and then reflects:

> In thoughts like these true wisdom may discern
>   Longings sublime, and aspirations high,
> Which some are born with, but the most part learn
>   To plague themselves withal, they know not why:
> 'Twas strange that one so young should thus concern
>   His brain about the action of the sky;
> If *you* think 'twas philosophy that this did,
> I can't help thinking puberty assisted.
>
> (I. xciii)

The couplet, with its grotesque Hudibrastic rhyme, scoffingly relates Juan's soulful longings and aspirations, and his philosophical questionings, to the physical processes of adolescence. It affirms the subjection – at least in some degree – of soul to body, mind to matter, spirit to flesh.

The dichotomy suggested by these terms is never far from our minds as we read *Don Juan*. It is humorously dramatized for us when the hero, watching the coast of Spain recede, utters a sad farewell to his 'dearest Julia', reads her letter, and cries,

'And oh! if e'er I should forget, I swear –
  But that's impossible, and cannot be –
Sooner shall this blue ocean melt to air,
  Sooner shall earth resolve itself to sea,
Than I resign thine image, Oh! my fair!
  Or think of any thing excepting thee;
A mind diseased no remedy can physic –'
(Here the ship gave a lurch, and he grew sea-sick.)

'Sooner shall heaven kiss earth –' (here he fell sicker)
  'Oh, Julia! what is every other woe? –
(For God's sake let me have a glass of liquor,
  Pedro, Battista, help me down below.)
Julia, my love! – (you rascal, Pedro, quicker) –
  Oh Julia! – (this curst vessel pitches so) –
Beloved Julia, hear me still beseeching!'
(Here he grew inarticulate with retching.)

                                        (II. xix–xx)

Seasickness seems to be winning. Three stanzas later, however, we receive an assurance that Juan's love for Julia, being perfect, survived the trial. This is all very well, but if it had survived we should have expected to hear more about it. In fact, there are only two more references to Julia in the entire poem. Each of these occurs in a context which draws attention to human weakness in the face of powerful physical pressures. One comes when the hungry men in the open boat, driven to cannibalism, take Julia's letter by force from Juan in order to draw 'lots for flesh and blood' (II. lxxiii). The other comes when Juan has fallen in love with Haidée, and Byron, asking whether he ought to have forgotten Julia so soon, decides that 'the moon/Does these things for us' (II. ccviii).

Haidée's prompt care for the 'almost famish'd, and half drown'd' Juan has twin motives. Her 'pity' and 'charity' are aroused – and allusions to Matthew 25:35 and I Corinthians 13:13 remind us of the authority for regarding this as the highest of motives – but she is also attracted by his looks. These motives are ironically juxtaposed when, on his opening his 'black eyes', Haidée and her maid Zoe find their 'charity increased' (II. cxxix, cxxxi).

When they visit the sleeping Juan on the following morning, the two young women assume complementary and almost emblematic rôles. Haidée bends over him,

> And thus like to an angel o'er the dying
>   Who die in righteousness, she lean'd; and there
> All tranquilly the shipwreck'd boy was lying,
>   As o'er him lay the calm and stirless air:
> But Zoe the meantime some eggs was frying,
>   Since, after all, no doubt the youthful pair
> Must breakfast, and betimes – lest they should ask it,
> She drew out her provision from the basket.
>
> (II. cxliv)

Byron likes to emphasize love's need for physical nourishment. He does so later in this same episode (II. clxx) and again in the description of Lord Henry's public dinner (XVI. lxxxvi). He appreciates that the climate can help, too:

> What men call gallantry, and the gods adultery,
> Is much more common where the climate's sultry.
>
> (I. lxiii)

Moreover, he likes to insist on love's need for physical satisfaction. He ridicules the idea of Platonic love:

> Oh Plato! Plato! you have paved the way,
>   With your confounded fantasies, to more
> Immoral conduct by the fancied sway
>   Your system feigns o'er the controlless core
> Of human hearts, than all the long array
>   Of poets and romancers: – You're a bore,
> A charlatan, a coxcomb – and have been,
> At best, no better than a go-between.
>
> (I. cxvi)

Juan's relationship with Julia provided an earlier occasion for such ridicule (I. lxxix–lxxx), and his transference of his affection to Haidée is to provide a later one (II. ccxi–ccxii).[1] At the same time, the spirits of Juan and Haidée were 'never bound/By the mere senses' (IV. xvi).

[1] Other jibes at Platonic love occur in I.cxi, V.i, IX.lxxiv–lxxv, X.liv, XI.xliii, and XIV.xcii.

Juan's fidelity to the memory of Haidée is tested on the slave-ship which is bearing him to Constantinople. He is chained to an attractive brunette, who is eager to please him. He remains indifferent, however, partly because he still grieves for Haidée, and partly for reasons of a strictly physical kind:

> But all that power was wasted upon him,
>   For sorrow o'er each sense held stern command;
> Her eye might flash on his, but found it dim;
>   And though thus chain'd, as natural her hand
> Touch'd his, nor that – nor any handsome limb
>   (And she had some not easy to withstand)
> Could stir his pulse, or make his faith feel brittle;
> Perhaps his recent wounds might help a little.
>
>   (IV. xcv)

He resists his next sexual temptation, too; and this time there is no reference to his 'recent wounds' as having helped. The imperious Gulbeyaz asks, 'Christian, canst thou love?' (V. cxvi). His thoughts of Haidée make him unresponsive, so

> She rose, and pausing one chaste moment, threw
> Herself upon his breast, and there she grew.
>
> This was an awkward test, as Juan found,
>   But he was steeled by sorrow, wrath, and pride:
> With gentle force her white arms he unwound, ...
>   And looking coldly in her face, he cried, ...
>
>   ... 'Love is for the free!'
>
>   (V. cxxv–cxxvii)

After so many demonstrations of the power of the flesh over the spirit, Juan's words and deeds claim that the spirit can successfully defy the flesh. Byron has stated as much a few stanzas earlier:

> Our souls at least are free, and 'tis in vain
> We would against them make the flesh obey –
> The spirit in the end will have its way.
>
>   (V. cx)

But Juan's claim is to some extent compromised by the fact that, as soon as Gulbeyaz starts to cry, his

> virtue ebbed, I know not how;
> And first he wondered why he had refused;
> And then, if matters could be made up now.
>
> (V. cxlii)

Fortunately, an unexpected interruption prevents the ebb from proceeding too far.

The conflict shifts to a new area in the war cantos, VII and VIII. Material considerations motivate heroism:

> each high, heroic bosom burned
> For cash and conquest, as if from a cushion
> A preacher had held forth (who nobly spurned
> All earthly goods save tithes);
>
> (VII. lxiv)

and the 'truly brave' exhibit in turn a bestial ferocity and a semidivine compassion:

> A mixture of wild beasts and demi-gods
> Are they – now furious as the sweeping wave,
> Now moved with pity: even as sometimes nods
> The rugged tree unto the summer wind,
> Compassion breathes along the savage mind.
>
> (VIII. cvi)

At the taking of Ismail, the low incidence of rape is sardonically ascribed to 'cold weather and commiseration' (VIII. cxxix).

But the appetite which, along with the sexual appetite, most frequently brings home to Byron the bondage of mind to matter is the appetite for food and drink.

> I think with Alexander, that the act
> Of eating, with another act or two,
> Makes us feel our mortality in fact
> Redoubled; when a roast and a ragout,
> And fish, and soup, by some side dishes backed,
> Can give us either pain or pleasure, who
> Would pique himself on intellects, whose use
> Depends so much upon the gastric juice?
>
> (V. xxxii)

The story supplies many instances of this dependence. During the storm at sea, those on board the endangered ship turn to two different sources of comfort:

> There's nought, no doubt, so much the spirit calms
>   As rum and true religion.
>
> (II. xxxiv)

When one of the small boats sinks with its personnel and its provisions, the survivors in the other

> grieved for those who perish'd with the cutter,
> And also for the biscuit casks and butter.
>
> (II. lxi)

While the eunuch Baba is leading Juan and Johnson as slaves into the palace in Constantinople, Juan suggests that they should overpower him and escape. Johnson replies:

> 'and when done, what then?
>   *How get* out? how the devil got we in? ...
> Besides, I'm hungry, and just now would take,
> Like Esau, for my birthright a beef-steak.' ...
>
> And nearer as they came, a genial savour
>   Of certain stews, and roast-meats, and pilaus,
> Things which in hungry mortals' eyes find favour,
>   Made Juan in his harsh intentions pause,
> And put himself upon his good behaviour.
>
> (V. xliv, xlvii)

Byron moves immediately into a short digression on the potent appeal made by the dinner bell. Later, he acknowledges the depressing effect indigestion can have upon metaphysical 'soarings' (XI. iii). His description of the guests at Norman Abbey leads to the reflection

> That happiness for Man – the hungry sinner! –
> Since Eve ate apples, much depends on dinner;
>
> (XIII. xcix)

and a reference to the 'substantial company engrossed/By Matter' at the public dinner produces the confession

> That one scarce knew at what to marvel most
> Of two things – how (the question rather odd is)
> Such bodies could have souls, or souls such bodies.
>
> (XVI. xc)

Several of the passages I have quoted make it clear that the bondage of spirit to flesh is less than complete – though authorial irony sometimes undercuts such claims for the autonomy of the spirit as they contain. Claims of the kind also occur elsewhere. Hope keeps alive the starving men in the open boat (II. lxiv–lxvi); the face of the dying Haidée seems so 'full of soul' that no one can believe that earth can claim the whole of her (IV. lx); and Byron later asserts that 'mind can never sink,/And 'gainst the body makes a strong appeal.' But this assertion is followed immediately by an expression of doubt:

And yet 'tis very puzzling on the brink
Of what is called Eternity, to stare,
And know no more of what is here than there.

(X. xx)

The assassination of the military commandant – an incident which happened while Byron was in Ravenna, and which he reports in letters dated 9 December 1820 – has already initiated sceptical ponderings of this kind:

it was all a mystery. Here we are,
And there we go:– but *where*? five bits of lead,
Or three, or two, or one, send very far!
And is this blood, then, formed but to be shed?
Can every element our elements mar?
And air – earth – water – fire live – and we dead?
We, whose minds comprehend all things? No more;
But let us to the story as before.

(V. xxxix)

Such ponderings grow more frequent in the English cantos, and early in the first of these there is a brilliantly outrageous stanza in which Byron tells how in attacks of sickness his flesh dictates to his spirit and compels the adoption, one after another, of the articles of the conventional creed:

The first attack at once proved the Divinity;
(But *that* I never doubted, nor the Devil);
The next, the Virgin's mystical virginity;
The third, the usual Origin of Evil;
The fourth at once established the whole Trinity
On so uncontrovertible a level,

    That I devoutly wished the three were four,
    On purpose to believe so much the more.

(XI. vi)

The irony here has the effect of making doubt more spiritual than faith itself.

Byron does not advance any thesis regarding this dichotomy between soul and body, mind and matter, spirit and flesh. As on other topics, he is content to set down whatever seems to him at the time of writing to be supported by experience, even if it does not easily square with what he has set down elsewhere. While one incident may show that the spirit is at the mercy of the flesh, another may show that it can assert itself against it; while the adolescent Juan is ridiculed because he is excessively soulful, the mature Lord Henry is criticized because

        there was something wanting on the whole –
    I don't know what, and therefore cannot tell –
    Which pretty women – the sweet souls! – call *Soul*.
      Certes it was not body; he was well
    Proportion'd, as a poplar or a pole,
      A handsome man, that human miracle;
    And in each circumstance of love and war
    Had still preserved his perpendicular.

(XIV. lxxi)

Nor does Byron try to treat the theme in a consistent and strictly defined terminology. He assumes that his readers are sufficiently conversant with the traditional and rather uncertain distinction he has in mind, and he proceeds to deal with it in such familiar terms as come to hand.

Watching him do so, we come to know him better. We see him as having an extraordinary liveliness and restlessness of mind and as having a taste for speculation, though no great determination in pursuing it. But the theme is not valuable merely because it helps him to impose himself on our imaginations. Its chief value is that it helps him to those startling contrasts and abrupt surprises which give so dramatic a texture to his monologue. In particular, it helps him to the incongruities which regularly precipitate his readers' laughter: for example, when Inez was parting from her son, 'A letter . . . she gave (he never read it)/Of good advice – and two or three of credit' (II. ix); and Catherine's generous gift of a 'monstrous diamond' to Juan was prompted by either 'love or brandy' (XI. xxxix). In most of the passages cited, the incongruities involve the comic subversion, by stubborn material facts, of various kinds of rarefied moralizing or sentimentalizing or idealizing. By bringing us down to earth, the author seeks to overthrow 'cant'. Even when he is at his least destructive, as in his account of Zoe's preparation of breakfast for Juan and Haidée, his incongruities work in such a way as to modify attitudes which are in danger of becoming divorced from physical reality.

Finally, through the story that is told and the digressions that accompany it, Byron in *Don Juan* expresses both his intense enjoyment of life and his disabused sense of its 'Nothingness' (VII. vi). The conventional antithesis between man's more ethereal and his more earthly part, though applied quite differently in different poetic contexts, yields many apt particular formulations for this double response to existence.

The stanza in which Byron speaks of 'the Nothingness of life' is one of two (I. xv, VII. vi) in which he quotes the well-known text, 'all is vanity', from Ecclesiastes 1:2. This 'Vanitas vanitatum' theme has already come to our notice in connexion with the digression in which he mentions Cheops's desire to keep 'his memory whole, and mummy hid' (I. ccxix). Here the alternating alliteration so cunningly links the Pharaoh's two disparate aims that the line lodges itself firmly in the memory as an essentially Byronic expression, at once ludicrous and pathetic, of the vanity of human wishes.[1] When contemporary critics accused Byron of misanthropy, he rightly resisted the charge (IX. xx–xxi). His conviction that 'all is vanity' is expressed sardonically, wryly, sometimes theatrically; but it is expressed with a pity for, rather than a detestation of, his fellow-men.

Fame, he declares, is transient. Posterity will forget a man's name (IV. cii, VII. xxxiv, XII. xix), or garble it (VIII. xviii), or doubt its connexion with the tomb erected to immortalize it (IV. ci), or stumble upon it without knowing to whom it belonged (III. lxxxix). 'Nought's permanent among the human race'; even 'the world of *eight* years past' has disappeared (XI. lxxvi–lxxxii). For time 'brings all beings to their level' (IV. ii), exposes such 'masonic folly' as pyramid-building (I. ccxix, V. lxiii), cuts short 'man's vain glory, and his vainer troubles' (XIII. lxv), and provides a perspective in which even 'the graves/Of Empires heave but like some passing waves' (XV. xcix).

These are explicit formulations of the theme from the digressions.

---

[1] Alliteration is employed in the same way and to the same effect in the third line of I.clxvii.

But the very action of the poem embodies it. Time could only have brought Juan and Haidée 'cruel things or wrong' (IV. xxvii), and what it quickly brings them in fact is their brutal separation and Haidée's death; Juan's enslavement by Lambro is one of the 'strange vicissitudes' of which the world is full (IV. li); Johnson's experiences have given him a realistic awareness of man's precarious state; and this precariousness is brought home to us as we read by the shipwreck, the siege of Ismail, the highway robbery, and other incidents. We witness as it were a demonstration that life is but

> A little breath, love, wine, ambition, fame,
> Fighting, devotion, dust, – perhaps a name.
>
> (II. iv)

Conclusion

For those who do not insist upon too purposeful an organization and too strict an economy, *Don Juan* is Byron's masterpiece. Untidily and unpredictably, it shows us life as viewed by a brilliant exponent of worldly commonsense. He is disillusioned and sceptical; impatient of cant; robust, high-spirited, and humane. Admittedly, he does not normally embody these attitudes and values in compact, highly-charged utterances, and this probably accounts for some neglect of his work today, when many readers favour short, pregnant poems or short, pregnant passages from longer poems. On the contrary, he is discursive. He holds forth at length, variously and fascinatingly. He teems with words, observations, and reflections. His verse is continuously readable, and not justified merely by its climaxes. Its very copiousness is an aesthetic asset.

Admittedly, he can lapse into carelessness. He meets the exigencies of rhyme and metre in II. cxxv–cxxvi and XIII. lix, for example, by quite shamelessly padding out his lines with clichés and other verbiage. But more commonly the octave stanza enables him firmly to control the tone and the emphases of his discourse. He frequently uses the six lines linked by alternate rhyming to develop a description or thought, or to report a series of speeches or events; the final couplet, with its new and therefore unexpected rhyme, then houses the culminating speech or event, the item which gives a surprising, often a ludicrous, turn to the whole description or line of thought. To be sure, not every stanza conforms to this account; but it does indicate the kind of pattern towards which Byron's stanzas of *ottava rima* are constantly tending.

As stanza follows stanza, we are overcome by his superb, infectious vitality. Few readers will suppose that Byron tells, or knew, anything like the whole truth about life. His experience was wide and often intense, but his social status certainly restricted it. He had, for example, no understanding of those areas of British life in which the evangelical revival was currently producing not 'cant moral' but a new morality. Nevertheless, in the best of his verse and prose, and above all in *Don Juan*, he voices the insights of a worldly, disillusioned, exuberant aristocrat of genius with a zest and a vitality which are all the more welcome in a century when many writers, in W. H. Auden's words,

> declare
> That they are in complete despair
> Yet go on writing.

7

The Vision of Judgment

Southey and Byron

In 1817 the Tory Poet Laureate, Robert Southey, was embarrassed by the unauthorized publication of a short drama, *Wat Tyler*, which he had written twenty-three years earlier while still a fervent supporter of the French Revolution. Byron heard of this while on a visit to Rome and wrote to Murray on 9 May:

> Southey's *Wat Tyler* is rather awkward; but the Goddess Nemesis has done well. He is – I will not say what, but I wish he was something else. I hate all intolerance, but most the intolerance of Apostacy. . . . It is no disgrace to Mr. Southey to have written *Wat Tyler*, and afterwards to have written his birthday or Victory odes (I speak only of their *politics*), but it is something, for which I have no words, for this man to have endeavoured to bring to the stake (for such would he do) men who think as he thought, and for no reason but because they think so still, when he has found it convenient to think otherwise.

Eight years earlier, Byron had jibed at Southey in *English Bards, and Scotch Reviewers* for writing 'too often and too long' (l. 226). Since then, they had met at Holland House 'with all becoming courtesy on both sides'. Each had admired the other's looks on this occasion, though neither liked the other's poetry (27 September 1813; and *New Letters of Robert Southey*, ed. K. Curry, 2 vols., New York and London, 1965, ii, p. 77 [28 September 1813]). But Byron's reaction to the issuing of *Wat Tyler* shows that he not only considered Southey an uneven and over-prolific poet ('Journal', 22 November 1813), but also disliked him as a renegade who was ready to persecute those who had remained true to the liberal cause.

152

Before long, a suspected personal grievance reinforced his literary and political objections to the Laureate. In 1818 someone told him that Southey had been saying, after a visit to Switzerland in 1817, that Byron and Shelley had lived there with two sisters in 'a League of Incest' (*Correspondence*, 11 November 1818). There was in fact no blood relationship between the two young women in question, one of them being William Godwin's daughter by his first marriage, and the other his second wife's daughter by a previous marriage; and, while the one was Shelley's mistress, later to become his wife, and the other Byron's mistress, there was no basis for the accusation of promiscuous intercourse. Byron's indignation was natural, though his belief that Southey was the slanderer appears to have been ill-founded.

Resentment, which he was never slow to feel, seems at once to have inspired his 'Dedication' of *Don Juan* to Southey 'in good, simple, savage verse, upon the Laureat's politics, and the way he got them' (19 September 1818). The decision to publish the first two cantos of *Don Juan* anonymously caused him to withhold this 'Dedication': 'I won't attack the dog so fiercely without putting my name' (6 May 1819). But Southey had already got wind of it. 'If it should sufficiently provoke me', he wrote to a friend, 'you may be assured that I will treat him with due severity, as he deserves to be treated, and lay him open, in a live dissection' (*Selections from the Letters of Robert Southey*; ed. J. W. Warter, 4 vols., London, 1856, iii, p. 137 [31 July 1819]).

Six months later, the death of George III imposed an official duty upon the Laureate which he discharged in April 1821 by publishing *A Vision of Judgement*. In his 'Preface' to this funeral ode, he attacked 'the Satanic school' of poetry in terms which made it clear that Byron was in his mind:

> Men of diseased hearts and depraved imaginations, who, forming a system of opinions to suit their own unhappy course of conduct, have rebelled against the holiest ordinances of human society, and hating that revealed religion which, with all their efforts and bravadoes, they are unable entirely to disbelieve, labour to make others as miserable as themselves, by infecting them with a moral virus that eats into the soul! The school which they have set up may properly be called the Satanic school; for though their productions breathe the spirit of Belial in their lascivious parts, and the spirit of Moloch in those loathsome images of atrocities and horrors which they delight to represent, they are more

especially characterised by a Satanic spirit of pride and audacious impiety, which still betrays the wretched feeling of hopelessness wherewith it is allied.

Byron retaliated in the 'Appendix' to the first edition of *The Two Foscari* (1821). Southey had spoken of the unavailing 'remorse of conscience' that might be felt by the author of a Satanic book when on his death-bed. Byron stigmatized this line of argument as cowardly, impudent, and blasphemous. He also alluded in general terms to the calumnies which he believed Southey to have uttered on his return from Switzerland.

Within a month, Southey retorted. In a letter to the *Courier*, dated 5 January 1822, he denied that he had uttered any such calumnies. He also pointed out that Byron had not answered his charges against 'the Satanic school'. Evidently feeling that the debate was going in his favour, he offered his opponent a piece of advice: 'When he attacks me again, let it be in rhyme. For one who has so little command of himself, it will be a great advantage that his temper should be obliged to *keep tune.*'

In saying this, Southey was ignoring a few passing jibes at himself occurring in the first four cantos of *Don Juan*, as well as the still unreleased 'Dedication'. He was sarcastically inviting a verse attack more sustained than any of these. Unknown to him, Byron had already acted in accordance with his recommendation. He had completed *The Vision of Judgment*, his devastating travesty of Southey's funeral ode, three months earlier and had sent it to Murray on 4 October 1821. After Southey's letter to the *Courier*, he was eager for its appearance in print. But his business relations with Murray had deteriorated by this time. So it was John Hunt who published it, as the opening item in the first number of *The Liberal*, on 15 October 1822.

A Vision of Judgement

In prose, Southey had had the advantage. Shortly after their only recorded meeting, his opponent had described his prose as 'perfect' ('Journal', 22 November 1813). Moreover, his confidence in his own righteousness made him a formidable antagonist.

In verse, however, things were to go very differently. Even among the official utterances of our Laureates, *A Vision of Judgement* deservedly occupies a bad eminence. Its metre is singularly ill-chosen. Southey devotes most of the 'Preface' in which he denounces 'the Satanic school' to a description and justification of the unrhymed accentual hexameters which he employs. A. H. Clough's *Bothie of Tober-na-Vuolich* (1848) and *Amours de Voyage* (1858) demonstrate the suitability of English hexameters for certain kinds of serio-comic writing, but none of our poets has yet used them with success in a serious long poem. Southey's seriousness is immaculate, and his hexameters proceed with a kind of stately limp that justifies Byron's description of them as 'spavined dactyls' (*The Vision of Judgment*, xci).

A Vision of Judgement consists of twelve short parts. In the first of these, 'The Trance', a supernatural Voice summons the poet, like Dante, to view the secrets of the grave; and in the next two, 'The Vault' and 'The Awakening', he passes beyond death:

> Then I beheld the King. From a cloud which cover'd the pavement
> His reverend form uprose: heavenward his face was directed,
> Heavenward his eyes were raised, and heavenward his arms were
>   extended.

The spirit of Spencer Perceval, the reactionary Prime Minister who had been assassinated in 1812 shortly after George III became permanently insane, greets his monarch, assures him that his son has ruled wisely and firmly as Prince Regent, and informs him of the defeat of Napoleon. The king asks whether the subversive spirit of Jacobinism has yet been quelled.

> Still is that fierce and restless spirit at work, was the answer:
> Still it deceiveth the weak, and inflameth the rash and the desperate.
> Even now, I ween, some dreadful deed is preparing.

In the fourth part, 'The Gate of Heaven', the king reaches the place of judgment.

> O'er the adamantine gates an Angel stood on the summit.
> Ho! he exclaim'd, King George of England cometh to judgement!
> Hear Heaven! Ye Angels hear! Souls of the Good and the Wicked
> Whom it concerns, attend! Thou, Hell, bring forth his accusers!

The 'Spirit by which his righteous reign had been troubled', the Fiend of revolution, produces two of these in the fifth part, 'The Accusers'. John Wilkes, the agitator, is one of them:

> Him by the cast of his eye oblique, I knew as the firebrand
> Whom the unthinking populace held for their idol and hero,
> Lord of Misrule in his day.

The unidentified political journalist 'Junius' is the other:

> Mask'd had he been in his life, and now a visor of iron
> Rivetted round his head, had abolish'd his features for ever.

'Wretched and guilty souls', they dare not accuse the king they have injured, so the Fiend hurls them back into hell. The sixth part, 'The Absolvers', shows how some of those who had wronged George III during their lives are now ready to admit their fault. George Washington is prominent among them, and he and the king praise each other's integrity.

Since the remainder of Southey's poem has no close parallel in Byron's, a brief review will suffice. The titles of the parts indicate its course. In 'The Beatification', the king drinks of the Well of Life and rises 'in a glorified body . . . to bliss everlasting appointed'. In the last five parts, he is welcomed by successive groups of beatified spirits. There are 'The Sovereigns', 'The Elder Worthies', 'The Worthies of the Georgian Age', and 'The Young Spirits'. Finally, in 'The Meeting', he is reunited with his own family.

Writing of *A Vision of Judgement*, Southey's own son, a clergyman, solemnly conceded 'that to speculate upon the condition of the departed, especially when under the influence of strong political feelings, is a bold, if not a presumptuous undertaking' (*Life and Correspondence of Robert Southey*, ed. C. C. Southey, 6 vols., London, 1849-50, v, p. 67). Southey seems to have confused membership of the heavenly host with membership of the Tory party. At the same time, he must have suspected that others would find the identification irreverent, or absurd. So he invests the persons and situations in his poem with a Miltonic vagueness; he makes them ideal manifestations of good and evil (or Toryism and Jacobinism) rather then clearly imagined people and places. But, whereas the power and the compact allusiveness of Milton's writing make his generalized presentations immensely suggestive, Southey lacks the literary resources to make his anything of the kind. His writing is flat and conventional; his 'spavined dactyls' jog us from cliché to cliché; he strives for dignity, and he achieves pomposity.

The Vision of Judgment

Byron seems to have objected to *A Vision of Judgement* on three counts Firstly, it was a presumptuous poem. Secondly, it was a Tory poem –

and, what was more, the work of a bigoted renegade. Thirdly, it was a bad poem, inflated, tame, stilted, and preposterous.

The Rev. C. C. Southey, the poet's son, has already come near to acknowledging for us the force of the first objection. Byron, while still very young, had felt that the anticipation of the Last Judgment by another poet, George Townsend, was 'a little too daring: at least, it looks like telling the Lord what he is to do' (27 August 1811). So perhaps we ought not to feel surprise when he denounces *A Vision of Judgement* as 'Southey's impudent anticipation of the Apotheosis of George the Third' (6 October 1821). At the same time, it may be asked on what grounds a man who professed a kind of eighteenth-century deism could make this objection. In reply, having recalled Byron's notorious self-contradictions, we may argue that along with the deist there persisted in him enough of the Calvinist for the objection to spring naturally to his mind. Alternatively, we may take the view that, apart from all theological considerations, Byron would instinctively resist any attempt to formulate a total and final judgment of a human life. But, whether his objection was Christian or humanist, it was sincere and strong and left him thinking *A Vision of Judgement* an impudent poem.

The Toryism of the work was equally offensive to him. He detested the Tory policies of the reign which had just ended: the attempt to bully the American colonies, the failure to remove the legal disabilities imposed on the Roman Catholics, the hostility towards the French Revolution, and the repressive measures adopted in the face of social unrest at home. He could not respect a king who lent his authority to such purposes. Even less could he respect a sycophantic Poet Laureate who complacently celebrated the reception into eternal bliss of a monarch who, whatever his domestic virtues, had in Byron's eyes been politically disastrous. In his 'Preface' to *The Vision of Judgment*, he declared, 'The gross flattery, the dull impudence, the renegado intolerance, and impious cant, of the poem by the author of "Wat Tyler", are something so stupendous as to form the sublime of himself – containing the quintessence of his own attributes.'

Southey's poetic failure constituted a warning against the use of hexameters. But Byron is unlikely to have needed it. For his counterblast, he naturally resorted to *ottava rima*, the form which by now had become his settled favourite, the form in which he could 'rattle on exactly as I'd talk/With any body in a ride or walk' (*Don Juan*, XV. xix) and in which the very relaxedness of his manner enabled him to spring the deadlier surprises on his readers.

He sets his poem where much of Southey's is set, just outside the gate
of heaven; but, instead of generalizing his setting and his characters,
he renders them in the most familiar and prosaic of particular terms.
This furthers his humorous and satirical purposes. The lock is 'dull',
the keys 'rusty', and Saint Peter a cantankerous janitor. Just as, in life,
the saint cut off the right ear of Malchus, the high priest's servant, in an
attempt to rescue Jesus (John 18:10), so in his present state he employs
force in an attempt to exclude Louis XVI from unmerited bliss; since
he was the first pope, he protests vehemently against the beatification of
such an enemy of Catholic Emancipation as George III; and as one of
the original twelve disciples he exhibits a snobbish hostility to a late-
comer, 'That fellow Paul – the parvenù!' (xx). Socially, he evidently
ranks below the archangel Michael and Satan, the spokesmen of heaven
and hell in the debate for the soul of the dead George III. Michael can
address him patronizingly as 'Good Saint!' and apologize to Satan for
the intemperate 'warmth of his expression' (li). But the superior breed-
ing of Michael and Satan is shown most convincingly at their first
encounter:

> though they did not kiss,
> Yet still between his Darkness and his Brightness
> There passed a mutual glance of great politeness.

> (xxxv)

Michael bows 'as to an equal, not too low,/But kindly' (xxxvi). Satan,
though he has fallen from his high estate, is mindful of his seniority;
he meets

> his ancient friend
> With more hauteur, as might an old Castilian
> Poor Noble meet a mushroom rich civilian.

> (xxxvi)

In contrast with Michael, 'A beautiful and mighty Thing of Light'
(xxviii), and Satan, 'Eternal wrath on his immortal face' (xxiv), Saint
Peter is something of a buffoon. He is even subjected to the indignity
of being prevented from dozing by a Cherub, who 'flapped his right
wing o'er his eyes' (xvii).

This Cherub announces to him the death of George III, who arrives
at the celestial gate in stanza xxiii. Before this, however, Byron turns
his eyes towards the earth and describes the burial of a king who had
died old, mad, and blind. He starts cynically enough by representing it

as 'a sepulchral melodrame', a 'show' (x), in which the tears were 'shed by collusion' and the elegies were 'Bought also' (ix). Performers and spectators flocked to it, but no genuine mourners.

> There throbbed not there a thought which pierced the pall;
>   And when the gorgeous coffin was laid low,
> It seemed the mockery of hell to fold
> The rottenness of eighty years in gold.   (x)

The corpse, contrasted with its ostentatious setting, becomes the object not only of disgust but also of pity. When Henry Crabb Robinson read *The Vision of Judgment* to Goethe in August 1829, this stanza, and especially its final couplet, won the particular admiration of the eighty-year-old poet (*Diary, Reminiscences, and Correspondence of Henry Crabb Robinson*, ed. T. Sadler, 3 vols., London, 1869, ii, p. 436).

The almost Shandian mobility of Byron's temperament again becomes apparent when he reflects upon the meaning of the loyal 'God save the king!' He comments sarcastically,

>   It is a large economy
> In God to save the like; but if he will
> Be saving . . .

if, that is, God is obstinately set upon saving even kings ('will' receives a telling emphasis), Byron is not going to exert himself in opposition. In fact, he can go further. He can allow that God's wish to save is 'all the better; for not one am I/Of those who think damnation better still' (xiii). Even if he is alone in doing so, he would like to oppose the cruel doctrine of eternal damnation.[1]

At once, he pretends to feel that he has gone too far. In a series of apparently concessive statements introduced by 'I know . . .', 'I know . . .', 'I know . . .', he reviews the arguments against such resistance to the doctrine of eternal punishment as he has just shown. But he does so with mounting irony. Acknowledging that he may be damned for his resistance, he makes it clear that in that case he will be damned for his charity; admitting that 'the best doctrines' are 'crammed' into us 'till we quite o'erflow', he lets the crude forcefulness of his language bring to our minds the revulsion that will naturally follow our compelled surfeit; and, recognizing that 'all save England's Church' have

---

[1] Cf. 'all punishment, which is to *revenge* rather than *correct*, must be *morally wrong*. And *when* the *World is at an end*, what moral or warning purpose can eternal tortures answer?' ('Detached Thoughts', 96).

fallen into hopeless error, he permits himself a couplet which, with its colloquial emphasis on '*damned*' and its ludicrous feminine rhyme, rounds off the stanza with hearty, scornful laughter:

> I know this is unpopular; I know
>   'Tis blasphemous; I know one may be damned
> For hoping no one else may e'er be so;
>   I know my catechism; I know we're crammed
> With the best doctrines till we quite o'erflow;
>   I know that all save England's Church have shammed,
> And that the other twice two hundred churches
> And synagogues have made a *damned* bad purchase.   (xiv)

'God help us all! God help me too!' (xv), he continues. He knows that he would be only too easy to damn, but he doubts whether he merits so much attention. On this rueful and self-depreciatory note, he concludes the only digression of any length in *The Vision of Judgment*.

Like the longer and more numerous digressions in *Don Juan*, this on eternal punishment helps to create in our minds an image of the narrator. In *The Vision of Judgment*, he is an aggressive but fundamentally kindly man; he has a taste for mockery and can indulge it recklessly; he does not exaggerate his own importance, however, and, though plain-spoken, he is abundantly good-natured.

George III having arrived, Satan and Michael come to claim him for hell and heaven respectively. Byron describes Satan in powerfully melodramatic terms; but a moment later he is indulging his delight in absurdity by saying that the hatred in Satan's glance makes Saint Peter sweat 'through his Apostolic skin' (xxv) and causes the Cherubs to form a protective circle around 'their poor old charge', the king, 'for by many stories,/And true, we learn the Angels all are Tories' (xxvi). Chief among these stories is presumably Southey's *A Vision of Judgement*. At Michael's invitation, Satan states his case for the king's damnation.

He speaks eloquently and judiciously. He recognizes the king's 'tame virtues' (xlvii) and admits that he was no more than 'a tool from first to last' (xliv). These concessions give an additional persuasiveness to his charge that, as a tool, George III helped to make his own reign as bloody as any in history and 'ever warred with freedom and the free' (xlv). Until almost the end of an oration that extends over more than ten stanzas, Byron avoids completely the feminine rhymes which are normally so prominent a feature of his writing in *ottava rima*. He evidently wished to avoid the levity which they tend to introduce. Satan's denunciation of the king is the serious political heart of the poem.

At its conclusion, we have another of Byron's sudden switches from the elevated to the absurd. When Satan, using his first feminine rhyme, describes George III as 'The foe to Catholic participation/In all the license of a Christian nation' (xlviii), Saint Peter flies into a rage, hoping that he may be damned himself if he ever opens the celestial gate to 'this Guelph' (xlix). Michael restores order, however, and invites Satan to call his witnesses. He does so. They are beyond number, and Byron revels in the opportunity of evoking their multitudinousness. Michael, though a trifle disconcerted by it, makes his protest with aristocratic politeness and suggests that Satan should content himself with 'two honest, clean,/True testimonies' (lxiii). Equally composed, Satan agrees.

Naturally, he summons the two who were prominent in Southey's *A Vision of Judgement*, John Wilkes and 'Junius'. Wilkes, a 'merry, cock-eyed, curious-looking Sprite' (lxvi), has a style of speech as distinctive as those of the comic gatekeeper and the two grandees. It is exuberant, racy, and irreverent, and Michael's more literary and dignified manner serves as an admirable foil to it. Wilkes thinks at first that an election meeting is in progress:

> The Spirit looked around upon the crowds
>   Assembled, and exclaimed, 'My friends of all
> The spheres, we shall catch cold amongst these clouds;
>   So let's to business: why this general call?
> If those are freeholders I see in shrouds,
>   And 'tis for an election that they bawl,
> Behold a candidate with unturned coat!
> Saint Peter, may I count upon your vote?'
>
> 'Sir,' replied Michael, 'you mistake; these things
>   Are of a former life, and what we do
> Above is more august; to judge of kings
>   Is the tribunal met: so now you know.'
> 'Then I presume those gentlemen with wings,'
>   Said Wilkes, 'are Cherubs; and that soul below
> Looks much like George the Third, but to my mind
> A good deal older – bless me! is he blind?'

'He is what you behold him, and his doom
   Depends upon his deeds,' the Angel said;
'If you have aught to arraign in him, the tomb
   Gives license to the humblest beggar's head
To lift itself against the loftiest.' – 'Some,'
   Said Wilkes, 'don't wait to see them laid in lead,
For such a liberty – and I, for one,
Have told them what I thought beneath the sun.'

'*Above* the sun repeat, then, what thou hast
   To urge against him,' said the Archangel. 'Why,'
Replied the spirit, 'since old scores are past,
   Must I turn evidence? In faith, not I.
Besides, I beat him hollow at the last,
   With all his Lords and Commons: in the sky
I don't like ripping up old stories, since
His conduct was but natural in a prince.'

(lxvii–lxx)

For all his scorn of the king, Wilkes is too little vindictive for his testimony to be of much use to Satan. His readiness to forgive contrasts pointedly with the mere shame that made Southey's Wilkes useless to Southey's Fiend. But the mysterious 'Junius' is more helpful: 'I loved my country, and I hated him' (lxxxiii). Satan is just suggesting that other witnesses should be called – including Washington, whom Southey had represented as one of 'The Absolvers' – when there occurs a sudden interruption which leads to the comic climax of the poem.

The devil Asmodeus bears in the poet Southey, whom he has arrested in the act of framing 'a libel – /No less on History – than the Holy Bible' (lxxxvi). Satan proposes, 'since he's here, let's see what he has done'.

'Done!' cried Asmodeus, 'he anticipates
The very business you are now upon,
   And scribbles as if head clerk to the Fates.'

(lxxxix)

A move by Southey to read aloud what he has been so presumptuously scribbling is halted by a general protest. Even the royal dotard comes to his senses sufficiently to utter his only speech in the poem. Mistaking Southey for the previous Laureate, the much-ridiculed H. J. Pye, he exclaims, with the repetitiousness that was habitual with him in life, 'What! what!/*Pye* come again? No more – no more of that!' (xcii).

Michael again restores order,

And now the Bard could plead his own bad cause,
With all the attitudes of self-applause.

He said – (I only give the heads) – he said,
  He meant no harm in scribbling; 'twas his way
Upon all topics; 'twas, besides, his bread,
  Of which he buttered both sides; 'twould delay
Too long the assembly (he was pleased to dread),
  And take up rather more time than a day,
To name his works – he would but cite a few –
'Wat Tyler' – 'Rhymes on Blenheim' – 'Waterloo'.

(xcv–xcvi)

Since contradictory attitudes towards politics and war inspire these three works, Southey's defence naturally shifts to his many changes of opinion. He then tries to solicit an order for a new biography to be written by himself – the subject being apparently a matter of indifference – and finally he renews his attempt to read aloud *A Vision of Judgement*. His long speech demands quotation in full, for short extracts cannot possibly do justice to a writer as profuse and uninhibited as Byron.

He had written praises of a Regicide;
  He had written praises of all kings whatever;
He had written for republics far and wide,
  And then against them bitterer than ever;
For pantisocracy he once had cried
  Aloud, a scheme less moral than 'twas clever;
Then grew a hearty anti-jacobin –
Had turned his coat – and would have turned his skin.

He had sung against all battles, and again
  In their high praise and glory; he had called
Reviewing 'the ungentle craft,' and then
  Became as base a critic as e'er crawled –
Fed, paid, and pampered by the very men
  By whom his muse and morals had been mauled:
He had written much blank verse, and blanker prose,
And more of both than any body knows.

He had written Wesley's life: – here turning round
   To Satan, 'Sir, I'm ready to write yours,
In two octavo volumes, nicely bound,
   With notes and preface, all that most allures
The pious purchaser; and there's no ground
   For fear, for I can choose my own reviewers:
So let me have the proper documents,
That I may add you to my other saints.'

Satan bowed, and was silent. 'Well, if you,
   With amiable modesty, decline
My offer, what says Michael? There are few
   Whose memoirs could be rendered more divine.
Mine is a pen of all work; not so new
   As it was once, but I would make you shine
Like your own trumpet. By the way, my own
Has more of brass in it, and is as well blown.

'But talking about trumpets, here's my "Vision!"
   Now you shall judge, all people – yes – you shall
Judge with my judgment! and by my decision
   Be guided who shall enter heaven or fall.
I settle all these things by intuition,
   Times present, past, to come – Heaven – Hell – and all,
Like King Alfonso. When I thus see double,
I save the Deity some worlds of trouble.'

                             (xcvii–ci)

This pert and presumptuous turncoat has, of course, only a limited resemblance to Robert Southey. But, from what he supposed to be the truth about his opponent, Byron has created in his poem a conceited literary timeserver who interests us both for his own sake and because he exemplifies a recurrent pattern of political behaviour.

Southey's public reading does not get very far. Angels, devils, and ghosts take flight in consternation. Saint Peter, living up to his reputation for impetuosity, fells the poet with his keys. The confusion enables Byron to bring his poem to a hilariously satisfying close. He must have wondered what he was to do with the king at the end of it. To send him to hell would be pettily vindictive; to send him to heaven would be to endorse Southey's verdict; to send him to either would also look like 'telling the Lord what he is to do'. Byron's solution was to allow the feeble-minded old man to slip unnoticed into heaven,

And when the tumult dwindled to a calm,
I left him practising the hundredth psalm.

(cvi)

In this way, good humour is maintained, and even charity, without any compromising of what would have been the just verdict on as bad a king as ever 'left a realm undone' (viii).

Some readers prefer *The Vision of Judgment* even to *Don Juan* itself. They admire the compactness and economy which result from Byron's concentration in it upon a clearly conceived purpose, and they note that even the one important digression from its plot is strictly relevant to its theme. Rendering the subject in more familiar and prosaic terms than those employed by Southey, Byron gives us varied and vital characters engaged in a lively action which develops unpredictably, even to the final stanza. His dialogue is excellent. If Satan's speech for the damnation of George III is the serious political centre of the poem, and Southey's personal appearance its comic climax, the work as a whole is remarkable for its controlled alternations of gravity and jest, of sardonic satire and nonsensical play. Our constant awareness of the humorous, relaxed narrator does much to prevent such variety from degenerating into mere miscellaneity. But the alternations of mood remain important. The highly dramatic patterning of light and shade, of cheerfulness and destructiveness, justifies Byron's own description of his poem as 'in my finest, ferocious, Caravaggio style' (*Correspondence*, 12 October 1821).

8

Cain: A Mystery

Though Byron's poems in *ottava rima* form his major achievement, they should not monopolize attention. The powerful descriptions and sombre broodings of *Childe Harold's Pilgrimage*, the harrowing recreation in *The Prisoner of Chillon* of the experience of a man long denied his freedom, and the poignant 'lyrical cry' of 'So We'll Go No More A-Roving' suggest something of the range of the best of his other works. Nor is the last of these unique among his shorter poems. 'She Walks in Beauty', 'Stanzas for Music', 'Epistle to Augusta', and others of his lyrics similarly unite great power and simplicity of feeling with utter clarity of style.

Few nowadays would claim a high place for *Cain*. In it Byron repudiates 'cant religious', just as in the *ottava rima* poems he repudiates 'cant political, cant poetical, . . . cant moral'. His doing so gave great offence to many who read *Cain* when it first appeared, and within ten months he was describing it as the Waterloo of his reputation (*Don Juan*, XI. lv–lvi). Admittedly, his heterodoxy had peeped out in earlier publications; in *Don Juan*, II. cxxxiv, for example, he had ventured to hint uncertainty regarding the orthodox Christian teaching on life after death. But *Cain*, making a frontal assault on received beliefs, provoked a sense of outrage so deep that both the work itself and its reception call for a more thorough consideration than its intrinsic merits would encourage.

Before Publication

On 28 January 1821, Byron recorded in his 'Diary': 'Pondered the subjects of four tragedies'. The second of these was 'Cain, a metaphysical subject, something in the style of Manfred, but in five *acts*, perhaps, with the chorus'. *Cain* was to have only three acts, and no chorus; but it was certainly to have a metaphysical subject, and up to a point it was to be in the style of *Manfred*.

Byron started to write it on 16 July 1821. He finished it in less than two months and sent it to Murray on 10 September. In the letter announcing it he described it as '*a Mystery*', explaining this word as meaning 'a tragedy on a sacred subject'. He expressed the view 'that it contains some poetry', demanded 'a proof of the whole by return of *post*', and ordered a dedication to Sir Walter Scott.

He wrote from Ravenna, where he had been living since late in 1819. Naturally, he was anxious to hear of the safe receipt of his manuscript in London. Two days after its dispatch, a second letter to Murray asked for a prompt acknowledgment of *Cain*'s arrival and supplied three lines to be appended to Eve's curse upon the murderer in III. i – 'as pretty a piece of Imprecation . . . as you may wish to meet with in the course of your business'. As usual, Byron was eager to know what Gifford thought of his new work, 'for I have a good opinion of the piece, as poetry: it is in my gay metaphysical style, and in the *Manfred* line' (12 September 1821). William Gifford, the editor of the *Quarterly Review*, was one of Murray's advisers. Byron had a profound respect for his literary judgment and left to him many final decisions regarding the published texts of his poems. The association was a strange one, between a Tory scholar of plebeian origin and a Whig poet of aristocratic birth.

While still awaiting news of his manuscript's arrival, Byron described the work to Moore (19 September 1821):

> It is in the *Manfred* metaphysical style, and full of some Titanic declamation; – Lucifer being one of the *dram. pers.*, who takes Cain a voyage among the stars, and afterwards to 'Hades,' where he shows him the phantoms of a former world, and its inhabitants. I have gone upon the notion of Cuvier, that the world has been destroyed three or four times, and was inhabited by mammoths, behemoths, and what not; but *not* by man till the Mosaic period, as, indeed, is proved by the strata of bones found; – those of all unknown animals, and known, being dug out, but none of mankind. I have, therefore, supposed Cain to be shown, in the *rational* Preadamites, beings endowed with a higher intelligence than man, but totally unlike him in form, and with much greater strength of mind and person. You may suppose the

small talk which takes place between him and Lucifer upon these matters is not quite canonical.

The consequence is, that Cain comes back and kills Abel in a fit of dissatisfaction, partly with the politics of Paradise, which had driven them all out of it, and partly because (as it is written in Genesis) Abel's sacrifice was the more acceptable to the Deity. I trust that the Rhapsody has arrived – it is in three acts, and entitled '*A Mystery,*' according to the former Christian custom, and in honour of what it probably will remain to the reader.

Baron Cuvier had recently interpreted the fossil record of the pre-history of the earth as pointing to a series of local catastrophes, after each of which the area concerned was repopulated by species coming in from other parts. Byron evidently imagined the process as involving a whole series of creations of life, each terminated by a total catastrophe, the creatures belonging to each successive age exhibiting a falling-off from those of earlier ages.

On the day after he described *Cain* to Moore, and again a week after that, Byron was asking Murray whether the manuscript had arrived (20 and 27 September 1821); and on 1 October, three weeks after dispatching it, he was still wondering, in a letter to Moore, 'if my *Cain* has got safe to England'. Once he knew it was there, he became impatient for the proofs. In his letters of 26 and 28 October, he chafes at Murray's dilatoriness in supplying them.

Within the next few days, he received an intimation of things to come. Murray asked him to alter two passages, evidently because he feared they would be offensive to orthodox Christian readers. Byron retorted (3 November 1821):

The two passages cannot be altered without making Lucifer talk like the Bishop of Lincoln – which would not be in the character of the former. The notion is from Cuvier (that of the *old Worlds*), as I have explained in an additional note to the preface. The other passage is also in character: if *nonsense* – so much the better, because then it can do no harm, and the sillier Satan is made, the safer for every body. As to 'alarms,' etc., do you really think such things ever led any body astray? Are these people more impious than Milton's Satan? or the Prometheus of Æschylus? . . . Are not Adam, Eve, Adah, and Abel, as pious as the Catechism?

Gifford is too wise a man to think that such things can have any *serious* effect: *who* was ever altered by a poem? I beg leave to observe, that there is no creed nor personal hypothesis of mine in all this: but I was obliged to make Cain and Lucifer talk consistently, and surely this has always been permitted to poesy. Cain is a proud man: if Lucifer promised him kingdoms, etc., it would *elate* him: the object of the Demon is to *depress* him still further in his own estimation than he was before, by showing him infinite things and his own abasement, till he falls into the frame of mind that leads to the Catastrophe, from mere *internal* irritation, *not* premeditation, or envy of *Abel* (which would have made him contemptible), but from the rage and fury against the inadequacy of his state to his conceptions, and which discharges itself rather against Life, and the Author of Life, than the mere living.

His subsequent remorse is the natural effect of looking on his sudden deed. Had the *deed* been *premeditated*, his repentance would have been tardier.

The three last MS. lines of Eve's curse are replaced from *memory* on the proofs, but incorrectly (for I keep no copies). Either keep *these three*, or *replace* them with the *other three*, whichever are thought least bad by Mr. Gifford. There is no occasion for a *revise*; it is only losing time.

Byron here advances two arguments in defence of *Cain* and, while doing so, states what he intended to be its central theme. One of his arguments – '*who* was ever altered by a poem?' – is merely an expression of his habitual disdain for his own sedentary trade. 'As to defining what a poet *should* be,' he had written three days after recording the original conception of *Cain*, 'it is not worth while, for what are *they* worth? what have they done?' ('Diary', 31 January 1821). For his main argument, however, he insists upon the autonomy of *Cain* as a dramatic poem. He maintains that the views expressed in it come from the *dramatis personae*, not from himself; that, while the characters may abide our question, the author is free. He was to make more use of this argument later.

Consideration of the characters, and in particular of the motivation of Cain, leads him to formulate the central theme of the work. Cain feels 'rage and fury against the inadequacy of his state to his conceptions', and these emotions discharge themselves 'rather against Life, and the Author of Life, than the mere living'. Romantic rebellion thus culminates in blasphemy. In a more atheistical climate of opinion, the outcome might have been an assertion of the absurdity of the human situation. But Cain does not for a moment question the existence of God. Nor did Byron. Not only did he profess a kind of eighteenth-century deism, but his early childhood in Aberdeen had left him more of a Calvinist than could easily have been suspected.

Before the end of September 1821, Moore had read *Cain* in manuscript and had written to Byron describing it as 'wonderful – terrible – never to be forgotten. If I am not mistaken, it will sink deep into the world's heart; and while many will shudder at its blasphemy, all must fall prostrate before its grandeur. Talk of Æschylus and his Prometheus! – here is the true spirit both of the Poet – and the Devil' (*The Letters of Thomas Moore*, ed. W. S. Dowden, 2 vols., Oxford, 1964, ii, p. 606). Byron thanked him in his letter of 16 November 1821. But one week later he was shocked by a thoroughly hostile verdict from Hobhouse, to which he replied as temperately as he could on the day of its arrival (*Correspondence*, ii, p. 205). Writing to Murray on the following day, he declared that Hobhouse had 'launched (uncalled for, for I did not solicit his opinion that I recollect at least) into a most violent invective upon the subject of *Cain* (*not* on *a religious* account at all as he says) and in such terms as make the grossest review in the lowest publication that ever I read upon any scribbler moderate in comparison' (24 November 1821).

A number of leading men of letters – notably Shelley, Scott, and Goethe – were in due course to join Moore in admiring *Cain*. But the reading public, as represented by its reviewers, sermon-writers, and pamphleteers was to a large extent to share Hobhouse's hostility to it. Publication took place on 19 December 1821. The nature and meaning of the dramatic poem which from that date gave such deep offence to so many of its readers will clearly repay attention.

Cain: A Mystery

The action of *Cain* occurs at a time when the disobedience of Adam and Eve has already resulted in the exclusion from Eden not only of the sinners themselves but also of their whole progeny. Their elder son Cain resents what seems to him the flagrant injustice of this sentence. Death, of which he is ignorant but which he fears, awaits alike his parents, himself and his wife, and all their descendants. An important irony in the play is that he is to be the instrument by which it will make its first appearance in the world.

The play opens with his refusal to join in the family worship of Jehovah: 'I have nought to ask.' Adam presses him: 'Nor aught to thank for?' 'No', retorts Cain. 'Dost thou not *live*?' asks Adam, only to receive the sour reply, 'Must I not die?' (I. i. 28–9). Cain can feel no gratitude to a deity who inflicted a cruel punishment on Adam and Eve after having himself exposed them to temptation, and who extended that punishment to their still unborn and unoffending progeny. Jehovah's goodness is far from evident; it certainly does not follow from his being all-powerful. 'I judge but by the fruits', says Cain, ' – and they are bitter' (I. i. 78).

Clearly, Cain does not need a tempter to lead him into revolt. All Lucifer will have to do is to encourage him in the revolt to which he has already committed himself. Lucifer is a highly articulate Manichæan. He claims that he and Jehovah reign over all things, over 'Life and Death – and Time –/Eternity – and heaven and earth' (I. i. 548–9); having 'nought in common' (I. i. 305) with Jehovah, he will neither serve him nor share with him; the two of them reign in division, conflicting and irreconcilable, 'the great double Mysteries! the *two Principles*!' (II. ii. 404).

Lucifer takes Cain's education in hand. He bewilders him by conveying him through the vast spaces of the Newtonian universe. He shows him in the realm of Death the beautiful, mighty, and intelligent beings formed in earlier creations and duly destroyed prior to the creation of the present world and the men who inhabit it. Jehovah, the 'Maker' and the 'Destroyer' (I. i. 266), is responsible for these creations and catastrophes. Lucifer, as Jehovah's eternal antagonist, assiduously fosters in Cain the resentment these sights provoke. He has himself preferred 'an independency of torture/To the smooth agonies of adulation' (I. i. 385–6) as a member of the heavenly host. He urges Cain to reject Adam's docile identification of Jehovah with goodness and to judge him in the light of experience: 'what have been his gifts/To you already, in your little world?' 'But few,' admits Cain, 'and some of those but bitter.' Lucifer exhorts him:

>   Back
> With me, then, to thine earth, and try the rest
> Of his celestial boons to you and yours.
> Evil and Good are things in their own essence,
> And not made good or evil by the Giver;
> But if he gives you good – so call him; if

Evil springs from *him*, do not name it *mine*,
Till ye know better its true fount; and judge
Not by words, though of Spirits, but the fruits
Of your existence, such as it must be.
One good gift has the fatal apple given, –
Your *reason*: – let it not be overswayed
By tyrannous threats to force you into faith
'Gainst all external sense and inward feeling:
Think and endure, – and form an inner world
In your own bosom.

(II. ii. 447–64)

Lucifer does not rely solely upon more or less rational argument. He brings emotional pressures to bear, too. When Cain professes his love for his brother, Lucifer taunts him for his meekness in not resenting the obvious favouritism of Abel by Eve, by Adam, and even by Jehovah himself, who finds Abel's sacrifices 'acceptable' (II. ii. 353). Cain acknowledges that he has known impulses of resentment.

His affection for his brother and sisters is genuine enough, however. In particular, his deep love for his wife and sister, Adah, and for his two children by her, is a principal condition of the hostility he feels towards a deity who has punished them for a sin they did not commit. In the third and last act of the play, when this ruthless and arbitrary deity manifests his habitual preference for Abel's offering of 'scorching flesh and smoking blood' (III. i. 299), Cain's indignation overcomes the meekness for which Lucifer taunted him. He goes to throw down the favoured altar, and, when Abel hinders him, he murders his brother. In his rage, he proclaims his deed a sacrifice to the god who 'loves blood' (III. i. 310).

Abel's dying words anticipate those recorded in Luke 23:34 as spoken on the Cross, 'Oh, God! receive thy servant! and/Forgive his slayer, for he knew not what/He did' (III. i. 318–20). Abel has been represented throughout as humble and 'gentle as the flocks he tended' (III. i. 505); his is a naturally Christian soul. 'Tamed down' (I. i. 180) is Cain's phrase for Adam, 'cheerful and resigned' is Eve's (I. i. 51). In fact, Adam and Eve have both submitted to their lot before the play opens. Cain is the only member of the family who cannot contentedly accept a lot 'inferior still to my desires/And my conceptions' (II. i. 82–3). He is a Romantic rebel:

It is not with the earth, though I must till it,
I feel at war – but that I may not profit
By what it bears of beautiful, untoiling,
Nor gratify my thousand swelling thoughts
With knowledge, nor allay my thousand fears
Of Death and Life.

(II. ii. 125–30)

This explains his responsiveness to a tempter who proclaims the 'nothingness' (II. ii. 422) of life as it is but declares that he would have made men gods, that he would have enabled them to live for ever, and that nothing can quell the indomitable mind:

Lucifer I tempt none,
    Save with the truth: was not the Tree, the Tree
    Of Knowledge? and was not the Tree of Life
    Still fruitful? Did *I* bid her pluck them not?
    Did I plant things prohibited within
    The reach of beings innocent, and curious
    By their own innocence? I would have made ye
    Gods; and even He who thrust ye forth, so thrust ye
    Because 'ye should not eat the fruits of life,
    And become gods as we.' Were those his words?
Cain They were, as I have heard from those who heard them.
    In thunder.
Lucifer Then who was the Demon? He
    Who would not let ye live, or he who would
    Have made ye live for ever, in the joy
    And power of Knowledge?
Cain Would they had snatched both
    The fruits, or neither!
Lucifer One is yours already,
    The other may be still.
Cain How so?
Lucifer By being
    Yourselves, in your resistance. Nothing can
    Quench the mind, if the mind will be itself
    And centre of surrounding things – 'tis made
    To sway.

(I. i. 196–216)

Lucifer pities Cain for loving 'what must perish'. 'And I thee', retorts Cain, 'who lov'st nothing' (II. ii. 337–8). This exchange epitomizes the difference between them. Lucifer embodies a principle. He has something of the grandeur and sadness of Milton's Satan, something of the sardonic truthfulness of Goethe's Mephistopheles. But he remains both more and less than human. Cain, however, knows love and pity and remorse. As well as a Romantic rebel, he is a hero of sensibility. Both sides of his nature contribute to make him the murderer and the exile who departs with Adah and their children at the end of the action.

But this differentiation between the two leading characters is not enough. From a dramatic point of view, Byron would have done well to have heightened the tension between them. If he had shown Lucifer seducing a pious but susceptible son of Adam into an eventual defiance of God, if he had shown him tempting a 'cheerful and resigned' Cain to crave for forbidden knowledge, he would have been providing the kind of conflict that is the life of drama. As things are, Cain is already defiant, already craving for knowledge, when we first see him. All Lucifer does is to encourage by spectacular means the revolt to which Cain has previously committed himself. He takes him on a grand tour of the universe and enables him to behold 'the history/Of past – and present, and of future worlds' (II. i. 24–5). The effect of these spectacles, and of the impresario's comments, is to bring home to Cain his own insignificance, his bondage to the flesh, and his mortality. The experience augments his existing 'rage and fury against the inadequacy of his state to his conceptions', until he is ripe to defy God in act and so commits the first murder.

By making Cain a humanized Lucifer – or Lucifer an apotheosized Cain – Byron establishes the defiance of God exhibited by his leading characters as the stance that is upheld by the play as a whole. In the neighbourhood of these two, the docility of Adam and Eve and the anticipatory Christianity of Abel seem merely ignoble. Byron was perhaps being a little disingenuous, and was assuredly in the wrong, when he argued that his characters speak only for themselves in such speeches as Lucifer's in praise of

> Souls who dare use their immortality –
> Souls who dare look the Omnipotent tyrant in
> His everlasting face, and tell him that
> His evil is not good!
>
> (I. i. 137–40)

There can be little or no doubt that Lucifer and Cain protest and blaspheme as spokesmen for the author himself. Byron went so far as to allow Lucifer to foretell the atonement (I. i. 163–6),[1] the descent into hell (I. i. 541–2), and the miraculous walking on the Sea of Galilee (II. i. 16–20). The accuracy of his foreknowledge has the effect of validating his more outrageous utterances.

Underlying these is his Manichæism. A Prince of Darkness who wishes to make his career intellectually respectable may well have a use for this dualistic theology, though he will no doubt define the two principles to suit himself. Thus Byron's Lucifer identifies God with tyranny and obscurantism, himself with freedom and enlightenment. Nowhere in the drama does its author suggest that these identifications are incorrect. Certainly the placid assurances of the conformist characters that God is good carry very little weight in the context of the play. Nor does Lucifer tempt Cain to the murder. He merely gives him knowledge and encourages him to believe in the self-sufficiency of the human mind. In fact, God himself seems more to blame for the crime than does Lucifer. For it is his cruel tyranny that provokes the proud but loving Cain to try to overthrow the favoured altar, and in trying to do so to commit an act as completely out of character as the murder of his brother.

Byron had a sincere and lively interest in theological and philosophical speculation but little taste or aptitude for sustained thinking. So *Cain* is remarkable less for intellectual profundity than for the lucidity and emphasis with which its leading ideas are formulated. Its verse seems to aspire to the virtues of prose. In many passages, weak endings are numerous enough to compromise the integrity of the separate metrical lines. When a stronger rhythm imposes itself, the usual result is a rather bare rhetoric. Admittedly, there are incisive formulations, such as Lucifer's harsh dismissal of the heavenly host's 'smooth agonies of adulation' (I. i. 386), but in general the verse of *Cain* lacks the resonance of that of *Childe Harold's Pilgrimage* and the exuberant virtuosity of that of *Don Juan* and *The Vision of Judgment*.

After Publication

Murray issued *Cain* in the same volume as two other new plays by

[1] This passage was omitted from the text in the first edition and in all subsequent editions until Coleridge restored it from the manuscript in 1901 (*Poetry*, v, p. 219n).

Byron, *Sardanapalus* and *The Two Foscari*. J. G. Lockhart briefly noticed all three for the sprightly Tory monthly, *Blackwood's Edinburgh Magazine*. His verdict was that *Cain* 'contains, perhaps, five or six passages of as fine poetry as Lord Byron ever wrote or will write; but, taken altogether, it is a wicked and blasphemous performance, destitute of any merit sufficient to overshadow essential defects of the most abominable nature' (January 1822).

A month later, 'Siluriensis' (John Matthews) contributed a longer article to the same magazine. He recognizes *Cain* as one of 'the effusions of the Satanic school', and with reference to Byron's 'Preface' he continues: 'The poet imagines that he cannot be censured for making his dramatis personæ speak in their proper characters, and supposes that he shelters himself from all blame in disseminating unreproved blasphemy, by asserting that he cannot make Lucifer "talk like a clergyman."' 'Siluriensis' complains of the 'slovenly haste' apparent in the writing of all three plays. But his main charge against *Cain* is that throughout it Byron's 'end and aim appears to be to perplex his readers by starting doubts necessarily inexplicable to human understanding, and insinuating opinions derogatory to the veneration we owe to the Divine Being, and filling their minds with discontent at the nature which it has pleased Infinite Wisdom to bestow on mankind.' He envies the Scots their good fortune in having, as their 'great bard', Sir Walter Scott, whose 'vivid pictures of life and manners' excite 'all the best feelings of our nature . . . , without once extorting a blush from modesty, or a frown from rational piety.'

In its issue bearing the same date, February 1822, the great Whig quarterly, the *Edinburgh Review* – derided in *Blackwood's* as 'the dull, stupid, superannuated, *havering* Edinburgh' (xi, p. 90) – came into action. Its review was anonymous, in accordance with custom, but Francis Jeffrey is known to have written it. As a youth, Byron had held Jeffrey responsible for the *Edinburgh*'s contemptuous treatment of his own first publication, *Hours of Idleness*, and he had attacked him in *English Bards, and Scotch Reviewers*. But when the *Edinburgh* praised *Childe Harold's Pilgrimage*, I and II, he repented of his petulance and wrote to Jeffrey to apologize for the attack. In a conciliatory reply, Jeffrey hinted that he had not been the author of the review of *Hours of Idleness*. (In fact, H. P. Brougham had written it.) During the years that followed, Jeffrey continued to review Byron favourably. But *Cain* was too much for him. Writing 'far more in sorrow than in anger', he had to admit that, although *Cain* abounds in beautiful passages, and shows more *power* perhaps than any of the author's dramatical compositions, we regret very much that it should ever have been published. It will give great scandal and offence to pious persons in general – and may be the means of suggesting the most painful doubts and distressing perplexities, to hundreds of minds that might never otherwise have been exposed to such dangerous disturbance. It is nothing less than absurd, in such a case, to observe, that Lucifer cannot well be expected to talk like an orthodox divine – and that the conversation of the first Rebel and the first Murderer was not likely to be very unexceptionable – or to plead the authority of Milton, or the authors of the old mysteries, for such offensive colloquies. The fact is, that here *the whole argument* – and a very elaborate and specious argument it is – is directed against the goodness or the power of the Deity, and against the reasonableness of religion in general; and there is no answer so much as attempted to the offensive doctrines that are so strenuously inculcated. The Devil and his pupil have the field entirely to themselves – and are encountered with nothing but feeble obtestations and unreasoning horrors. Nor is this argumentative blasphemy a mere incidental deformity that arises in the course of an action directed to the common sympathies of our nature. It forms, on the contrary, the great staple of the piece – and occupies, we should think, not less than two-thirds of it; – so that it is really difficult to believe that it was written for any other purpose than to inculcate these doctrines – or at least to discuss the question upon which they bear.

While Jeffrey completely exonerates Byron from the charge of writing with 'any mischievous intention', he insists that such works as *Cain* are mischievous in tendency. Byron has only one superior among living authors; but that one, Scott, provides Jeffrey, as he provided 'Siluriensis', with his example of how great literary gifts can be used for the benefit of mankind.

Byron heard of this adverse criticism some time before he saw it. On 17 May 1822, he wrote to Murray: 'nothing that has or may appear in Jeffrey's review can make me forget that he stood by me for ten good years, without any motive to do so but his own good will.' Three weeks later, after having read the article, he assured Moore that he would not retort, 'for I owe him [Jeffrey] a good turn still for his kindness bygone' (8 June 1822). When Hobhouse visited him four months later, however, Byron confessed that he had been 'much hurt' (L. A. Marchand, *Byron: A Biography*, p. 1031). By this time, he was working on Canto X of *Don Juan*, and he there addresses Jeffrey, saying that their 'little feuds' are now over, and adding:

> Here's a health to 'Auld Lang Syne'!
> I do not know you, and may never know
> Your face, – but you have acted on the whole
> Most nobly, and I own it from my soul.

(X. xvi)

Later still, when he was writing Canto XII, he made a jocular reference to Jeffrey's invidious contrast between Scott and himself (XII. xvi).

Long before this the Tory *Quarterly Review* – characterized in *Blackwood's* as 'the cold, well-informed, heartless, witless, prosing, pedantic Quarterly' (xi, p. 90) – had joined in the attack. The anonymous article published in its issue dated July 1822 was the work of Reginald Heber. Shortly to become Bishop of Calcutta, and today best known as the author of the hymn 'Holy, Holy, Holy, Lord God Almighty!', Heber aims in this review 'to unmask the sophisms which lurk under his [Byron's] poetical language; and to show how irrelevant to the truths of natural and revealed religion are those apparent irregularities in the present course of things, which he makes his objection to the being or the benignity of the Creator'. Not that Heber is much impressed by the 'poetical language' or the dramatic power of *Cain*: 'we close the book with no distinct or clinging recollection of any single passage in it, and with the general impression only that Lucifer has said much and done little, and that Cain has been unhappy without grounds and wicked without an object.' But even an unimpressive work may call for refutation. Heber seeks to provide it:

> The sarcasms of Lucifer and the murmurs of Cain are directed against Providence in general; and proceed to the subversion of every system of theology, except that (if theology it may be called) which holds out God to the abhorrence of his creatures as a capricious tyrant, and which regards the Devil (or under whatever name Lord Byron may chuse to embody the principle of resistance to the Supreme) as the champion of all which is energetic and interesting and noble; the spirit of free thought and stern endurance, unbrokenly contending against the bondage which makes nature miserable.

To Heber, this amounts to a 'deification of vice', a 'crazy attachment to the worser half of Manicheism'. Byron infers a malevolent Creator 'from the mixture of evil and sorrow which the world presents'. Before we do likewise, Heber would have us enquire, 'first, whether *more* good than evil, *more* happiness than misery is not found, after all, in the world with which we are so much displeased; and, secondly, whether the good which exists is not, apparently, the result of direct *design*, while the evil is *incidental* only'.

The italicized word '*design*' announces that Heber will be borrowing his weapons from the armoury of William Paley. His doing so makes further summary of his argument unnecessary. For present purposes, it will suffice to say that he concludes with a recommendation to Byron 'to abstain from compositions of which the only effect can be to offend the honest prejudices, and unsettle the most estimable principles of the great majority of that nation who would gladly find a blameless delight in his volumes, and express a patriotic pride in his renown'.

Though Byron was now refusing to read reviews, a reprint of the earlier half of Heber's article forced itself on his attention in a French publication. Heber says little about *Cain* in this earlier half; Byron's description of the criticism as 'extremely handsome, and any thing but unkind or unfair' (25 December 1822) relates mainly to what is said about his other plays. Heber objects to much in these, too. But a year's exposure to hostile comment had evidently left Byron ready to welcome any criticism that was temperate in tone.

Hostile comment had not been limited to the great reviews. As early as 9 February 1822, Moore told Byron that the play '*has* made a sensation' (*The Letters of Thomas Moore*, ii, p. 618). Eight days later, the liberal *Examiner* reported that 'the very highest authority in the land', George IV himself, had 'expressed his disapprobation of the blasphemy and licentiousness of Lord Byron's writings' (*Poetry*, v, p. 204). Three days later still, Byron was well aware that 'the parsons are all preaching at it, from Kentish Town and Oxford to Pisa, – the scoundrels of priests, who do more harm to religion than all the infidels that ever forgot their catechisms!' (20 February 1822). Meanwhile, a cheap pirated edition was not only threatening Murray's profits but alarming Tories and churchmen by making the subversive drama available to members of the lower orders.

One churchman, the Rev. H. J. Todd, writing under the pseudonym 'Oxoniensis', produced early in 1822 a pamphlet entitled *A Remon-*

strance Addressed to Mr. John Murray, Respecting a Recent Publication.
'Oxoniensis' remonstrates with the publisher because he considers the
author incorrigible. Byron knew of the *Remonstrance* by 6 February
1822 and conjectured that its clerical author 'wants a living'. Two days
later he wrote to Murray his much-quoted letter from Pisa:

> Attacks upon me were to be expected; but I perceive one upon
> *you* in the papers, which I confess that I did not expect. How,
> or in what manner, *you* can be considered responsible for what *I*
> publish, I am at a loss to conceive.
>
> ... *Cain* is nothing more than a drama, not a piece of
> argument: if Lucifer and Cain speak as the first Murderer and the
> first Rebel may be supposed to speak, surely all the rest of the
> personages talk also according to their characters – and the
> stronger passions have ever been permitted to the drama ...
>
> The Attempt to *bully you*, because they think it won't succeed
> with me, seems to me as atrocious an attempt as ever disgraced
> the times ... I can only say, *Me, me, adsum qui feci*; that any
> proceedings directed against you, I beg, may be transferred to me,
> who am willing, and *ought*, to endure them all; that if you have
> lost money by the publication, I will refund any or all of the
> Copyright; that I desire you will say, that both *you* and *Mr.
> Gifford* remonstrated against the publication, as also Mr. Hobhouse;
> that *I* alone occasioned it, and I alone am the person who, either
> legally or otherwise, should bear the burthen. If they prosecute,
> I will come to England – that is, if, by meeting it in my own
> person, I can save yours. Let me know: you shan't suffer for me,
> if I can help it. Make any use of this letter which you please.

Murray availed himself of this permission to show the letter to others.
An outcome was the appearance in *Blackwood's* for the following
month, March 1822, of an amusing verse paraphrase of it in the metre
and style of *Don Juan* by 'Ensign Odoherty' (probably J. G. Lockhart).

In his *Remonstrance*, 'Oxoniensis' makes much of Byron's indebtedness to earlier freethinkers. He assures Murray 'that this poem, this
Mystery with which you have insulted us, is nothing more than a
Cento from Voltaire's novels and the most objectionable articles in
Bayle's Dictionary, served up in clumsy cuttings of ten syllables, for
the purpose of giving it the guise of poetry' (p. 10). Byron certainly
owed a lot to the authors named. But 'Oxoniensis' exaggerates too
noticeably when he asserts 'that there is not a single passage, – not a

point of sentiment, imagery, or incident, which he [Byron] has not repeated from himself, or stolen from some other writer' (p. 12).

This is not his main charge against *Cain*, however. Though 'Oxoniensis' believes the doctrines it embodies to be derivative and invalid, he fears that 'they may mislead the ignorant, unsettle the wavering, or confirm the hardened sceptic in his misbelief' (p. 13). The poem is dangerous because in it Byron 'quarrels with the very conditions of humanity, rebels against that Providence which guides and governs all things, and dares to adopt the language which had never before been attributed to any being but one, "Evil be thou my good"' (pp. 18–19).

To *Cain*, 'Oxoniensis' opposes *Paradise Lost*. Had Byron been willing to learn, Milton could, he argues, have shown him how 'a really powerful mind grapples with those difficulties, which Bayle and Voltaire have taught him to consider as insurmountable' (p. 11). His comparison provoked another pseudonymous pamphleteer, 'Harroviensis', to step forward immediately in Byron's defence. *A Letter to Sir Walter Scott*, published like the *Remonstrance* early in 1822, develops an interpretation of *Cain* as an orthodox Christian poem by the simple expedient of insisting that all the heterodox speeches belong to Lucifer and Cain and ought no more to be ascribed to the poet than ought similarly heterodox speeches by the diabolical and other fallen characters in *Paradise Lost*.

This argument echoes Byron's repeated assertion – for example, in letters dated 3 November 1821 and 4 March 1822 – that his characters speak for themselves and not for their author. Naturally, the *Letter to Sir Walter Scott* delighted him. He thought it 'conclusive', asked Murray to identify 'Harroviensis', and suggested that the pamphlet should be appended to the next edition of *Cain* (13 and 18 April, 1 and 4 May 1822). Murray brushed aside 'Harroviensis' as 'a tyro in literature' (6 June 1822). But five months later Byron was still mentioning him with gratitude (? November 1822).

Meanwhile, a third pamphleteer had contributed to the debate. His pseudonym, 'Philo-Milton', and his title, *A Vindication of the Paradise Lost from the Charge of Exculpating 'Cain,' a Mystery*, declare his aim. He argues that the comparison of heterodox speeches from *Cain* with heterodox speeches from *Paradise Lost* does not prove what 'Harroviensis' wishes it to prove. The heterodox speeches in *Paradise Lost* occur in a context which implicitly or explicitly invites us to scrutinize them critically; those in *Cain* so dominate their contexts that they are themselves rightly taken to embody the central doctrines of the poem.

As a result, the temptation in the one case exists for Adam and Eve alone, but in the other it exists 'for *us* as well as for' Cain (p. 20). Like other hostile critics, 'Philo-Milton' deplores Byron's publication of a poem so eligible for piracy and therefore so capable of disseminating its sceptical and subversive doctrines among the populace.

For more than twenty years, pamphlets and books, in verse and in prose, continued to offer refutations of the obnoxious drama. But Byron had lost interest in them well before the end of 1822. His most characteristic comment on the consternation he had provoked comes in the letter to Moore, dated 8 March 1822, that was quoted early in Chapter III. This is characteristic in its rapid alternations of earnestness, ruefulness, and irreverence. Basically, *Cain* is one more expression of Byron's 'detestation/Of every despotism' (*Don Juan*, IX. xxiv); it voices, however imperfectly, his detestation of the despotism of the Old Testament Jehovah. In the religious and political climate of 1821-2, to publish such a protest was to ask for trouble. As we have seen, Byron got it.

9

Reputation

'I awoke one morning', wrote Byron, 'and found myself famous' (*Letters and Journals*, ii, p. 106, *note*). This was in 1812. *English Bards, and Scotch Reviewers* had been a success, but the first two cantos of *Childe Harold's Pilgrimage* were a triumph. The Turkish tales quickly added to this and developed the image of the Byronic hero in the public mind. Shortly after Byron left England for the last time, the reception of *The Prisoner of Chillon, Manfred*, and the later cantos of *Childe Harold's Pilgrimage* showed that he still had a large and receptive following.

Many orthodox and conservative members of this had felt misgivings about the moral, political, and religious tendencies of the works which fascinated them. After the scandal of the separation, their unease hardened into condemnation. Byron, finding that reviewers and others who had previously favoured him were more and more liable to denounce his scepticism and political liberalism, became increasingly defiant and reckless. He was irreverent and subversive in *Don Juan*, deliberately impious in *Cain*.

He had always both delighted and shocked his readers, and during these later years many of them were distinctly more shocked than delighted. Nevertheless, he remained a popular author, though rather less so than when he had been writing the Turkish tales. His dramas, apart from *Cain*, were unsuccessful, but readers took up his other works eagerly enough, even if only to be outraged by what they found. 'Do *not* take it into your head, my dear B.', Moore wrote to him on 9 February 1822, 'that the tide is at all turning against you in England. Till I see some symptoms of people *forgetting* you a little, I will not believe that you lose ground. As it is, . . . nothing is hardly talked of but you; and though good people sometimes bless themselves when they mention you, it is plain that even *they* think much more about you than, for the good of their souls, they ought' (*The Letters of Thomas Moore*, ii, p. 618). Nor did Byron lack defenders.

Andrew Rutherford's 'Introduction' to *Byron: The Critical Heritage* gives an excellent survey of the vicissitudes of Byron's reputation between 1808 and the twentieth century, a survey well illustrated by the numerous documents that make up the remainder of his substantial book. He points out that Byron's defenders did not necessarily divide from his opponents along party lines, even though Leigh Hunt and Southey might be held to exemplify some such correlation. Hobhouse was a Radical who disapproved of *Don Juan* and *Cain*; J. W. Croker was a Tory who enjoyed *Don Juan*. While Hazlitt's republicanism and Bonapartism could not conquer his literary and social distaste for Byron's writings, Scott's conservatism and piety did not inhibit his admiration for even the most provocative of them.

Can the death of a man of letters ever have had the effect upon his contemporaries that Byron's had? Jane Welsh learned of it suddenly in a crowded room. 'My God,' she wrote to Thomas Carlyle, 'if they had said that the sun or the moon had gone out of the heavens, it could not have struck me with the idea of a more awful and dreary blank in the creation than the words, "Byron is dead!"' (*The Love Letters of Thomas Carlyle and Jane Welsh*, ed. A. Carlyle, London, 1909, i, p. 369). A boy of fourteen, Alfred Tennyson was so moved by the news that he climbed up to a quarry near his home and scratched the words 'Byron is dead' upon the sandstone. Byron's self-sacrifice in the cause of Greek independence deeply affected public opinion throughout Europe. Without it, the British, French, and Russian navies might never have united in the same cause at Navarino in 1827. Goethe had Byron and his last adventure in mind when he introduced Euphorion into the second part of *Faust*.

For Byron's reputation was more than merely British. It spread rapidly over the whole of Europe and throughout the English-speaking world. Musset was his disciple in France, Pushkin in Russia. During the nineteenth century, at least forty-one translations of one or more cantos of *Childe Harold's Pilgrimage* appeared in no fewer than ten different languages, and as many as thirty-four translations of *Manfred* in twelve different languages. These two works inspired musical compositions by Berlioz, Schumann, and Tchaikovsky. Painters, too, took subjects from them and from other poems by Byron.

Even during his lifetime, he was read and discussed far beyond

Europe. On 15 January 1821 he recorded in his 'Diary' that in 1814 he
and Moore were once

> going together, in the same carriage, to dine with Earl Grey, the
> *Capo Politico* of the remaining Whigs. Murray . . . had just sent
> me a Java gazette – I know not why, or wherefore. Pulling it out,
> by way of curiosity, we found it to contain a dispute (the said
> Java gazette) on Moore's merits and mine. I think, if I had been
> there, that I could have saved them the trouble of disputing on
> the subject. But, there is *fame* for you at six and twenty! Alexander
> had conquered India at the same age; but I doubt if he was
> disputed about, or his conquests compared with those of Indian
> Bacchus, at Java.
>
> It was a great fame to be named with Moore; greater to be
> compared with him; greatest – *pleasure*, at least – to be *with* him;
> and, surely, an odd coincidence, that we should be dining
> together while they were quarrelling about us beyond the
> equinoctial line.

In June 1815 he took great pleasure in what an American visitor told
him about his transatlantic fame, and seven years later he was gratified
to find himself described as 'the favourite poet of the Americans' (*His
Very Self and Voice*, ed. E. J. Lovell, pp. 124, 298).

In his own country, Byron's reputation declined during the half-
century following his death. He remained popular with working-class
Radicals: Friedrich Engels says as much in *The Condition of the Working
Class in England*, and Philip Collins has assembled evidence tending to
support the view (*Thomas Cooper, the Chartist: Byron and the 'Poets of
the Poor'*, Nottingham, 1969). But Giuseppe Mazzini and Charles
Kingsley were unusual among more sophisticated readers in speaking
up for him during the early Victorian period.

Rutherford distinguishes five main themes in Victorian criticism of
Byron. First, there was the question of his sincerity both as a man and
as an artist. Second, there was the question of his pessimism, its origins
and implications. Third, critics debated the truth or falsity of his poetic
vision. Fourth, they discussed his rebelliousness. Fifth, they considered
his poetic art. When, from about 1870 onwards, Byron's reputation
began very slowly to rise again, critics tended to concede his deficiencies
as an artist but to insist upon the truth of his poetic vision and the
admirable nature of his revolt. This is roughly what Matthew Arnold
did. While deploring the frequent slovenliness and tunelessness of

Byron's verse, he praises the 'irreconcilable revolt and battle', to which Byron was roused by the 'falsehood, cynicism, insolence, misgovernment, oppression, with their consequent unfailing crop of human misery' characteristic of the aristocratic rule of his time ('Byron', *Essays in Criticism: Second Series*, London, 1888):

> The old order, as after 1815 it stood victorious, with its ignorance and misery below, its cant, selfishness, and cynicism above, was at home and abroad equally hateful to him. 'I have simplified my politics,' he writes, 'into an utter detestation of all existing governments' ['Journal', 16 January 1814]. And again: 'Give me a republic. The king-times are fast finishing; there will be blood shed like water and tears like mist, but the peoples will conquer in the end. I shall not live to see it, but I foresee it' ['Diary', 13 January 1821].

Arnold was not alone in praising Byron at this date. Swinburne had written appreciatively of him in 1865, sixteen years before the first publication of Arnold's essay. But when Arnold ranked Byron above Keats and Shelley, the current favourites, Swinburne switched from eloquent appreciation to shrill abuse. Nevertheless, Arnold's praise, together with that of John Ruskin, John Morley, Alfred Austin, and others, ensured a steady, if slow, rise in Byron's stock.

It still does not stand anything like as high as it once stood; and his reputation today derives not from the works that gave rise to the Byronic hero but from the serio-comic poetry of his later years. There is now general agreement that he vacillated between going along with contemporary romantic trends and remaining loyal to eighteenth-century classical principles, that the former tendency was dominant during his years of fame in England, and that the latter tendency prevailed when he found contentment in Italy. W. J. Calvert in *Byron: Romantic Paradox* (New York, 1935) was influential in establishing this view. He regards *Don Juan* as Byron's masterpiece in that it is the work in which his strength and sincerity at last found adequate expression.

This preference was developing slowly in England during the latter part of the nineteenth century. It developed equally slowly on the Continent, where Byron's earlier writings enjoyed a degree of popularity that diverted attention from his masterpieces, where readers and critics were so resolved to see him as a champion of Romanticism against Classicism that they overlooked other aspects of his achievement, and where his personal legend by its nature so much more easily exportable than any specifically literary achievement – as a critic of perfidious Albion and a fighter for liberty was of tremendous political importance.

In the twentieth century, the most severe onslaught upon Byron's reputation seems to have come from Bertrand Russell in Book III, Chapter xxiii, of his *History of Western Philosophy* (1946). He sees Byron as a typical aristocratic rebel, committing himself to Titanic cosmic self-assertion and to Satanism and indulging in hero-worship of Napoleon, and by his example promoting that revolt of unsocial instincts which has troubled Europe ever since. Russell admits that his remarks apply more closely to the myth than to the writer or the man. But he insists that, like many other prominent men, Byron 'was more important as a myth than as he really was. As a myth, his importance, especially on the Continent, was enormous.'

Ought not our aim to be to demythologize such reputations by determining as precisely as possible the attitudes, insights, and beliefs embodied in each particular work by Byron or any other writer? That has been my aim in the present book. Do I need to add that no reader is obliged himself to adopt a particular set of attitudes, insights, and beliefs as the price of accepting a work of imaginative literature? We read such a work mainly to share for the time being, by a willing suspension of disbelief, the vision, the outlook upon life, the sense of values, of a man different from ourselves and living in circumstances different from our own. These differences may occasionally be so slight that our reading does little more than strengthen our own stance and so becomes, one may say, devotional. But normally our stance will differ appreciably from that implicit or explicit in the work before us. The experience of that work will be valuable not because it reinforces or undermines our own positions but because it makes us aware of the consequences of other positions as occupied by other men and so extends our sense of the possibilities of life. Byron's experience was varied and often intense, but it was limited; and it was the experience of a man whose own development had rendered him hypersensitive in some areas and insensitive in others. We should be foolish to receive him as a guru. But we can enlarge our own awareness by permitting him to communicate to us his ardent love of liberty and detestation of cant; his keen enjoyment of the pleasures offered by a life in which, nevertheless, 'all is vanity'; and his honesty and courage.

o

Principal Publications of Work by Byron

Hours of Idleness, Newark, 1807.
English Bards, and Scotch Reviewers, London, 1809.
Childe Harold's Pilgrimage, Cantos I and II, London, 1812.
The Giaour, London, 1813.
The Bride of Abydos, London, 1813.
The Corsair, London, 1814.
Lara (with Samuel Rogers's *Jacqueline*), London, 1814.
Hebrew Melodies, London, 1815.
The Siege of Corinth and *Parisina*, London, 1816.
Childe Harold's Pilgrimage, Canto III, London, 1816.
The Prisoner of Chillon, and Other Poems, London, 1816.
Manfred, London, 1817.
Beppo, London, 1818.
Childe Harold's Pilgrimage, Canto IV, London, 1818.
Mazeppa, London, 1819.
Don Juan, Cantos I and II, London, 1819.
Marino Faliero and *The Prophecy of Dante*, London, 1821.
Don Juan, Cantos III–V, London, 1821.
Sardanapalus, The Two Foscari, and *Cain*, London, 1821.
The Vision of Judgment, in *The Liberal*, i (London, 15 October 1822).
Heaven and Earth, in *The Liberal*, ii (London, 1 January 1823).
The Age of Bronze, London, 1823.
The Island, London, 1823.
Don Juan, Cantos VI–VIII; Cantos IX–XI; Cantos XII–XIV; London, 1823.
The Deformed Transformed, London, 1824.
Don Juan, Cantos XV and XVI, London, 1824.

The Works of Lord Byron: Poetry, ed. E. H. Coleridge, 7 vols., London, 1898–1904; *Letters and Journals*, ed. R. E. Prothero, 6 vols., London, 1898–1901.

Principal Publications of Work by Byron

Byron: Poetical Works, ed. F. Page, Oxford Standard Authors, London, 1904 (revised by J. D. Jump, 1970).

The Poetical Works of Lord Byron, ed. E. H. Coleridge, London, 1905.

The Complete Poetical Works of Lord Byron, ed. P. E. More, Cambridge Edition of the Poets, Boston, Mass., 1905.

Lord Byron's Correspondence, ed. J. Murray, 2 vols., London, 1922.

Byron's 'Don Juan', ed. T. G. Steffan and W. W. Pratt, 4 vols., Austin (Texas) and Edinburgh, 1957.

Lord Byron's Cain, ed. T. G. Steffan, Austin (Texas) and London, 1968.

Byron's Hebrew Melodies, ed. T. L. Ashton, London, 1972.

Bibliographical Notes

Chapter 1: An Age of Revolutions

The English history of the period surveyed in this chapter receives authoritative attention in volumes xii and xiii of the Oxford History of England: J. Steven Watson's *The Reign of George III 1760–1815*, 1960; and Sir Llewellyn Woodward's *The Age of Reform 1815–1870*, 1938 (second edition, 1962). The standard account of the influence of the French Revolution in England is P. A. Brown's *The French Revolution in English History*, 1918 (reprinted with a Bibliographical Note, 1965); the corresponding account for Scotland is H. W. Meikle's *Scotland and the French Revolution*, 1912 (reprinted 1969). Henry Collins contributes a short Marxist study, 'The London Corresponding Society', to *Democracy and the Labour Movement*, edited by John Saville, 1955. E. P. Thompson's *The Making of the English Working Class*, 1963, also calls for mention. I have drawn on several of these in my description of life in Regency England and have also made use of Arthur Bryant's *The Age of Elegance 1812–1822*, 1950, and the appropriate chapters in G. M. Trevelyan's *English Social History*, 1944. In *The Making of Italy 1796–1870*, 1968, D. Mack Smith has assembled many of the most important documents relating to the process of Italian unification; and Robert E. Zegger has an interesting article, 'Greek Independence and the London Committee', in *History Today*, xx (1970), pp. 236–45.

The long chapter on Byron in Carl Woodring's *Politics in English Romantic Poetry*, Cambridge (Mass.), 1970, is scholarly and perceptive but could have been more clearly written.

Chapter 2: George Gordon, Lord Byron

I have relied greatly upon L. A. Marchand's *Byron: A Biography*, 3 vols., 1957, which is detailed, accurate, and judicious, and supersedes most of the earlier biographical studies. The same author's *Byron: A Portrait*, 1971, is a single-volume abridgment, with some revision, of the original work. Among such predecessors as Marchand's work has not totally eclipsed, Iris Origo's *The Last Attachment*, 1949 (reissued 1971), describes Byron's liaison with Teresa Guiccioli

191

and his life in Italian society and prints 156 letters and short notes; while Harold Nicolson's *Byron: The Last Journey*, 1924 (new edition, 1948), offers a cool but finally sympathetic appraisal of the Greek adventure. G. Wilson Knight's *Lord Byron's Marriage*, 1957, is a speculative account of the marriage and separation; Malcolm Elwin's *Lord Byron's Wife*, 1962, is the first to be based upon unrestricted access to the Lovelace Papers. John Buxton's *Byron and Shelley*, 1968, is an attractive history of the friendship between the two poets, and W. H. Marshall's *Byron, Shelley, Hunt, and 'The Liberal'*, Philadelphia, 1960, a scholarly account of the episode to which its title refers.

In addition to these biographical studies, I have used the various collections of Byron's letters and other prose (see Notes on the Text, p. xiii), and also, for the sake of the new material contained in it, Peter Quennell's selection, *Byron: A Self-Portrait*, 2 vols., 1950. Similarly, I have used the three volumes in which E. J. Lovell has edited the extant records of Byron's conversation: *Medwin's 'Conversations of Lord Byron'*, Princeton, 1966; *Lady Blessington's 'Conversations of Lord Byron'*, Princeton, 1969; and *His Very Self and Voice*, New York, 1954, this last being a collection of all the conversations apart from those in the other two volumes.

Chapter 3 :   Byron's Prose

While biographers of Byron and critics of his poetry have made use of his prose writings, these writings have received very little critical attention on their own account. Two short studies are G. Wilson Knight's *Byron's Dramatic Prose*, Byron Foundation Lectures, Nottingham, 1953, and my own 'Byron's Letters' in *Essays and Studies 1968*, ed. Simeon Potter, London, 1968. Most of the latter has been incorporated in the present chapter.

One obstacle to the serious critical study of Byron's prose is the unreliability of the printed texts. Comparison of the letter dated 12 August 1819 as given in *Letters and Journals* with L. A. Marchand's version of part of it (*Byron: A Biography*, p. 807), in which omissions have been supplied from the manuscript, illustrates how far the texts available for our analysis may differ from what Byron wrote. Marchand is now preparing what should be the definitive edition of Byron's letters.

Chapter 4 :   Heroes and Rhetoric, 1812–18

In *The Byronic Hero: Types and Prototypes*, Minneapolis, 1962, P. L. Thorslev traces the descent of Byron's heroes from various eighteenth-century and Romantic hero-types and by so doing provides a useful corrective to sweeping generalizations about 'the Byronic hero'. R. F. Gleckner's *Byron and the Ruins of Paradise*, Baltimore, 1967, concentrates mainly upon the earlier poems as expressing 'the misery and lostness of man, the eternal death of love, and the repetitive ruination of paradise' (p. 251). These poems also receive attention in a number of the general studies mentioned below under Chapter 6: *Don Juan*. In particular, Rutherford's treatment of most of them is as severe as Gleckner's is sympathetic. J. J. McGann devotes more than one-third of *Fiery Dust: Byron's Poetic Development*, Chicago and London, 1968, to *Childe Harold's Pilgrimage*, which he sees as a pioneering example of confessional poetry. My remarks on the changes of narrator in *The Giaour* owe something to T. S. Eliot's analysis in his essay, 'Byron' (1937), reprinted in his *On Poetry and Poets*, 1957.

Chapter 5: *Beppo* and the Octave Stanza

An authoritative monograph on *Whistlecraft* and its relationship to the tradition of Italian medley poetry on the one hand and to *Beppo* on the other introduces R. D. Waller's useful edition of J. H. Frere's *The Monks and the Giants*, 1926. In *Italy and the English Romantics: The Italianate Fashion in Early Nineteenth-Century England*, 1957, C. P. Brand has naturally more to say about Byron and Shelley than about any of their contemporaries. His elucidation of what Byron learned from Casti is especially welcome. All the authors of the general studies mentioned below under Chapter 6: *Don Juan* give some attention to *Beppo*; Rutherford and Marchand devote complete chapters to it.

Chapter 6: *Don Juan*

Like everyone else who now writes on *Don Juan*, I owe much to the edition of it by T. G. Steffan and W. W. Pratt, 4 vols., Austin (Texas), 1957. In this, the text occupies volumes ii and iii. Volume i, entitled *The Making of a Masterpiece*, contains Steffan's introduction to the poem and a number of valuable supporting appendices; volume iv contains Pratt's notes. Other books devoted to *Don Juan* include E. F. Boyd's *Byron's 'Don Juan'*, New Brunswick (N.J.), 1945, an informative study of the personal and literary elements that went to its composition, and G. M. Ridenour's *The Style of 'Don Juan'*, New Haven, 1960, a study that differs from my own in emphasizing the coherence and unity of the work.

In several general studies, *Don Juan* receives fuller attention than any other poem. Notable among these are Paul West's lively *Byron and the Spoiler's Art*, 1960, Andrew Rutherford's judicious *Byron: A Critical Study*, 1961, M. K. Joseph's eclectic *Byron the Poet*, 1964, and L. A. Marchand's methodical *Byron's Poetry*, 1965. *Don Juan* has also an important place in W. W. Robson's brilliant essay, 'Byron as Poet', which he includes in his *Critical Essays* 1966.

Chapter 7: *The Vision of Judgment*

In the book mentioned in the last paragraph, Rutherford describes *The Vision of Judgment* as 'Byron's masterpiece, aesthetically perfect, intellectually consistent, highly entertaining, and morally profound' (p. 237). His views on the poem have certainly influenced my own.

Chapter 8: *Cain: A Mystery*

In *The Byronic Hero: Types and Prototypes*, Minneapolis, 1962, P. L. Thorslev writes interestingly on *Cain*. But the most nearly exhaustive treatment of this dramatic poem is T. G. Steffan's *Lord Byron's 'Cain': Twelve Essays and a Text with Variants and Annotations*, Austin (Texas) and London, 1968. Steffan's estimate of the poem's intrinsic value is higher than mine. His book is extremely informative, though misleading in what it says about metre.

Chapter 9: Reputation

I owe much in this chapter to S. C. Chew's *Byron in England: His Fame and After-Fame*, 1924; to W. W. Pratt's 'Survey of Commentary on *Don Juan*', printed as an Appendix to volume iv of *Byron's 'Don Juan'*, edited by T. G. Steffan and W. W. Pratt, 4 vols., Austin (Texas), 1957; and to *Byron: The Critical Heritage*, an anthology of criticism from 1808 to 1909 edited by Andrew Rutherford, 1970. Rutherford reprints the important pronouncements of most of the nineteenth-century critics whom I mention. Philip Collins's *Thomas Cooper, the Chartist: Byron and the 'Poets of the Poor'*, Byron Foundation Lectures, 1969, presents evidence of working-class interest in Byron during the early Victorian period.

Index

Index

Index